Translation and the Making
of Modern Russian Literature

Literatures, Cultures, Translation

Literatures, Cultures, Translation presents a new line of books that engage central issues in translation studies such as history, politics, and gender in and of literary translation, as well as opening new avenues for study. Volumes in the series follow two main strands of inquiry: one strand brings a wider context to translation through an interdisciplinary interrogation, while the other hones in on the history and politics of the translation of seminal works in literary and intellectual history.

Series Editors
Brian James Baer, Kent State University, USA
Michelle Woods, The State University of New York, New Paltz, USA

Editorial Board
Rosemary Arrojo, The State University of New York, Binghamton, USA
Paul Bandia, Concordia University, Canada, and Harvard University, USA
Susan Bassnett, Warwick University, UK
Leo Tak-hung Chan, Lingnan University, Hong Kong, China
Michael Cronin, Dublin City University, Republic of Ireland
Edwin Gentzler, University of Massachusetts Amherst, USA
Carol Maier, Kent State University, USA
Denise Merkle, Moncton University, Canada
Michaela Wolf, University of Graz, Austria

Translation and the Making of Modern Russian Literature

Brian James Baer

Bloomsbury Academic
An imprint of Bloomsbury Publishing Inc

B L O O M S B U R Y

NEW YORK • LONDON • OXFORD • NEW DELHI • SYDNEY

Bloomsbury Academic

An imprint of Bloomsbury Publishing Inc

1385 Broadway	50 Bedford Square
New York	London
NY 10018	WC1B 3DP
USA	UK

www.bloomsbury.com

BLOOMSBURY and the Diana logo are trademarks of Bloomsbury Publishing Plc

First published 2016

© Brian James Baer, 2016

Library of Congress Cataloging-in-Publication Data

A catalog record for this book is available from the Library of Congress.

ISBN: HB: 978-1-6289-2799-3
PB: 978-1-6289-2798-6
ePub: 978-1-6289-2801-3
ePDF: 978-1-6289-2802-0

Series: Literatures, Cultures, Translation

Typeset by Integra Software Services Pvt. Ltd.
Printed and bound in the United States of America

For Rosemary and Bill

Contents

Acknowledgments   viii

Introduction: Born in Translation   1

1   Reading Between, Reading Among: Poet-Translators in the
Age of the Decembrists   21

2   The Translator as Forger: (Mis)Translating Empire in
Lermontov's *Hero of Our Time* and Roziner's
A Certain Finkelmeyer   49

3   The Boy Who Cried "Volk"!: (Mis)Translating the Nation in
Dostoevsky's "Peasant Marei" and Iskander's "Pshada"   69

4   Refiguring Translation: Translator-Heroines in
Russian Women's Writing   87

5   *Imitatio*: Translation and the Making of Soviet Subjects   115

6   Reading Wilde in Moscow, or *Le plus ça change*:
Translations of Western Gay Literature in Post-Soviet Russia   133

7   Unpacking *Daniel Stein*: Where Post-Soviet Meets Postmodern   163

Bibliography   181

Index   207

Acknowledgments

It is a great privilege for me to open the Bloomsbury Series Literatures, Cultures, Translation. In this regard, I would like to thank Haaris Naqvi of Bloomsbury Press for his unwavering support of the series and for his general advocacy for providing high-quality academic volumes at a reasonable price. With this series, my coeditor, Michelle Woods, and I seek, humbly, to continue the groundbreaking work accomplished by the series Translation Studies, coedited by Andre Lefevere and Susan Bassnett in the 1990s. In that spirit, we hope to promote work that, like the writings of Lefevere and Bassnett, is sophisticated without being jargon-laden, provocative without being sensationalist, and focused without being narrow. As interest in World Literature continues to grow and departments throughout the Humanities and Social Sciences begin to take the "translation turn," we hope that this series will be a place to contemplate in a rigorous and profound way the implications involved in reading the world "in translation."

This book has evolved over the course of many years, enriched by the generous support and feedback of many friends and colleagues in the fields of Translation Studies and Russian Cultural Studies, such as Michelle Woods, Klaus Kaindl, Claudia Angelelli, Rosemary Arrojo, Judy Wakabayashi, Michaela Wolf, Yana Hashamova, and Helena Goscilo, to name but a few. Certain conferences, too, played a key role in developing my thinking on the topic of this book, specifically, the Transfiction conferences held at the University of Vienna in 2011 and at the University of Tel Aviv in 2013, and the Translation in Russian Contexts Conference, held at the University of Uppsala in 2014, where a spirit of true intellectual exchange provided a perfect venue for presenting my work in progress. A special thanks goes out to the students in my doctoral seminar Current Trends in Translation Studies, who helped me wrestle with some of the more complex philosophical and methodological questions raised by post-structuralist scholarship on translation. Last but not least, I would like to thank the Kent State Office of Research and Sponsored Programs and the Institute for Applied Linguistics at Kent State University, which have been so supportive of my research over the years.

Notes on Transliteration

The Library of Congress transliteration system is used in this book whenever Russian sources are cited or unfamiliar Russian words are introduced. For the sake of readability, however, I have chosen to use in the body of the text the established English versions of the surnames of well-known Russian writers, politicians, and cultural figures, hence Tolstoy rather than Tolstoi, and Ulitskaya rather than Ulitskaia. All translations are mine unless otherwise indicated.

Introduction

Born in Translation

The literature of most nations begins with translations.

Tomas Venclova (1979)

*No comprehensive study of Russia can afford to ignore the contribution
made by translators and translation in the development of its literature,
and concomitantly in the evolution of its cultural and social identity.*

Leo Burnett and Emily Lygo (2013:1)

In 1897, the Russian writer and religious philosopher Vladimir Solov'ev
(1853–1900) published a poem entitled "The Birthplace [or Homeland]
of Russian Poetry" [Rodina russkoi poezii], which he dedicated to
Vasilii Zhukovsky's 1802 translation of Thomas Gray's "Elegy Written in
a Country Churchyard."[1] In a footnote to his poem, Solov'ev comments:
"Despite the foreign origin of the poem and the lack of sentimentality in
certain places, 'A Country Churchyard' can be considered the beginning of
truly *human* poetry in Russia after the relative rhetorical triumphs of the
Derzhavin period" (1900:151).

By situating the origin of modern Russian poetry, and by extension,
Russia's national identity, in a translation, figured as the transformation of a
graveyard into a birthplace, Solov'ev re-presents translation not as a symptom
of Russia's dependence on the West, a manifestation of what Jean-Jacques
Rousseau described dismissively as "le génie imitatif" of modern Russia, but
rather, as a vehicle for overcoming that dependence, for asserting Russia's

---

[1] Solov'ev's title may be an intertextual reference to the critic Vissarion Belinsky's famous
description of Aleksandr Pushkin as "the sun of Russian poetry" (*solntse russkoi poezii*).
Zhukovsky's translation was first published in 1802 in Nikolai Karamzin's Western-
leaning journal *Vestnik Evropy* [Messenger of Europe]. Karamzin had rejected an earlier
version of the translation, which Zhukovsky revised following the untimely death of his
beloved friend Andrei Turgenev, at the age of twenty three, which marked the revised
version with a very personal pathos.

national difference, suggesting several decades before Walter Benjamin the productive, or in this case re-productive, possibilities of translation.[2]

In so doing, Solov'ev presents a distinctly post-Romantic vision. Rather than the manifestation of a transcendent—and original—national spirit that reveals itself through time, Russian identity, Solov'ev implies here, is constructed dialogically, in and through contact with the foreign. It is performed in the act of translation. As Andrew Wachtel notes, "Russia's manifest destiny was built *not on any inherent quality of Russian culture itself* but rather on its ability to absorb and perfect what it had taken from outside" (1999: 54; italics mine). Only in Russia, Wachtel asserts, is the national poet "praised for his ability not to epitomize but to transcend his native culture" (1999: 57).

And yet, at the same time, the discourse of mourning and loss invoked by Solov'ev betrays a quintessentially Romantic melancholic structure. By announcing the birth of modern Russian culture not with a triumphant ode, as Derzhavin would have done, but with an elegy, a lyric genre dedicated to the contemplation of death and separation, Solov'ev posits loss, or nostalgia for a mythic origin(al), as the enabling condition of that identity. And so, with his elegy to a translation of an elegy, Solov'ev does not "fix" the origin of Russianness; he succeeds only in inscribing that origin, in the language of deconstruction, within an endless deferral of meaning—underscored by his use of a footnote, a perfect example of a Derridean supplement, which, instead of completing the thing to which it is appended, exposes the semantic lack at its core.[3] The birth of the nation and of Zhukovsky's poem is, one could say, haunted by the specter of translation. Moreover, by joining translation and nationalism within a common melancholic structure, Solov'ev displays a precocious insight into the constitutive role played by mourning in modern nationalism, as discussed by Benedict Anderson and Vincente Rafael, among others (for more on this, see Chapter 3).

---

[2] I am referring here to Walter Benjamin's essay "The Task of the Translator," in which he puts forward the idea that translations grant the original a kind of afterlife, however ghostly. For more on this notion, see Bella Brodski's *Can these Bones Live? Translation, Survival, and Cultural Memory* (2007). Rousseau's critique of Russia as a culture of imitation is from Book 2, Chapter 8 ("The People") of *The Social Contract*.

[3] Rosemary Arrojo's remark regarding translators' footnotes, namely, that they challenge "the fantasy of the author's 'original' as a closed, stable object, identifiable as some sort of reliable presence," applies, of course, to all footnotes, as demonstrated most famously by the Russian novelist and translator Vladimir Nabokov who pioneered the conspicuous use of footnotes as a modernist device in his fictional works, most notably *Pale Fire*, as well as in his translations of Mikhail Lermontov's *A Hero of Our Time* and, more (in) famously, of Pushkin's *Eugene Onegin*, where Nabokov's footnotes are at least three times the size of the translation proper.

Translation, therefore, represents a double bind insofar as "the 'irreducibility' of translation, the otherness and hybridity at its core" (Hermans 2010:210) problematizes the nationalist project of establishing a transcendent and *sui generis* national identity, which many Russians believed to be a necessary precondition for competition in the European literary field. In other words, translation made it very difficult to forget the essential strangeness of Russia's national origins. And so, while translation was central to Russia's nationalist project, it threatened the very tenets of that project to the extent that "the persistent need for translation, and the risks and opportunities it entailed—renders the nation's borders constantly open to the coming of something alien and other than itself" (Rafael 2005:xviii). And so, the task of achieving the "authenticity of the original" through translation is an impossible one (Buden 2013:193).

Although this double bind is not unique to Russia—as Tomas Venclova puts it, "the literature of most nations begins with translations" (1979)—it was, I will argue, felt more acutely by Russians for two basic reasons: first, the "belatedness" of Russia's modern nation-building project and, second, Russia's complicated identity as an "imperial nation." These two phenomena, moreover, are thoroughly entangled.

Translation and belatedness

The Russian experience of belatedness—accompanied by the need to "liberate" Russian culture from the shackles of French cultural imperialism—bears a striking resemblance to the postcolonial condition as described by David Chioni Moore: "the cultures of postcolonial lands are characterized by tensions between the desire for autonomy and a history of dependence, the desire for autochthony and the fact of hybrid, part-colonial origin, between resistance and complicity, and between imitation (mimicry) and originality" (2001:112). Animated by all the tensions delineated by Moore, translation then is the perfect lens through which to examine the troubled discursive construction of national identity in imperial Russia.

Russia's "belated" entry onto the European cultural scene following Peter the Great's policy of forced Westernization in the early eighteenth century, which resulted in an intense accumulation of cultural capital—accomplished largely through translations and adaptations—occurred at precisely the time when Romanticism was positing original genius as the defining characteristic of literary texts—and of nations. This problematized the Russian nationalist project in a way it had not in France or England centuries before.[4] Jean-Jacques Rousseau, Western Europe's perhaps greatest Romantic thinker, attributed to Russia's Peter I "a genius for imitation," defining *true* genius as "the kind that creates and makes everything out of nothing" ([1762]1997:73). This view of Russia's imitative nature reflected a broader Enlightenment-era project that constructed Eastern Europe within a developmental model as the internal, backward Other of the West, as documented by Larry Wolff in *Inventing Eastern Europe: The Map of Civilization on the Mind of the Enlightenment* (1994).

Members of Russia's cultural elite reacted to the charge of belatedness in two basic ways. Some bought into the developmental model and sought to overcome Russia's belatedness—to catch up with the West—through translation. In this model, translation is seen as a necessary component of a nation's education, or *Bildung*. As Zhukovsky put it, "Translations enrich a language. [...] In a word, translation is for a language what travel is for the education of the mind" ([1810]1985:81, 82). This was a view echoed by the critic Vissarion Belinsky, who declared translation to be "necessary" [*neobkhodimo*] for the development of Russia's language and literature ([1835]2013:33). In this scenario, translation is a temporary stage on the developmental path toward an "original" literature.

Aleksandr Pushkin, too, believed translations to be essential to the development of Russian literature, referring to the Russian translation of Homer's *Iliad* as a "heroic task" and to the Russian translation of Benjamin Constant's *Adolphe* as an "important event" in Russian literary history ([1825, 1830]1986:147, 232). Nonetheless, he encouraged Zhukovsky, his friend and mentor, to use "his own imagination and [take] his subjects from domestic sources" ([1822]1986:48)—that is, to move beyond translation.

Others, however, challenged the developmental model altogether, offering a sustained critique of the Romantic rules of the game, according to which originality served "as the guarantor of individual subjectivity" (Gutbrodt 2003:19). Translation was put forward as an ethical and aesthetic alternative to the Western cult of original authorship. The promotion of Russia's translation tradition in this scenario often carried within it an attack on what Russians saw as core Western values, such as individualism, private ownership, and the worship of novelty, embodied in the figure of the Romantic author.

---

[4] In the pre-Romantic period, debates between the Ancients and Moderns centered on *how* to translate, not, as in the Romantic period, on *whether* to translate. The association of translation with loss makes translation for Romantics into the textual counterpart of the architectural ruin.

The Russian critique of Western Romantic authorship went hand in hand with a reevaluation of imitation, and by extension, translation, which had been so denigrated by Romantics, such as Rousseau and Edward Young.[5] In Pushkin's words, "Our talent is not a free agent and imitation is not a shameful form of stealing—a sign of mental dullness, but a worthy trust in one's own powers, a hope of finding new worlds, following in the steps of genius, or the experiencing, even more lofty in its humility, of a desire to study one's model and thus give it a second lease of life" ([1836]1986:401). In the debate over the origins of the poetry of Ossian, for example, Pushkin considered the whole question of whether the work was "a translation, an imitation, or his own composition" to be largely irrelevant given the fact that "everyone read and re-read [Ossian] with delight" ([1830]1986:276);[6] he also coined the phrase "a genius of translation"— provocatively oxymoronic in the Romantic Age—to describe Zhukovsky. Belinsky followed suit, repeatedly describing Zhukovsky's translations as "original" ([1841]2013:32). Indeed, this critique of Romantic authorship is alive and well today, as evident in the remarks of the Russian writer and translator Boris Buden: "Caught in the deadlock of transition, the East was translating itself into the idiom of the West by desperately striving to achieve the impossible—the authenticity of the original. *But this is not what translation is about*" (Buden 2013:193; italics added).

Russian ambivalence toward the Western Romantic cult of originality was also reflected in the enormous moral and social burden placed on the shoulders of its writers, expressed so succinctly by the nineteenth-century poet and Decembrist leader Kondraty Ryleev, who famously declared: "I am a Citizen not a Poet" (qtd. in Pushkin 1986:52n). This, too, enhanced the status of translation in Russian culture, which since Peter the Great's policy of forced Westernization was seen as a vital service to the nation. In light of this, Lev Tolstoy's rejection of novel-writing at the very height of his fame in favor of didactic literature and translation can be said to reflect a certain cultural logic. So, too, does Mikhail Bakhtin's concept of polyglossia— that we speak with the words of others, words shot through with previous meanings and associations—and Lev Vygotsky's notion that knowledge is acquired through the construction of meaning in dialogue. In official

---

[5]   See, in particular, Young's 1759 essay "Conjectures on Original Composition."

[6]   More than a century later, the Russian novelist Vladimir Nabokov would express a similar attitude toward the heated debates over the legitimacy of the medieval manuscript *The Lay of Igor's Campaign*. For him, its importance lay in its status as a work of art, not as a legitimate historical document. (For more on Nabokov's attitudes toward translation, see Baer 2011.)

Soviet culture, too, suspicion of "original" writing led to the privileging of translators as model cultural workers (see Chapter 5).

Translating the imperial nation

Russia's nationalist project was also complicated by the fact that this project lay in the hands of a thoroughly cosmopolitan elite, many members of which were in fact ethnically non-Russian. In addition, Russia was since the sixteenth century an enormous multilingual, multiethnic empire. The external otherness of Russia's elite combined with the internal otherness represented by the various peoples of the Russian empire made the construction of a modern national identity an especially fraught endeavor, requiring not only the invention of traditions but also, as Ernst Renan put it, many acts of forgetting.[7]

Since the fall of the Soviet empire, many scholars have addressed Russia's problematic dual identity (Hosking 1997, Condee 2009, Clowes 2011, and Etkind 2011), as illustrated in the somewhat oxymoronic-sounding phrases "empire of nations" (Hirsch 2005) and "imperial nation" (Clowes 2011:70). Scholars largely agree that these two aspects of Russia's identity were at odds with one another.[8] As Geoffrey Hosking argues, the exigencies of maintaining the empire impeded the emergence of a Russian national consciousness (1997). Or, as Nancy Condee puts it, "Historical attempts at theorizing Russian national identity have been confounded by this mismatch of—at the risk of hyperbole—Russia's hypertrophic empire and relative absence of nationhood" (2009:12).

While this is important to keep in mind and helps to explain why Russia has been largely ignored in postcolonial studies, we should also recognize that modernist theories of the nation as an "imagined community" with "invented traditions" have blurred the conceptual boundaries between nation and empire.[9] While nationalists may attempt to define nations

---

[7]   To the extent that nation and empire represent two, for the most part, mutually exclusive ways to "imagine community," Russians have had trouble accommodating the two identities. Later in the introduction I discuss Russian literary works that stage the split between Russia's national and imperial identities.

[8]   While Russia, then the Soviet Union, long held the distinction of being "Europe's last multi-national empire, the third largest empire in human history" (Condee 2009:5), it differed in many crucial ways from the empires of its Western European neighbors. Russia's empire was a contiguous territorial empire, in which many of Russia's colonized peoples—at least those in the Western part of the empire—lived better than the Russians themselves. For example, serfdom was only practiced in Russia proper.

[9]   The concept of "invented traditions" was popularized by E. J. Hobsbawn and T. O. Ranger in their 1983 collected volume, *The Invention of Tradition* (Cambridge University Press).

against empires in essentialist biological and geographical terms, no nation, Anderson points out, is so small that every member will ever "know most of their fellow-members, meet them or even hear them, yet in their minds lives the image of their communion" (1991:6). Or, as Liah Greenfeld puts it, "the only foundation of nationalism as such, the only condition, that is, without which no nationalism is possible, is an idea; nationalism is a particular perspective or a style of thought. The idea that lies at the core of nationalism is the idea of the 'nation'" (1992:3–4). The bonds that link citizens within a national community are therefore no less "imagined" than those that join imperial subjects, although the former may be more horizontally figured, i.e., fraternal, and the latter more vertically, around a sacred center. As Anderson concludes, "Communities are to be distinguished, not by their falsity/genuineness, but by the style in which they are imagined" (1991:6).[10]

That being said, a fundamental distinction between nations and empires can nonetheless be drawn in terms of their respective relationships to translation. Simply put, while nations construct translation as a threat— a scandal, to use Lawrence Venuti's (1998) term—empires rely on translation to sustain their multiethnic, multilingual polity, both on the level of everyday administration and on a more abstract, metaphorical level. And so, while many nations invest, often heavily, in the translation of their canonical literature, they have an enormous emotional investment in the ultimate untranslatability of that literature, which serves as proof of the national genius. To paraphrase Robert Frost's famous remark about poetry, one could define national identity as that which is *lost* in translation. As Alexandra Jaffe puts it, "When translators talk about the untranslatable, they often reinforce the notion that each language has its own 'genius', an essence

---

[10] Moreover, as the French historian Fernand Braudel insists in his seminal *The Identity of France*, the origins of the modern nation are not, as nationalists would like us to believe, shrouded in the mists of time; they are in fact very recent: "The *modern* notion of *la patrie*, the fatherland, had scarcely appeared in the sixteenth century; the nation took on its first explosive form with the Revolution: and the word *nationalism* first appears only from the pen of Balzac—when everything was still to be played for" (1988:18). Moreover, the emergence of the modern nations is predicated on the overcoming of subnational identities (regions, provinces, *pays*), which, Braudel insists, "long maintained and still do maintain a significant degree of autonomy" (1988:20). Braudel presents modern French "identity" as forged from diversity, a diversity that persists and challenges the idea of a French nation to such an extent that "the unity of France," he writes, "is hard to keep in sight" (1988:35)—hard to keep in sight because it is imagined. This is not to deny the many real differences between nations and empires, but it does allow us to recognize that nations, too, must accommodate the otherness, the diversity, within in order to imagine an identity that transcends some boundaries while enforcing others, underscoring the essential arbitrariness of both identities.

that 'naturally' sets it apart from all other languages and reflects something of the 'soul' of its culture or people" (2010:271).

The cosmopolitan emigré writer Vladimir Nabokov asserted the essential untranslatability of Pushkin's novel in verse *Eugene Onegin* with his decision to "sacrifice everything (elegance, euphony, clarity, good taste, modern usage, and even grammar) that the dainty mimic prizes higher than truth" (1975:I, viii) in his translation, which was roundly criticized for being unreadable. Nabokov's approach to this beloved text, largely considered to be a founding work of modern Russian literature, was one, incidentally, he did not take with his previous translations of Russian poetry into English, which were strictly rhymed and metered (see his *Three Russian Poets: Selections from Pushkin, Lermontov and Tyutchev in New Translations* 1944). Paradoxical, too, is the fact that Nabokov makes the claim of untranslatability for a work that he himself describes as a kind of translation:

> [...] at best the picture of a tiny group of Russians, in the second decade of the last century, crossed with all the more obvious characters of western European romance and placed in a stylized Russia, which would disintegrate at once if the French props were removed and if the French impersonators of English and German writers stopped prompting the Russian-speaking heroes and heroines. (1975:7)[11]

The Russian émigré poet and writer Vladimir Veidle makes a similar claim for the untranslatability of Russian poetry—and by extension, Russian national identity—in an essay of 1960 entitled "On the Untranslatable":

> To analyze the untranslatable it is better to turn to poems that consist entirely or almost entirely of an untranslatable remnant (*ostatok*) and that, like the poems "On the Hills of Georgia" or "Beneath the Blue Sky of One's Native Land," you will never be able to carry over with "your own words" (svoimi slovami). (1973:147–148)

For Veidle, the impossible task of translating Russian poetry—in particular, these two mature lyric poems by Pushkin, both written, incidentally, while the poet was in the Caucasus—rewrites the border between *svoi* and

---

[11] Nabokov's translation approach was also, as Burnett and Lygo point out, a clear rejection of the Soviet School's practice of "free translation" (2013:25).

chuzhoi, "us" and "them," which allows the exiled poet to relocate himself, metaphorically, beneath the blue sky of his native land.[12]

Empires, however, have a very different relationship to translation insofar as they rely on translation for their very existence, which requires transcending linguistic, cultural, and geographic barriers. The close association of empires with translation is suggested in the concept of *translatio imperii*—suggesting that empires themselves can be "translated," in the sense of "carried over." And so, while nations are defined by their geographic specificity, empires are defined by their geographic expansiveness. Imperial borders, one could say, are made to be extended while national borders are made to be defended, for, as Anderson points out, "No nation imagines itself coterminous with mankind. The most messianic nationalist does not dream of a day when all the members of the human race will join their nation in the way that it was possible, in certain epochs, for, say, Christians to dream of a wholly Christian planet" (1991:7). The greatest empires, on the other hand, aspire to be precisely that, "coterminous with mankind." Empires, therefore, have an enormous investment in the idea of translatability, while nations are deeply invested in the untranslatable, which serves as evidence of a nation's uniqueness. The tension between these two contradictory claims, which reflect what Naomi Seidman refers to as the "double edged potential of translation"— to establish differences (translation is necessitated by linguistic difference) and to overcome those differences (linking cultures in dialogue)—animates much of modern Russian thinking on Russian identity.

A number of early works of modern Russian literature in fact stage the essential incompatibility of these two, for the most part, mutually exclusive imagined communities. Consider, for example, Gavrila Derzhavin's poem "Life at Zvanka" ["Zhizn' zvanskaia"], in which the poet tacks onto an idyllic Horatian representation of Russian country life, in which "everything is neat and represents Rus" ["opriatno vse i predstavliaet Rus'"], a Pindaric ode celebrating Russian imperial glory, replete with references to classical mythology and Russian military conquests. In Bakhtinian terms, the cyclical chronotope of the Horatian idyll (nation/motherland) is abruptly replaced by the chronological chronotope of the ode (empire/fatherland), shifting from an appreciation of the anonymous and everyday to a celebration of

---

[12] This concept of untranslatability would be deployed by Russian nationalist writers in the post-Stalinist Soviet Union as an act of resistance to the universal translatability promoted by communist internationalism. See, in particular, the 1963 essay by Varlaam Shalamov "The National Borders of Poetry and Free Verse" (2013:118).

great men and extraordinary deeds. Similarly unresolvable is the opposition of the national to the imperial found in Pushkin's poem "The Bronze Horseman," which opens with a paean to the glory of the Russian empire and to the imperial might of Peter the Great followed by a narrative poem that presents that imperial power as oppressive and demonic.

The tension between primordialist and modernist conceptions of the nation is illustrated in what is considered to be the first modern history of Russia, written by the Romantic writer cum historian Nikolai Karamzin. In his monumental *History of the Russian State* (1816–1826), Karamzin betrays a primordialist orientation in the body of the text where he claims that the root *slav-*, denoting the Slavic peoples, is etymologically related to the word *slava*, meaning "glory." But, then, in a footnote, he betrays a modernist orientation, admitting that this is probably a false etymology, offering the more likely—and less heroic—explanation that Slavic was derived from the word *slovo*, meaning "word" (Karamzin [1816]1993:129). He subverts the primodialist orientation of his project even more blatantly, however, in Book 12, where he includes the "Voyage beyond the Seas," an account by the Russian merchant Afanasii Nikitin of his journey to India in the fifteenth century. This text, as Catriona Kelly observes, ends with "an almost exact transcription of the prayer spoken by converts to Islam," revealing "the uncertainty at the center of Russian national identity" (2001:126).

We also see a tension between translatability and untranslatability in Solov'ev's somewhat contradictory claim that Zhukovsky's translation of Gray's elegy could somehow be both "truly human" and quintessentially Russian. While the triumphant (imperial) discourse of translatability offers a utopian solution to the problem of Russian national identity, mystifying the cosmopolitan otherness at the heart of Russian imperial culture, every act of translation nonetheless carries with it a reminder of Russia's belatedness (translations typically come second) and of its imitative position vis-á-vis the West (as source or model). Hence, the many tragicomic "copy clerks" featured in the fiction of Russian nineteenth-century writers such as Gogol and Dostoevsky. Like the translator, the copy clerk serves as a trope for the imitative nature of Russian culture, an embodiment of a deeply interiorized "anxiety of influence." As Kirill Medvedev, a contemporary Russian poet and translator, notes, "translators have the psychology of the 'little person.' Every work they translate becomes [Akakii Akakievich's] overcoat for them" (qtd. in Kalashnikova 2008:338).

Gregory Jusdanis, writing about the "belated modernity" of modern Greece, argues that, "the antinomies of nationalist discourse, which could not be overcome in reality, could be resolved in the utopian space of literary culture" (1991:74). I would make a somewhat different argument, focusing on the ways in which Russian writers attempted the rather more slippery task of resolving the antinomies of their imperial nation in the utopian space of *translated* literature. As in Solov'ev's elegy to Zhukovsky's translation of Gray's elegy, the idea of a truly *Russian* translation mystifies the native/ foreign opposition that structures Romantic nationalist thought, while the description of Russian poetry as "truly *human*" mystifies the distinction between the national and the international, or the universal, which has dogged Russian nationalist discourse for more than two centuries.[13]

In this utopian scenario, the successful translator is seen as an the embodiment of the universal translatability that underpinned the Russian empire. Consider, for example, the words of the great nineteenth-century Russian translator and poet Vasilii Zhukovsky, who claimed in a letter to the writer Nikolai Gogol, "My mind is like flint that needs to be struck against a rock in order for a flame to ignite. Almost everything in me is foreign, or related to the foreign, although at the same time everything is my own" ([1847]1960:544). Gogol, in turn, celebrated Zhukovsky's "translated" identity:

> Everything of this kind he took from foreigners, mostly from Germans— and almost all in translation. But that inner yearning that is imprinted on his translations lends them such vitality that even Germans who have mastered the Russian language acknowledge that the originals seem like copies and the translations like true originals. *You don't know what to call him—a translator or an original poet.* A translator loses his own individuality, but Zhukovskii revealed his more than all our other poets. If you were to glance over the table of contents of his poetry, you would see that one is taken from Schiller, another from Uhland, a third from Walter Scott, and a fourth from Byron, and all of them are the truest copies, word for word, in which the identity of every poet is preserved

---

[13] But translation was never simply a technic of empire. It soon became a trope that could reconcile the contradictions underlying Russia's problematic identity as a "national empire." As Andrew Wachtel explains: "This group recognized that Russianness could not successfully be defined by ethnicity, relation, or political traditions. Rather, the nation was to be imagined on the basis of a few carefully chosen qualities of Russian culture and the Russian language in particular. As opposed to the elites of other imperializing nations, whose explicit or implicit assumption of cultural superiority caused them to view their own values as universal and as something to be imposed on others, members of the Russian cultural elites proposed a model that emphasized their nation's peculiar spongelike ability to absorb the best that other peoples had to offer as the basis for a universal, inclusive national culture" (1999:52). This was, Wachtel insists, "a genuinely alternative view and not merely a transvaluation of Western European signs" (1999).

and nowhere does the translator thrust himself forward. But if you were to read several poems at one sitting and then ask yourself whose poems you'd read, neither Schiller, nor Uhland, nor Walter Scott would appear before your eyes but rather the poet who alone from all others is worthy to sit not at their feet but beside them as their equal. How does his own identity pass through the identities of all these poets? It is a mysterious phenomenon, but one that is visible to everyone. There is not a single Russian who is unable to assemble a true portrait of Zhukovskii's soul from his works. ([1846]2013: 28–29)[14]

(One could also say that, as the illegitimate son of a Russian nobleman, Ivan Bunin, and a Turkish maidservant, Zhukovsky served as a literal embodiment of empire.) This utopian discourse of translatability would be heavily exploited in the Soviet era in the official policy of "friendship of peoples."

Denationalizing literary studies

The idea of Russian national identity being constructed through translation anticipates postmodern notions of identity as performed, not given, and of translation as a transformative event in the target culture, not a pale copy of an original. Postmodern thinkers have advocated for translation to be moved from the margins to the very center of the humanities as both a metonym and a metaphor for the iterability, supplementarity, and polyglossia inherent in all writing. As Octavio Paz put it so eloquently, "No text can be original because language itself, in its very essence, is already a translation—first from the nonverbal world, and then, because each sign and each phrase is a translation of another sign, another phrase" (1992:154). Reconceived in this way, translation becomes an important site from which to critique the Romantic cult of originality and the attendant privileging of origin(al)s. As Mona Baker put it, "Translation can no longer

---

[14] Interestingly, Gogol made similar remarks about Russia's leading "original" poet and writer of the time, Aleksandr Pushkin: "In Spain he is a Spaniard, with a Greek, a Greek—in the Caucasus—a free mountaineer, in the full sense of the term; with an older person he breathes the passage of time in olden days; should he glance toward a peasant in his hut—*he is completely Russian from head to toe*: all the features of our nature were echoed in him . . . . Our poetry has tried all the chords, was nurtured by the poetry of all the peoples, listened to the lyres of all the poets, attained some sort of *world-wide language*, so that it could prepare everyone for a more meaningful service" (qtd. in Wachtel 1999:57).

be understood as the reproduction of a stable, bounded 'original' but has to be reconceptualized as an ongoing rewriting of an already pluralized 'original' " (Baker 2010:435).

While many literary scholars would acknowledge the constitutive role played by translation in the development of modern literary traditions, translated and hybrid texts nevertheless remain marginalized if not entirely invisible absent in most departments of language and literature in the West, a symptom of the *monolingualization* of culture produced by the modern nation-state and the sacralization of origin(al)s. As André Lefevere notes:

> Literary histories, as they have been written until recently, have had little time for translations, since for the literary historian, translation has had to do with "language" only, not with literature—another pernicious outgrowth of the "monolingualization" of literary history by Romantic historiographers intent on creating "national" literatures preferably as uncontaminated as possible by foreign influences. (1992:24).

Johan Heilbron makes a similar point in regard to a monumental survey of French publishing: "In the remarkable project directed by Roger Chartier and Henri-Jean Martin (1982–86) on the French book trade, which contains more than 3,000 pages, there is not a single chapter on translations or translators. Literary history also tends to ignore translation since it is commonly conceived as national history" (2010:316). Emily Apter makes a similar point in *Against World Literature,* where she points out, "literary history's cartographic catalogue is [...] either constrained by the national habitus or by the agglomerative rubric of World Literature" (2013:40).

Even in the Soviet Union, a country that heavily promoted translation in furthering both its domestic (imperial) agenda and its internationalist (communist) aspirations, departments of Russian language and literature were resistant to incorporating translations into the curriculum. As the Ukrainian translation scholar Aleksandr Leites noted in 1955:

> Issues of literary translation are often addressed in isolation from the general problems facing socialist realist literature. In articles by literary scholars and critics there appear, at best, random, impressionistic comments on individual issues of literary translation. A sharp disproportion exists between the place occupied by literary translations in our literary life and the attention paid to it in literary criticism. (1955:100)

Leites here echoes a complaint leveled by the critic Nikolai Chernyshevsky in 1856, that "Only when more attention is paid to translated literature than it is today will works of literary history lose their biased, one-sided perspective" (2013:58). This was a view shared by his contemporary Vissarion Belinsky, who insisted that "translations into Russian belong to Russian literature" ([1838]2013:31).

Recognizing the "tyranny of the national" that continues to organize departments of language and literature helps to explain a number of phenomena in the field of Russian literary studies, such as why the generation of Russian women who wrote exclusively in French in the late eighteenth and early nineteenth centuries were utterly ignored until the 1980s when Juri Lotman "discovered" them—they simply didn't fit into the national canon;[15] why in doctoral seminars on Dostoevsky, the author's first published work—a translation of Balzac's *Eugénie Grandet*— is rarely discussed; why Mikhail Mikhailov, the Russian translator, writer, and publisher, whose translations of Heine and of US antislavery poetry played such an enormous role in the political life of Russia in the 1860s and in the consolidation of the radical left, is left entirely out of courses on nineteenth-century Russian literature; why students in seminars on Pasternak are not assigned his translations of Shakespeare; and why there are no courses offered on, say, Shakespeare in Russia, which could easily fill two semesters.[16] To examine a nation's literature through the lens of translation, then, is to interrogate the continued investment of literary studies in Romantic nationalism and to challenge the imperative to monolingualize cultures. In this sense, I could have titled this book *Translation and the Unmaking of Modern Russian Literature*.

Challenging the monolingualization of literary studies is, one could argue, especially important in the context of Russian culture, where Peter's reforms and imperial realities produced an enormous number of bilinguals and a culture marked by hybridity. The nationalist privileging of the monolingual through the ideology of one language-one people has, however, constructed this hybridity, at least among Russia's elite, as a problem, a symptom of the elite's "split identity," of its alienation from the folk, and of Russia's failed nationalist project. Even the cosmopolitan Lotman, in his work on Russian elite culture of the late eighteenth and early nineteenth century, promoted the "conviction that the French-speaking

---

[15] I am referring here to Lotman's article published under the oxymoronic-sounding title "Russkaia literature na frantsuzskom iazyke" [Russian Literature in French].The study reflects a general interest on Lotman's part in works typically ignored in the national canon, which for him best revealed the social meaning or function of aesthetic forms.

[16] "La tyrannie du national" is a term coined by Gerard Noiriel in his study of asylum laws in modern France, *La tyrannie du national: Le droit d'asile en Europe, 1793-1993* (Paris: Calmann-Levy, 1991).

nobility lacked an authentic cultural identity" (Marrese 2010:719n)—with *authentic* here meaning *national*. Recent scholarship, however, has begun to challenge the marginalization of bilingualism in early modern Russia as alien and inauthentic. Michelle Larouche Marrese's research into the private correspondence of members of Russia's elite, for example, has revealed not a traumatic split in their identity but instead "an unproblematic cultural bilingualism" (2010:705). And so, to liberate literary studies from the tyranny of the national is to deconstruct the exclusive binaries produced by Romantic nationalism that relegate not only translation to the margins but bilingual identity and multilingual texts, as well.

That being said, translation is not a simple add on to the curriculum insofar as it forces us to rethink the nature of identity itself in nonessentialist, fundamentally relational terms. I should also note that translation and multilingualism per se cannot challenge or destabilize the institutions and conceptual categories created by Romanticism and institutionalized to this day. Here, I am in full agreement with Emily Apter's position challenging the assumption within the field of World Literature that translation is "a good thing *en soi*" (2013:8). Bakhtin, for example, described the social life of language as characterized by a struggle between centripetal and centrifugal forces, with polyglossia being an inherently centrifugal force, and monoglossia, an inherently centripetal one. Despite the fact that translation involves at least two languages and so might qualify in that sense as polyglossic, it does not, I would argue, *necessarily* belong to either set of forces. Within a traditional mimetic model of representation, translation is sooner a centrifugal force, its status as an imperfect copy serving to consecrate the source text as a complete, unified, and stable source of meaning and to erase the double-voicedness of translated texts.[17] And so, as paradoxical as it may seem, translations can and do contribute to the *monolingualization* of cultures. Indeed, the whole institutionalization of translation in language pairs—composed of standard "national" languages—supports the idea of one language-one nation, effectively marginalizing dialects and nonstandard forms and accents. As Reine Meylerts contends, every time we read "Translated from X" on the frontispiece of a book, it confirms "reigning notions of the unitary status of the source and target languages/texts and related notions of fidelity and equivalence" (Meylaerts 2010:227).

---

[17] Here, we see a rather direct connection between the phenomenon of *monolingualization*, described by Lefevere, and Bakhtin's concept of the *monologic*, as elaborated in the essays in *The Dialogic Imagination* (1981).

Therefore, only when translation is deployed as a centrifugal force can it truly challenge the assumptions that continue to organize the study of "national" literatures. As Michael Cronin argues in *Translation and Identity*, "Rather than considering translation as an issue which only arises when one goes *outside* the national language or the national literature, is it not time to actively consider translation as a phenomenon *inside* the language?" (2006:31). That is, to study not only *literature in translation* but *translation in literature*. Only then can translation serve as a "useful site from which to launch critical studies of culture and the cultural discourses that have structured colonial modernity" (Selim 2010:323); only then can "the politics of linguistic difference [be] availed to unhorse language nationalisms" (Apter 2013:25), allowing translation to expose "the complex heteronomy that inheres in all of our constructed solidarities" (Bermann 2005:3). From this, a more complex and dynamic model for the "evolution of [Russia's] cultural and social identity" (Burnett and Lygo 2013:1) can emerge, with identity now understood not in essentialist but in relational terms. But, in order to unleash the centrifugal force of translation, we must first liberate translation from a Romantic discourse that posits fullness of meaning in origin(al)s, or, as Cronin puts it, "mov[e] away from the Romantic notion of an 'original', *sui generis* national genius which is transported unchanged through time (immutable mobile) to a notion of literature that is networked beyond national borders through the intrinsic duality and mutability of translation (mutable mobile)" (2006:32). This book represents an attempt to write such a transnational history of Russian literature by rereading Russia's rich literary culture through the lens of translation.

The lens of translation

By displacing a nationalist optic, I hope in the seven chapters of this book to bring into focus various aspects of Russia's literary culture that have until now been if not entirely overlooked then understudied and, in so doing, produce new readings of canonical literary works (Chapters 2 and 3) alongside studies of popular literary works (Chapters 4 and 7), and new readings of Russian and Soviet translation discourse (Chapters 1, 5, and 6), which reveal translation to be at the very center of Russian thinking about literary production and national identity. By mixing analysis of literary representations of translators and translations with analysis of translation flows and of Russia's culture of translation at various historical moments, I hope to show what is gained by fully integrating "the problematics of translation" (Damrosch 2009:8) into the study of literature and culture.

Although the essays that follow are placed in a rough chronological order, this book does not pretend to be a history of translation in Russia. There are already several excellent works on Russian translation history in English, most notably Maurice Freidberg's *Literary Translation in Russia: A Cultural History* (1997), and Lauren Leighton's *Two Worlds, One Art: Literary Translation in Russia and America* (1991), as well as countless works in Russian by Soviet-era scholars of translation, such as Efim Etkind, Iurii Levin, Andrei Fedorov, Vilen Komissarov, and Ilya Serman, to name but a few. Rather than retrace that history, I mingle micro-histories with analysis of fictional translators to explore the ambivalent relationship between translation and Russian national identity and between original writing and translation in modern Russian culture. As a method, it is closer to what Naomi Seidman refers to as "translation stories," which embed translation within "the material, political, cultural, or historical circumstances of its production, that it in fact represents an unfolding of those conditions" (2006:9). In so doing, I reveal translation in Russia to be a highly contested site where Russians negotiated the tensions and contradictions at the heart of their modern nation-building project, and where the heterogenous origins of the Russian nation were both expressed and repressed.

Chapter 1 begins in the turbulent period leading up to the Decembrist Revolt of 1825, a time when translation emerged as a highly politicized practice that was "safer" than original writing and provided progressive-minded, "cosmopolitan" Russians of the time with a model for an engaged civic literature, which was largely unknown in Russia before then. A relatively small, highly homogenous polyglot elite, the Russian educated classes of the two capitals, relied to a great extent on translations of Western literature to lay the foundations of modern Russian literature. The chapter explores the alterity and elitism of this group's literary activities, which were motivated by the will to create an "original" Russian literary tradition. Specifically, I will examine Russian translations of French revolutionary verse by such poets as André Chénier, Arnault, and Pierre-Jean de Béranger. These translations were important in the creation of an intelligentsia that has throughout its existence been in varying degrees of opposition to the state. Russia's intelligentsia, which began as a cosmopolitan, multiethnic, French-speaking elite, followed a tradition of looking to foreign literature for solutions to Russia's political, social, and artistic problems.

Chapter 2 examines scenes of mistranslation in works of modern Russian literature, focusing on the nineteenth-century novel *A Hero of Our Time*, by Mikhail Lemontov, and the twentieth-century novel *A Certain Finkelmeyer*, by Felix Roziner. Scenes of failed or erroneous translation function, I argue, to highlight the disconnect between individual speakers and national and imperial "unities." This motif is especially well-developed in the two novels discussed and reflects the complex cultural politics of the Russian, then Soviet, empire, which contained over 100 different ethnic groups and languages. These scenes of mistranslation contribute to the history of Russian writers' critical engagement with empire.

Chapter 3 continues the investigation of mistranslation but in the context of nationalist discourse, focusing on the kinds of linguistic slips and blockages described by Sigmund Freud in Chapter 2 of his classic *The Psychopathology of Everyday Life*. Reexamining a key text by Fyodor Dostoevsky, "The Peasant Marei," which has been analyzed by a numbers of scholars as revealing aspects of the author's personal psychology, I suggest how the complex play with language in the short story says more about the "political unconscious" of Russia's creative intelligentsia than it does about the author's libidinal unconscious. Reflecting deep ambivalence over Russia's split identity as nation and empire, these acts of mistranslation shed light on what Ashis Nandy refers to as "the psychological biography of the modern nation-state" (1994:ix). Dostoevsky's story from the late nineteenth century is compared with a short story by Fazil Iskander "Pshada," which reexamines those same contradictions but from the point of view of an Abkhazian general in the Soviet army against the backdrop of the fall of the Soviet Union. Both stories stage the ambivalent position of Russia's polyglot imperial elite and expose the fissures in Russia's imperial identity.

The subject of Chapter 4 is gender, and the central role it plays in both translation and national discourse. I examine the extent to which discussions of gender and translation in the West, such as Lori Chamberlain's seminal essay "Rethinking the Gendered Metaphorics of Translation," can be applied to Russia, which has often been troped as feminine and, by extension, more spiritual, in relation to a masculine, that is, more aggressive and violent, West. Focusing on the gendering of translation in Dostoevsky's novel *Crime and Punishment*, and in works by three Russian woman writers, Nadezhda Khvoshchinskaia's novella *The Boarding School Girl*, Nina Gabrielyan's short story *Master of the Grass*, and Aleksandra Marinina's detective novel *The Stylist*, I explore traditional Russian associations of male and female not within an opposition of original writing and translation, respectively, as is typical in the West, but within a discussion of different modes of translation, which in turn reflect different ways of imagining the Russian nation. In this way, I hope to expand the scholarly discourse on translation as a gendered practice and, specifically, on the gendered ethics of translation.

Related to the question of gendered identities is the notion of subjectivity, a much-debated topic in contemporary Translation Studies. Traditional views of translators as invisible and disempowered have been complicated by studies of cultures outside the developed West, suggesting that such fundamental concepts as individuality and subjectivity are culturally constructed and so may be reflected in a different valuation of originality and imitation. In Chapter 5, I examine the discourse surrounding translation in Soviet-era Russia as part of a larger project to de-individualize authorship. Examining key texts on translation in the Soviet period, alongside the promotion of bardic authorship and the official critique of formalism, I seek to integrate translation discourse into a broader cultural context in which the translator emerged as an ideal cultural worker. Informed by revisionist Soviet history, which looks beyond the rigid dichotomies of the Cold War, I offer a Foucauldian rereading of translation as resistance in Stalinist Russia and establish continuities with pre-Soviet discourse on translation and the role of the translator in Russian society.

In Chapter 6, "Reading Wilde in post-Soviet Russia," I examine the reception of Western gay literature in post-Soviet Russia, exposing how post-Soviet translation and publishing practices reflect the deep ambivalence in contemporary Russian society regarding the West as a model for post-Soviet Russia. At first glance, the enormous popularity of Wilde in today's Russia appears as an anti-Soviet gesture—the regime was deeply suspicious of Wilde's work—as a way to reconnect with Russia's immediate prerevolutionary past, referred to as the Silver Age of Russian culture, and as indicative of a reevaluation of the creative individual in post-Soviet society. However, careful analysis of publishing records and the paratextual materials accompanying these post-Soviet editions reveals strong continuities with the Soviet and pre-Soviet reception of Wilde, which largely avoided any discussion of Wilde's sexuality and presented his repentant prison works—*De Profundis* and *On Reading Goal*—as the key texts in his oeuvre, works that can be easily fit within the Russian literary canon and its celebration of the redemptive aspects of suffering. Comparing the Russian reception of Wilde to his reception in the West, I present the packaging of Wilde in post-Soviet Russia as an example of a complex cultural positioning in regard to foreign cultural values, suggesting on the one hand a new "openness" to Western literature and culture while on the other hand replicating Soviet-era treatment of the author that would render him almost unrecognizable to a Western audience.

In Chapter 7, I explore the opposite position, examining how the desire of Western readers to see Liudmila Ulitskaya's best-selling novel *Daniel Stein, Intepreter* as a postmodern paean to tolerance and inclusion blinded them to an important homophobic subplot in the novel, which has its roots in an earlier work by the author that has yet to be translated into English. Ignoring this subplot, Western critics fail to see the degree to which this novel is an assertion of Russian exceptionalism and a reflection of Russian cultural politics in the Putin era. I then inscribe this critical lapse within a tradition of Western misprisions of Russia, built on the conflation of post-Soviet with postmodern.

This very brief overview of translation in Russia, I hope, suggests that while translation is by definition an international phenomenon, crossing languages and cultures, it is imagined and practiced in very culture-specific—and often nationalist—terms. It is a site at which national identity is both constituted and challenged, and, in nations of "belated modernity" that grow up in the shadow of the developed West, that site is intensely contested. Nevertheless, I would not argue that Russia represents a "unique," or dare I say "original," case but rather an *extreme* case of the constructive/deconstructive potential of translation, for perhaps in no other culture was translation provided as much material (and moral) support as in modern Russia while at the same time being subjected to often severe censorship restrictions. Translation, in that sense, can be considered a privileged site for the staging of the struggle between Russia's cosmopolitan aspirations and imperial ambitions, and its desire—and the desire of its colonial possessions—to be a nation.

This book is meant to appeal to two distinct audiences—that of Slavists, who have long acknowledged the important role played by translation in the development of modern Eastern European cultures but may not have considered the implications of this for the study of literature and nationalism. It is also meant for Translation Studies scholars, for whom modern Russia's rich—and very visible—culture of translation is little known or studied due to the dearth of translated materials on the subject. Far from a definitive literary history, this book aspires to generate discussion of how to denationalize literary studies by recognizing the constitutive role of translation in the making of modern literatures.

1

Reading Between, Reading Among: Poet-Translators in the Age of the Decembrists

Translation as a technic of promising novel connections can promote the formation of new publics attuned to other modes of publicity that often exceed the borders of the imperial public sphere.

Vincente Rafael (2007:242)

If a reliance on translation problematized Russia's Romantic nation-building project in the years following the Napoleonic Wars, it also offered unique opportunities for artistic expression, for intercourse with other cultures and ways of life, and for world-making. The translation of poetry was particularly important in the turbulent Age of the Decembrists, given the potential of poetry both to evade censorship and to foster solidarity. As the Czech poet Miroslav Holub put it, "Poetry was the language, poetry was the communication, not only because it could be more loaded with hidden meanings than prose. Poetry was higher above the heads of censors, but it was not so much found in the words as in the suggested tacit solidarity, in the silence between words, between lines and between poems" (Holub 1994:5). This chapter explores the role of translation among Russia's Decembrist poets [*poety-dekabristy*] as a prime example of the phenomenon of productive censorship and of all that can be gained in translation.[1]

Indeed, one of the defining features of Russian culture in the Age of the Decembrists was the attention paid to issues of translation. As the Soviet literary critic Ol'ga Kholmskaia put it, "Characteristic of the first third of the nineteenth century was an unusually keen interest in theoretical issues related to literary translation. Journals of the time were filled with articles

---

[1] There are two excellent works that deal with the social functions of literature in the Age of Pushkin: Todd (1986) and Debreczeny (1997). Neither book, however, treats the role of translation in any sustained fashion. An exception is Greenleaf (1998), who explores the constitutive role played by translation in the evolution of Konstantin Batiushkov's lyric voice.

and notes on recently published translations, while translators themselves affixed forewords to their translations, in which they polemicized with their opponents and defined their own positions" (Kholmskaia 1959:305).

The use of translation as a venue for the discussion of politically risky subjects and for the creation of solidarities under conditions of censorship was not, however, invented in the Age of the Decembrists.[2] Already in the late eighteenth century, for example, the writer and dramaturge Denis Fonvizin translated into Russian the Neo-Confucian text *Ta Hsüeh* (from a French translation), which "provided a language in which to articulate the reflections on imperial legitimacy and political opposition that had preoccupied him since the late 1760s" (Burson 2005)—that is, a somewhat safer way to speak truth to power. A century later, members of the Russian freemason movement, which swept the Russian elite in the late eighteenth and early nineteenth centuries and promoted progressive Enlightenment values of freedom and democracy, translated works not only by the organization's founder, John Mason, but by other politically progressive writers, such as the Americans Thomas Paine and Benjamin Franklin, as well as politically charged poems that exposed the injustice and tragedy of aristocratic privilege, such as Oliver Goldsmith's "The Deserted Village."[3] Schiller mania gripped the progressive Russian elite in the early nineteenth century, inspiring multiple translations of the German author's work, especially those focused on Romantic ideas of political equality and freedom, such as the tragedy *Don Carlos*. That being said, the use of translation to imagine new worlds and to create the communities necessary to bring those worlds into being was, one could say, perfected in the Age of the Decembrists.

Reading under conditions of censorship

Much of the research and commentary on censorship in the contemporary West has focused on the most repressive aspects of the practice: censorship as silencing, erasure, and blockage.[4] This focus is, perhaps, not surprising,

---

[2] Loseff includes a chapter on pseudo-translations in his monograph but fails to discuss the fact that translations proper also provided a de facto screen through which writer-translators could express politically sensitive views.

[3] For more on the role of the Russian Masons in the evolution of the Russian creative intelligentsia, see Baiburova (2000).

[4] For an overview of the scholarship on censorship in the field of Translation Studies, see Merkle (2002); Sturge (2004); Seruya (2008); and Chuilleanáin, Ó Cuilleanáin, and Parris (2009).

given the general consensus in the West that freedom of speech is a basic human right. In countries outside the developed West, however, freedom of speech may not be an expectation for most citizens. In fact, as Leon Twarog points out, "Tsarist Russia developed its system of censorship in the late eighteenth century when most of the other countries of Western Europe were already free of censorship" (1971:99). In such societies, where modern literature developed under the shadow of censorship, we find not only blatantly repressive practices but also what Francesca Billiani has referred to as, following Foucault, *productive* censorship (2007:10). This term refers to the phenomenon of authors, translators, and readers who develop often elaborate means of evading censorship both within texts themselves, in the form of Aesopian language and intertextual references, and outside texts, through the invocation of certain background knowledge.[5] In Russia, Nabokov notes, "the censor's task was made more difficult by his having to disentangle abstruse political allusions instead of simply cracking down upon obvious obscenity" (1981:4). That task was further complicated in the case of translated literature, where knowledge of a foreign language was necessary in order fully to decode the meaning behind translation shifts, as well as "the silence between words, between lines, between poems" (Holub 1994:5).

The study of productive censorship reorients scholarly attention by focusing on the role of readers for, without readers to decode embedded allusions, an author or translator's work is like the proverbial tree that falls in the forest.[6] People who live or have lived under harsh censorship conditions understand well the important role of the reader. Nabokov, for example, opens his book of lectures on Russian literature with an essay entitled "Russian Writers, Censors *and Readers*" (1981:1; italics mine), in which he notes: "For just as the universal family of gifted writers transcends national barriers, so is the gifted reader a universal figure, not subject to spatial or temporal laws. It is he—the good, the excellent reader—who has saved

---

[5] By examining works of productive censorship, I do not mean to downplay in any way the very real hardships that censorship in Russia presented to writers and translators. As Simon Karlinsky noted of Marina Tsvetaeva, who was forced to translate when she could no longer publish her own writing, "[These translations] kept her from writing any poetry of her won, but they also testify to what extent her poetic ability had survived all trials. […] But these translations, for all their excellence, are also a monument to the waste of talent in the Stalin years, when the best Russian poets […] were prevented by the regime from making their own creative contribution and were forced to put their gifts into the service of other literatures" (Karlinsky 1986:232). On the other hand, I feel that J. M. Coetzee fails to appreciate the complex sociological functions of encoding and decoding when he writes, "the game of slipping Aesopian language past the censor is ultimately a sterile one, diverting writers from their proper task" (1996:vii).

[6] An excellent example of research on productive censorship is Tomaszkiewicz (2002).

the artist again and again from being destroyed by emperors, dictators, priests, puritans, philistines, political moralists, policemen, postmasters, and prigs" (11). And, while the gifted reader may belong to a universal species, the Russian reader of the past, Nabokov asserts, "in sentimental retrospect, [...] seems to me to be as much of a model for readers as Russian writers were models for writers in other tongues" (11). Insofar as conditions of censorship schooled the Russian reader in the hermeneutic arts, there may be more to Nabokov's statement than simple patriotism.

In his study of Aesopian language in Soviet literature, *On the Beneficence of Censorship: Aesopian Language in Russian Literature* (1984), Lev Loseff also points out the essential role of the reader under conditions of censorship. Through the decoding of Aesopian texts, the "shrewd reader" constructs herself as more intelligent than the censor (read: the government), whom Nabokov described as possessing "one outstanding virtue—a lack of brains" (1981:4). Although an unjust characterization of Russian censors in many cases—after all, the Russian poet Fedor Tiutchev was a censor for many years—Nabokov's remark alludes to a point that Loseff develops more fully.[7] The act of "besting the censor," Loseff argues, functions not so much to relay information—for what "information" does a poem contain?—but rather, in more anthropological terms, as a kind of social ritual through which individuals, in this case, readers, are initiated into a select interpretive community (Loseff 1984:222-223). Similarly, Leo Strauss suggests that his classic study of censorship and philosophy, *Persecution and the Art of Writing*, be placed within the sociology of knowledge (1952:7). My approach in examining the Russian reading public during the Age of the Decembrists as an interpretive community that reproduced itself through the encoding and decoding of Aesopian language, covert allusions, and intertextual references in both original and translated tests is rather a foray into the sociology of group formation. More important, I would argue, than the subtlety and baroque style generated by productive censorship (Stavans 2005:19-20) are the alternative, and at times oppositional, interpretive communities generated by practices of encoding/decoding, which underscore the world-making potential of translated poetry in the Age of the Decembrists.

What binds these interpretive communities are the hermeneutic strategies and approaches they share. Studies of literary production

---

[7] The censor A. V. Nikitenko's diary provides an excellent look at the complex social role of the censor in tsarist Russia. Nikitenko, who was highly educated, saw his role as that of a cultural mediator. See Nikitenko (1975).

under conditions of censorship suggest that readers develop particular hermeneutic strategies and approaches to produce unofficial readings. Two works, in particular, have contributed to our understanding of the particular hermeneutic practices that develop under conditions of censorship. One is Lev Loseff's *On the Beneficence of Censorship* and the other is Annabel Peterson's *Censorship and Interpretation: The Conditions of Writing and Reading in Early Modern England* (1984). Loseff describes works written and read under conditions of censorship as characterized by the presence of what he calls screens and cues. The screens deflect the attention of the censor away from politically daring or oppositional meanings while the cues help the "shrewd reader" to construct those very meanings. Patterson, like Loseff, attempts to codify the "highly sophisticated system of oblique communication, of unwritten rules whereby writers could communicate with readers or audiences (among whom were the very same authorities who were responsible for state censorship) *without producing a direct confrontation*" (1984:53; italics added).

While Loseff discusses pseudo-translations as a kind of screen, neither he nor Patterson discusses the specific role of translated texts in these literary economies shaped by political censorship. This is somewhat surprising given that the double-voicedness of translated texts complicates the question of authorial responsibility for the text, offering some degree of protection. In this way, we could say that the status of a text as a translation is itself a kind of screen. This is something Efim Etkind implied when he noted that many Soviet writers exploited translation work in order to express their own aesthetic and moral concerns: "During a certain period, particularly between the 19th and 20th [Party] Congresses, Russian poets were deprived of the possibility of expressing themselves to the full in original writing and spoke to the reader in the language of Goethe, Oberliani, Shakespeare, and Hugo" (Etkind 1978:32)—in other words, through their translations.[8] And so, I will attempt below to adapt Loseff's and Patterson's very useful descriptive categories to the reading of translated literature in early nineteenth-century Russia to show how the study of translated texts not only confirms their descriptive models but also expands them.

Patterson describes four elements as central to the system of oblique communication that developed in early modern England. First, she notes the role of timing, that is, "the importance of an exact chronology to determine

---

[8]   Etkind was punished for having included this statement in the introduction to a volume of poetry translations. The passage was then excised from the introduction, lending credence to Michael Holquist's assertion that "censorship is like the house of the undertaker, in which one never speaks of death" (1994:14).

what any given text was likely to mean to its audience at the time of its appearance" (1984:55). Consider the case of Pushkin's review of the memoirs of the notorious French police informer Vidocq, which functioned as a covert attack on the contemporary Russian publisher and censor Faddey Bulgarin. As Sydney Monas describes it, "Vidocq and Bulgarin were so successfully equated that a Petersburg bookseller offered a portrait of Bulgarin for sale over the title 'M. Vidocq.' Before the police could interfere, his entire stock was sold out" (Monas 1961:211).

One can relate the element of timing to the hermeneutic strategy of drawing historical parallels between a literary work and contemporary events. Having grown up "amid the phantasmagorial stage set of Petersburg classicism, where the emperor played Augustus, and where one's very sense of self and gentlemanly status depended on one's participation in a system of signs that was deliberately foreign" (Greenleaf 1998:54), the Russian reading public of the time was, one might say, schooled in the art of historical parallelism by the regime itself. Alexander I, who quite consciously cultivated parallels with Augustus and the Roman Golden Age, unwittingly handed the educated Russians of his day a two-edged sword. During the hopeful, liberal years of his early reign, historical parallels with the ancient world seemed to work in Alexander's favor. In the more repressive years following the Napoleonic Wars, however, it provided Russians with the tools necessary to interpret this shift in less favorable historical terms: Julius the Senator becomes Julius Caeser, the tyrant. Lotman notes that Aleksandr Pushkin's exclamation "Here is Caesar—so where is Brutus" "was easily deciphered as the program for a future act" (Lotman 1984:88). Kondraty Ryleev, who would become a leader of the Decembrists, was known as the Brutus of the Decembrist movement, and in his short story "The Dagger," Pushkin celebrates the great assassins of history: Brutus, Marat, Charlotte Corday, and Karl Ludwig Sand (Leighton 1994:15, 20).

The role of timing is evident, too, in Mikhail Mikhailov's (1829–1865) decision to translate Schiller's drama *Love and Intrigue*, which featured a scene in which 7,000 German peasants are sold into the US army—those who objected were shot. As Mikhailov's Soviet biographer comments, "This scene had special significance for the translator who was filled with indignation against the selling of Russian peasants into the army. This scene tied the entire tragedy to Russian reality" (Fateev 1969:182).

Second, Patterson suggests that "provocation is given, or signification promoted, by some kind of a signal in the text itself" (Patterson 1984:55). This is what Loseff refers to as a "cue." Key words or references to key figures or places, such as Byron or Greece, were popular political cues in the Age of the Decembrists. As early as the late eighteenth century, US abolitionist literature functioned as a covert way to address—in a public forum—the problem of serfdom in Russia. The politically progressive publicist and translator Mikhail Mikhailov's translations of Longfellow's antislavery poems are exemplary in this regard. It is very likely that Mikhailov's decision to translate the title of Longfellow's antislavery cycle *Songs on Slavery* as *Songs of the Negros* [Pesni negrov] was a way to deflect the censor's attention from a reading that would implicate the Russian institution of serfdom while making the text available to like-minded progressives. This particular signal, or set of signals, can be traced back to the first Russian translations of Auguste Von Kotzebue's drama *The Negro Slaves*.[9]

Critical literature, including introductions, notes, and reviews about literary works and translations, also contained the necessary signals to prompt a subversive reading of a literary work. As General Beckendorff, the head of the Ministry of Police, commented to Count Lieven, the head of the Interior Ministry, which was then in charge of censorship, regarding an article by the literary critic Ivan Kireevsky, "The Nineteenth Century": "One has only to apply a certain amount of attention to perceive that the author, discussing literature as it were, has something quite different in mind: that by the word *enlightenment* he means *liberty*, that *the mind's activity* means for him *revolution*, and the skillfully contrived *middle ground* nothing if not a *constitution*" (quoted in Monas 1961:154). Discussion of literature—domestic and foreign, in translation and in the original—came to serve "as a vehicle for social and moral criticism" (166), especially when works by a foreign author were banned but works about that author were not. And so, while advocating for socialism outright could endanger a critic, doing so by praising the works of George Sand or the natural school of Gogol was easily done (194). Indeed, critics often worked hand in hand with writers and translators to encourage, or signal, subversive readings. This was the case with Mikhailov's popular translations of the works of the German poet Heinrich Heine. In order to avoid censorship, Mikhailov made sure to dilute his selection of Heine's more politically charged verses by including a good number of his early nature poems. Progressive critics, however, in their reviews of the volume drew the attention of their readers to the political poems, describing Heine not as a romantic but as a "negator," without specifying exactly what he was negating (Fateev 1969:175).

Another hermeneutic signal or cue, which is, perhaps, unique to literary translation, is repetition. (A parallel phenomenon among writers might be the repeated return to a theme.) When translators produce

---

[9]   It is possible that Kotzebue, who worked for many years in Russia and married a Russian, had from the start intended his play about Negro slaves to be a kind of allegory about Russian serfdom.

multiple translations of a single text, this may function, particularly under conditions of censorship, to focus readerly attention on that text.

Third, Patterson notes that "censorship confers a greater importance on prohibited views than they would otherwise have had" (56), so that the very act of censorship can serve, in a sense, as a signal or cue to the reader, directing them to look for prohibited views. As Michael Holquist argues, censorship has the effect of transforming the censored text into a kind of palimpsest: "One of the ironies that defines censorship as a paradox is that it predictably creates sophisticated audiences. The reader of a text known to be censored cannot be naïve, if only because the act of interdiction renders a text parabolic. [...] The patent aspect of a censored text is only part of a totality that readers must fill in with their interpretations of what was excluded" (1994:14). Translation creates a similar effect to the extent that it also assumes the existence of two textual layers, that of the source text and that of the target. And so, one could argue, meaning in translated literature under conditions of censorship is overdetermined. Of course, this encouraged a hermeneutics of suspicion on the censor's part, as well. Consider, for example, Zhukovsky's translation of Sir Walter Scott's lyrical ballad "On the Eve of St. John." It was held up by the censor who charged that Zhukovsky's choice to translate the word *monk* with the Old Russian word *chernets* (rather than *monakh*) might function as a cue to readers to find in Scott's ballad of revolt historical parallels with contemporary Russia (Rudd 1982:43).

Finally, Patterson lists the "indeterminacy" of literary texts as another challenge for censors insofar as "topical (and hence exciting) meaning may be present but *cannot be proven to be so*" (1984:56; italics mine), underscoring the ultimate futility of the censor's task. As Holub notes, this indeterminacy is only heightened in poetic works.

A hermeneutic convention that Patterson does not mention in the context of early modern England is one that was especially important in the Russian context. I will refer to it simply as shared background knowledge among readers, which allows for a high degree of implicitation, which is likely to be inscrutable to the censor. Background knowledge, especially involving the author's—and translator's—biography may be included in paratextual material accompanying a translation or it may circulate orally among the members of an interpretive community, helping to shape the interpretation of a text. For example, the biographies of the French Revolutionary poets André Chénier, Pierre-Jean de Béranger, and Jean-Vincent Arnault, who were all imprisoned or exiled for their political beliefs, offered inspiring life models for the young Decembrist poets. Chénier, in fact, continued to write poetry while in prison up to the very day of his execution, having the poems smuggled out with the laundry. These poems functioned as a kind of palimpsest, through which the reader could glimpse the writer's defiance in the face of persecution, creating a chain of identifications between author, translator, and reader.

The question of the writer's—and translator's—biography was an especially acute one in early nineteenth-century Russia, when the national literature was only decades old. The translation of established Western authors provided Russian writers of the time with role models, and Russian writer-translators were often drawn to the work of writers whose biographies appeared to parallel their own and whose work, in turn, reflected that biography. Larisa Vol'pert makes the point that Russian writers and translators of the early nineteenth century consciously connected themselves with some of the great writers of the Western tradition—Ovid, Dante, and Byron—through the motif of exile (Vol'pert 2010:240). This association served to elevate the personal life stories of these writers and translators, as well as the history of the Russian nation.

While such translations did not function *merely* as palimpsests, background knowledge about the poet-translator lent literary works a greater poignancy and relevance to the Russian audience. And, it was a largely safe practice to the extent that this biographical information was not inscribed in the text. Even the most innocuous poem could assume a political resonance when read with the knowledge that it was composed by a poet who was either in prison or political exile. This particular mode of reading was especially popular in the Romantic period, when the boundary between an author's life and work was blurred in the concept of *zhiznetvorchesto*, or "life creation."

The Decembrists as an interpretive community

The Russian reading public in the Age of the Decembrists represents a rather unique interpretive community or, to use the term coined by Holub, "a solidarity network" (1994:5). The term "Decembrist" refers to a group of elite young Russians who were members of secret political societies—the Northern Society and the Southern Society—formed to bring about political reform and progress in Russia following the Napoleonic Wars. These men, who had been to Western Europe during the war and had seen the greater freedoms enjoyed by society there, hoped to bring those freedoms to Russia. Upon Alexander's death, members of the Northern Society attempted to force Alexander's purportedly more liberal-leaning brother, Constantine, to assume the throne in place of his younger brother, Nicholas, and to adopt a constitution. They assembled in St. Petersburg on Palace Square before the Winter Palace on December 14, 1825, to force a coup. The revolt failed for a variety of reasons, and Nicholas I acted decisively to crush the liberal movement that had given birth to it. Five of the conspirators were executed and many more were sent into internal exile in Siberia. They—and their wives who followed them there—would become heroes for generations of Russians. As Lauren Leighton comments, "The Decembrists were admired not only by the radicals of the revolutionary movement that led to 1917, but by almost all whose dignity was expressed in the word intelligentsia" (1994:21). In this study, I will use Decembrist in a broad sense to refer to the "free-thinking Russian aristocratic circles of the time" (Sandler 1983:187).

The Decembrists themselves were a close-knit, fairly homogeneous group of elite young men, mostly from the imperial capital of St. Petersburg, many of whom were educated at the Lycée at Tsarskoe Selo, located on the grounds of the tsar's summer palace. In fact, many of the Decembrists were linked by blood. As Juri Lotman notes in his essay "The Decembrist as a Way of Life": "In no other Russian political program do we encounter such a quantity of kinship ties" (1984:111). And those Decembrists not related by blood often enjoyed long-term family friendships and social ties with their co-conspirators. With so much shared experience and background knowledge, the Decembrists formed an exceptionally cohesive interpretive community, making it possible "to talk about the Decembrist not only as the bearer of a particular political programme, but also as a specific cultural-historical type" (73). That cohesion was further enhanced by the Decembrists' "cult of brotherhood, based on the unity of spiritual ideals and the exaltation of friendship, [...] often at the expense of other connections" (110). The Russian reading public at the time, which was centered in the two capitals—Moscow and St. Petersburg—was only slightly less homogeneous.

The Age of the Decembrists in Russia was also marked by government censorship. As a consequence of Russia's belated entry onto the European cultural scene, Russians relied heavily on foreign works in all realms of the arts and sciences, which were in turn subject to approval by the censor. As Marianna Tax Choldin notes, "[Russian rulers] covet Western technology and know how, but are uneasy with Western values and ideas, and because the latter always seem to infiltrate along with the former, the government is confronted constantly with the problem of dealing with those troublesome foreign intruders" (1985:1) Fully one third of the books published by the Russian Academy of Sciences in the eighteenth century were translations (Rosslyn 2000:13).

The government deployed a variety of strategies to deal with foreign literature—in the original and in translation. In general, a foreign work could be imported or even published in Russia in the original language. This was a way to limit the diffusion of a given text to an elite audience of readers. Texts that were not permitted to be imported or published often circulated—at times with the censor's tacit approval—in manuscript form—*samizdat* avant la lettre. Finally, the work could be approved for translation, with or without suggested cuts or revisions. The "esteem" in which the censor held the translator is evident in the report of the committee on censorship established by Nicholas I in 1831, which reconsidered the question of an author or translator's responsibility for a work that had officially passed the censor: "such a rule could, and does not, exempt authors *or translators* from legal persecution in all cases" (quoted in Monas 1961:151; italics added). At other points in Russian history, however, authors and translators were dealt with differently. For example, the Russian translator of Peter Chaadaev's incendiary "First Philosophical Letter"—Chaadaev wrote it in French—got off scot-free while Chaadaev was declared mad and subjected to medical observation.

The Russian censor's treatment of foreign literature shifted with every major turn of political events. The Decembrists came of age in the early part of Alexander I's reign, which was filled with the promise of liberal reform. Alexander lifted the very strict censorship laws instituted by his father, Paul I, and reassigned the duty of censorship from the police to the Ministry of Education. Following the Napoleonic Wars, in the second half of Alexander's reign, the tsar became less interested in the liberal agenda and became engrossed in spiritualism. This shift was in turn reflected in his censorship policy; in 1819, he placed censorship once again under the Ministry of the Interior.

In the aftermath of the Decembrist uprising, the new tsar instituted much stricter censorship laws. These measures, known as the Shishkov reforms after their author, the conservative Admiral Aleksandr Shishkov, were adopted in 1826. Among other things, the reforms sought to replace academics with professional bureaucrats as censors and to guarantee that all publications would have a social benefit. Opposition led the tsar to relax these laws somewhat in 1828. Under the new laws, "any work which endangered the primacy of the church or the state remained outlawed. However, the ability of the government to hold authors accountable for their words was limited" (Zerbe 1997:695).

At the same time, liberal-minded Russian elite readers of the time were trained in the art of evading censorship through their exposure to esoterism, a popular movement in the reign of Alexander I, which was institutionalized in a variety of secret and not-so secret organizations, ranging from Freemasonry to Pietism. As Georges Florovsky points out, "Freemasonry did not signify a passing episode, but rather a developmental state in the history of modern Russian society. Toward the end of the 1770s freemasonry swept through nearly the entire educated class" (1979:online). Many of the Decembrists were Freemasons, and so were practiced in the art of encoding and decoding and believed in the added value of secrecy. This was especially important following the failed Decembrist revolt, when Nicholas I adopted his "cast-iron" censorship policy, leaving the survivors to express their views and feelings "covertly, [which] is why they turned to the skills of arcane, sub-rosa, secret communication provided them by the esoteric tradition" (Leighton 1994:21). Even within their literary clubs, such as The Green Lamp and Arzamas, a shared, private idiom emerged. "This language," notes Lotman, "rich in unexpected juxtapositions and stylistic combinations, became a kind of password, a means of recognition. The existence of a linguistic password, of a strongly marked circle jargon, is a characteristic feature of both 'The Lamp' and 'Arzamas'" (Lotman 1984:105).

The discussion of Freemasonry and Pietism, however, should not be restricted to a set of hermeneutic strategies. On a more profound level, they represent the empowerment of individual readers, which connects mass readership with the emergence of the modern citizen. No longer beholden to the official interpretations of the Church and State, readers began to pursue—often in groups of like-minded individuals—alternative interpretations. The threat posed by these newly empowered readers, however, was not lost on the powers that be. As Admiral Shishkov put it in reference to the Russian Bible Society, "this reading of the sacred books aims to destroy the true faith, disrupt the fatherland and produce strife and rebellion" (Florovsky 1979:online). Freemasonry was banned in 1822, three years before the Decembrist Revolt, and the Russian Bible Society was closed in 1826, one year after the revolt.

Because the sources of Freemasonry and Pietism were for the most part Western European, Russian followers sponsored or themselves produced an enormous number of translations (ibid.). "Scarcely by accident," Florovsky notes, "did the Rosicrucian A. M. Kutuzov translate Edward Young's 'Complaint, or Night Thoughts.' Young's book did not merely serve as a confession of a sentimental man, but as a guide for this newly awakened and sensitive generation" (ibid.). Moroever, a "great deal of reading was done in the lodges according to a strictly prescribed order and under the supervision and guidance of the masters [and] those outside the lodges read with equally great avidity" (ibid). Such reading honed Russian readers' skill in the decoding of symbolism, allusion, and historical parallels.

Lauren Leighton has demonstrated that the great Romantic translator Vasilii Zhukovsky repeatedly inserted references to the Masonic symbol of the "star of hope" into his translations, while referencing the symbol only once in his original work. While Zhukovsky's political views were more conservative than those of the Decembrists and for him the star of hope signaled the cult of friendship and the path to spiritual perfection, the symbol was radicalized in the works of other writers of the time, such as V. F. Raevsky, known as "the first Decembrist." In his poetry, "the metaphor of the Star of Hope also signifies freedom, but in the Weltanschaung of this poet, [...] freedom is a fully developed philosophical and political theme of liberation, even revolution" (Leighton 1994:59).

Another important condition that made possible the evasion of censorship through translation in the Age of the Decembrists was the fact that the Russian elite reader of the time was at least bilingual in Russian and French, and many also knew German, and others, English. Therefore, translators—and almost all the great writers of the period engaged in translation work in a serious and sustained manner—needn't worry about transmitting all the semantic details of the target text, for their readers had access to the source text. The purpose of translation at this time was instead to develop the Russian language and the Russian poetic repertoire, and target texts were expected to exist as self-sustaining, independent works of literature (Etkind 1997:6). This inaugurated a rather free approach to translation, giving the translator a certain license to alter the source text. It also produced a unique practice, which I refer as "double readership." The fact that readers could read and compare both source and target texts made it possible for them to appreciate fully the translator's textual manipulations.

What emerged was a very select interpretive community based on what Savely Senderovich refers to as the "symposium spirit" (1982:132–137). As Monika Greenleaf notes:

> Poets wrote poems for other poets, that is, for their friends and colleagues; every "friendly epistle" in verse was a fragment of that ongoing polylogue with other poets. Above all, the symposium practice established "dialogicity" as the hidden spring of lyric poetry .... Even the most intimate genres such as elegy and anthological epigram manifested their common origins in the "symposium"—by their allusiveness to a common fund of events, utterances, and written texts shared by the circle of writer/readers, their adherence to a shared (if often self-parodying) classical code, and their associative logic. (1998:70)

The act of writing—and translating—poetry became in the early nineteenth century a way to earn entry into an interpretive community, which served as a small-scale version of the society readers sought to create throughout Russia.

Translating resistance

The experience of the Napoleonic Wars, coupled with the birth of modern Russian nationalism that followed Napoleon's invasion, produced a generation of idealistic, civic-minded poets and authors in Russia for whom Byron was a revolutionary hero and the struggle for independence in Greece, a rehearsal for Russia's own struggle for freedom. And so, it would have been evident to the educated Russian reader of the time that the subtext to Decembrist Vil'gel'm Kiukhel'beker's poems dedicated to Byron or to Greece ("Grecheskaia pesn'" [Greek Song] or "Smert' Bairona" [The Death of Byron]) was the cause of liberty.[10] Russians who had been exposed to the relative freedom of Western Europe in the course of the Napoleonic Wars returned to Russia with a liberal political agenda. Writers sought to contribute to that agenda by developing a civic, or civic-minded, literature in Russia, one that raised various political issues while asserting the existence of an autonomous civil society.

Many of the Decembrists, such as A. Bestushev, K. F. Ryleev, V. K. Kiukel'beker, and A. I. Odoevsky, and those who were Decembrist-sympathizers, such as Pushkin,[11] were gifted men of letters who saw literature, and poetry, in particular, as an important vehicle for the expression of their liberal political aspirations. The Russian term *poety-dekabristy* (poet-Decembrists) is recognition of that fact. The poetic works of the Decembrists were characterized by "a mixture of romantic elements and classical imagery and devices [...and] thematically they show a sympathy with popular movements of resistance to despotism, love of civic freedom, a cult of heroism" (Glasse 1985:241).

Moreover, the Decembrists did not see literature as simply a venue for the dissemination of their views and aspirations. They looked to literature to give significance, historical meaning, to their actions through literary precedents. "The real-life behavior of an individual of the Decembrist circle," Lotman explains, "takes the form of an encoded

---

[10]   All translations are mine unless otherwise indicated.

[11]   Pushkin, the greatest poet of his time, was a close friend and schoolmate of many of the Decembrists. He clearly sympathized with their cause. On December 14, 1825, however, Pushkin was in exile on his estate at Mikhailovskoe, so whether he would have participated in the failed coup is one of the great unanswered questions of history.

text, and a literary plot is the code which enables us to penetrate its hidden meaning" (Lotman 1984:93). It was commonplace for Decembrists and those in their circle to refer to contemporary cultural and political figures in literary terms, as Brutus from Shakespeare's *Julius Caesar* or as the Marquis de Posa from Schiller's *Don Carlos*.

In their search for a civic literature, Russian writers looked to foreign models. As Leighton notes, "For political idealists like the Decembrists the impetus came from the French revolution as one model, the American as another. For the literary romantics, dreams of freedom were aroused by Lamartine, Chénier, Schiller, especially by the verse tales of Byron, and even more by the liberating effects of the free romantic imagination" (Leighton 1994:71). Translations and imitations of French literature and, in particular, the literature of the French Revolution were especially important to Russians attempting to develop a civic literature (Danilin 1973:319). Mikhail Zetlin explains the special relevance of eighteenth-century France to early nineteenth-century Russians as a kind of historical anachronism, a defining feature of Russia's belated entry onto the European cultural scene:

> While in the West the romantic era was coming into its own, in Russia Pushkin still read Voltaire's *La Pucelle* and the sentimental poems of Parny. Whereas Paris raved about Chateaubriand and de Maistre, St. Petersburg was only just beginning to discover Adam Smith and Montesquieu. At a time when throughout the Western world people were seeking to adjust themselves to post-Napoleonic reaction, in Russia there was growing up a generation kindred in spirit to that which, a score of years earlier, had made the French Revolution. (Zetlin 1958:14)

Consider Pushkin's reference to "vozvyshennaia Galla" [sublime Gaul] in his 1820 ode "Vol'nost'" [Liberty], the poem that led to his internal exile. The association of French literature—and poetry, in particular—with politics is obvious, too, in Prince Viazemsky's survey of contemporary French poetry, published anonymously in the journal *Moscow Telegraph* in 1826: "You ask what poetry is doing in France? It is doing politics" (quoted in Staritsyna 1969:16). He then goes on to offer a definition of civic literature as "any popular or civic poetry that contains lofty, social truths," which he then promotes: "And why shouldn't the poet be the equal of the orator as the guardian of popular interests and the public welfare?" (16).

Three French poets who were caught up in the politics of the Revolutionary period played an especially important role among liberal Russian writers as models of the civic-minded poet: André Chénier, Pierre-Jean de Béranger, and Antoine-Vincent Arnault. Through translations and imitations of these authors' works, Russian writers and translators introduced a civic-minded literature into Russian letters. Because such literature was especially suspect in the eyes of the autocratic regime, however, writers and translators developed unwritten codes to allow for the circulation of texts and paratextual materials that opened these texts to unofficial, often oppositional, interpretations.

The three French poets—André Chénier, Pierre-Jean de Béranger, and Antoine-Vincent Arnault—who exerted an especially important influence on liberal-minded Russian writers in search of a civic literature in the Age of the Decembrists were all deeply involved in the revolutionary events set off by the French Revolution of 1789. Chénier was imprisoned and executed just two days before the end of the Reign of Terror, and both Arnault and Béranger would be exiled for their political loyalties. Also important to Russian poets of the time was the fact that these men expressed their political aspirations in their poetry.

Aleksandr Pushkin was one of the Russian poets of the period who looked to Chénier as a model for understanding the role of the poet in society. As Stephanie Sandler notes, André Chénier "was seen in the 1820s as an impassioned champion of political liberty who had been martyred for his ideals during the French Revolution" (Sandler 1983:187), and the fact that Chénier's works were published for the first time in French in 1819 made them appear contemporary. Pushkin's fascination with Chénier, "who symbolizes the heroic demise of a poet" (188), was expressed in the fact that he translated or adapted four of the French poet's poems into Russian and wrote an original poetic work entitled "Andrei Shen'e" [André Chénier]. These works were crucial for Pushkin, Sandler asserts, in "working out a formula for asserting his independence as a poet" (187).

While the first three translations from Chénier appeared to address Pushkin's stylistic and aesthetic concerns of the time, his fourth and final translation of the elegy "Près des bords où Venise est reine de la mer" [Near the Shores Where Venice is Queen of the Sea], which was not contained in the original 1819 volume of Chénier's work, speaks to larger concerns on Pushkin's part about the role of the poet in society.[12] In this poem, notes

---

[12] This poem, which was first published in French only in 1826, is believed to have been written by Chénier while in exile in England (see Chénier 1862:412n). The other poems by Chénier translated by Pushkin were: the first twenty five lines of "L'Aveugle," the fragment "Oeta, mont ennobli par cette nuit ardente," and Chénier's fifth elegy. While these verses are less politically charged than "Près des bords où Venise est reine de la mer," the "theme of Hercules' suffering and horrible death and the triumph of his immortal spirit," which Pushkin intensifies in his translation of the fragment "Oeta, mont ennobli par cette nuit ardente," speaks to Pushkin's personal and poetic interest in the unique heroic individual (elsewhere in his work, the poet) who is destroyed by society (Sandomirskaia 1978:97).

V. B. Sandomirskaia, "Chénier turned out to be close to and in harmony with the mood and feelings of Pushkin, who had experienced persecution and exile. [...] The image of the solitary singer blazing a path for himself above the abyss and comforting himself with his song, was biographically close to Pushkin" (Sandormirskaia 1978:104). It is perhaps no coincidence that, while translating the poem in exile at his family estate at Mikhailovskoe, Pushkin intensified the theme of solitude (105).

On the whole, however, Pushkin takes relatively few liberties in his translation, which, according to Sandomirskaia, attests to the fact that the meaning and the images of the poem were so very close to him, aesthetically, biographically, and, one might say, politically. Indeed, Chénier's image of the "awesome and indomitable ocean, only favorable to man on a whim" had already entered Pushkin's poetry ("K moriu" [To the Sea], 1824) by the time he undertook this translation (105), and it is a theme that he developed later in *The Bronze Horseman* [*Mednyi vsadnik*, 1833], in which the destructive power of the sea is directly associated with autocratic power. Moreover, Sandomirskaia points out, "The events of 1825–1826— the Decembrist uprising, its failure, the crushing defeat of the entire movement, the death of 'friends, brothers, comrades'—lent this image [of the sea] a particular, tragic meaning" (105).

The first four lines of Pushkin's translation offer a statement of the poet's role, solitary and heroic, which is also reflected elsewhere in Pushkin's original verse:

Na more zhiznennom, gde buri tak zhestoko
Presleduiut vo mgle moi parus odinokoi,
Kak on, nad bezdnoiu bez ekha ia poiu
I tainye stikhi obdumyvat' liubliu.
[On the living sea, where storms so violently
Pursue in the gloom my solitary sail,
Like him, above the echo-less abyss I sing
And like to contemplate mysterious verses.]

The use of the first person subject pronoun establishes lines of identification between the gondolier, Chénier, and Pushkin. Moreover, the use of the verb *presleduiut* in line two, which can mean "pursue," "torment," and "prosecute," brings out the political implications of the metaphor of the violent sea.

Pushkin's identification with Chénier and the central role played by Chénier in Pushkin's thinking on the social role of the poet are also reflected in Pushkin's original poem "André Chénier," of 1825. The poem, which in Greenleaf's characterization, "dramatizes the duel between the private, elegiac impulse and the poet's public, odic responsibility" (Greenleaf 1994:87), is dedicated to Nikolai Raevsky, son of General Raevsky, who, it was rumored, had pledged to support the Decembrists, while in the poem itself Pushkin praises the poets Dante and Byron as "holy exiles." The French epigraph to the poem ("Ainsi, triste et captive, ma lyre, toutefois/ S'éveillait ....") is taken from a late poem by Chénier *La jeune captive* and "gives the first clue that Pushkin draws a parallel between his exile and Chénier's imprisonment: both poets are like the captive who sings despite her lack of freedom, and both have written poems about a sad captive who nevertheless sings on" (Sandler 1983:189). Approximately half of the poem's first, more liberal, soliloquy was censored, and that soliloquy subsequently circulated in manuscript form with a title referencing the Decembrist Revolt: "On December 14." While Pushkin denied giving the poem this title—he had completed the poem before the Decembrist uprising—"it none the less caused him much trouble," as Tatyana Wolff and John Bayley comment (Pushkin 1986:129n), which points to the fact that literary works can be co-opted by interested readers to their own ends. That "unofficial" version of the poem makes explicit the political implications of Chénier's verse and of Pushkin's interest in the French poet.

Another French poet who played an important role in the development of a civic poetry in Russia was Pierre-Jean de Béranger, who by the end of the nineteenth century would become far more popular in Russia than in his native France. Like Chénier, Béranger was deeply involved in politics and suffered the effects of that involvement, experiencing both imprisonment and exile. Béranger's poetry is often divided into two groups: his frivolous, Anacreontic verses celebrating the joys of private life, on the one hand, and his politically charged verses and political satires, on the other. The latter verses had little chance of passing the Russian censor in the Age of the Decembrists. In fact, the collections of Béranger's works *Chansons* [Songs] and *Nouvelles Chansons* [New Songs] were forbidden as early as 1825. The 1831 collection of Béranger songs was also forbidden, with the St. Petersburg Committee on Foreign Censorship noting its "revolutionary, profane and immoral spirit" (Danilin 1973:324).

This did not, however, prevent the circulation of Béranger's works—in French and in Russian translation—within informal networks of readers. Moreover, as poems and songs, Béranger's works could be performed at gatherings. As Zoia Staritsyna notes, "The poetry of Béranger was known to the Decembrists and to Pushkin; his songs rang out in the student groups of Moscow University in the 1830s, at the secret meetings of the Petrashevtsy, and in the 1850–60s Béranger became one of the most popular foreign poets in Russia" (Staritsyna 1969:5). Béranger was also mentioned occasionally in the critical literature of the time, although in very coded language. For example, in 1819, in the progressive journal *Syn Otechestva* [Son of the Fatherland], the mouthpiece of Decembrist circles, an anonymous essay was published under the title "A Review of French Literature of 1818," in which the following mention of Béranger was made: "The witty songs of Mr. Béranger, which can be compared in their dignity to odes, deserve to be placed among the best of our songs and would make a valuable collection for lovers of refined poetry and philosophy" (qtd. in Staritsyna 1969:10). Crucial here is the reference to the lofty public genre of the ode, which marks Béranger's work as civic-minded. As Staritsyna comments, "By naming some of Béranger's songs odes, the journal asserted the civic-mindedness of his early satirical songs in the first 1815 collection" (10). This connection was reinforced by Prince V. A. Viazemsky in a critical article of 1826, "Letters from France," in which he writes: "Béranger, believing himself to be writing simple songs, is writing lofty odes" (17). Later in that same article, Viazemsky makes a rather daring reference to Béranger's imprisonment:

> You probably know some songs of Béranger, but not only because the carefree Anacreon leads him at times from the path to the temple of glory, and as willingly [skol'ko voleiu] or twice as unwillingly [i vdvoe nevolieu] (as they say in our folk tales), he enters the prison of the holy Pelagia, and there he fasts for the immodesty of his Muse, which is too outspoken for its time. But he lives there, humming, and many of his songs, *written behind the prison bars*, are as free and as pleasant as before. (Qtd. in Staritsyna 1969:16–17, italics mine)

Here, the mention of Béranger's Anacreontic verses serves as a screen; the reader of the time, however, would have understood that the poet was not imprisoned for those light verses, and the short passage is peppered with references to his incarceration, including the phrase *nevoleiu*, which can mean both "unwillingly" and "as a captive." Viazemsky's subsequent mention of prison bars signals Béranger's political verse.

The second collection of Béranger's work appeared in 1821 and contained songs that sharply satirized the Restoration. For this, Béranger was tried and imprisoned, which made the poet even more popular among liberal circles in Russia. In fact, following his second arrest in 1828, a letter urging the French government to release the poet was sent from Russia, signed by a great number of readers (Staritsyna 1969:18). The cause of popularizing Béranger's work in Russia was taken up by Viazemsky, who, although not a member of the Decembrist societies, was of an oppositional mood. His first *Zapisnaia kniga* [Notebook] (1813–1823), a kind of literary diary or album, contains hand-written versions of many politically charged songs of Béranger. As Staritsyna notes, "Viazemsky copied songs that, clearly, were in harmony with his personal views, but he didn't just copy them, he circulated and promoted them, and sent them to friends" (11). In 1818, he sent two songs by Béranger to his friend A. I. Turgenev, encouraging him to have the song "La fée Urgande" translated. Turgenev wrote back, telling him that "their mutual friend Pleshcheev had already set one of the two poems to music and performed it at Karamzin's birthday" (11–12). Staritsyna conjectures that Viazemsky may himself have translated some songs of Béranger, "but anonymously, without reference to Béranger, making such translations very difficult to locate in the journals of the time" (12). A. A. Del'vig's translation of "Le bon Dieu," a biting political satire aimed at the church and the monarchy, circulated in manuscript form during the 1820s and was especially popular among the Decembrists, but it was published for the first time in London only in 1861, in a collection edited by A. I. Herzen and N. P. Ogarev under the title *Russkaia potaennaia literatura* [Russian Secret Literature] (14). A nameless copy of Del'vig's translation was found among the papers of the Decembrist Mikhail Lunin.

A third French poet who attracted the attention of Russian liberal or progressive writers of the Decembrist period was Antoine-Vincent Arnault. His poetic miniature "La Feuille" [The Leaf] enjoyed enormous popularity in tsarist Russia during the Decembrists' lifetime. As Vol'pert notes:

> This short poem had an unusual fate in Russia—the original was anthologized, it was committed to memory, eagerly recited, and actively translated (Zhukovskii, V. L. Pushkin, Davydov, S. Durov, [Lermontov] and Briusov). Significantly, it was highly valued by political exiles: "The fate of this little verse," wrote Pushkin, "is wondrous. Kostiushko recited it before his death on the shore of Lake Geneva; Alexander Ipsilanti translated it into Greek." (2010:244)

Pushkin's comment that Ipsilanti, the hero of the Greek independence movement, had translated the poem and that the exiled Belarussian Tadeush Kostiushko, a Freemason who fought for the rebels in the American War for Independence and was a leader of the Polish uprising in 1794, recited it on the banks of Lake Geneva—where he spent the last fourteen years of his life in exile—suggests the strong political associations the poem had acquired for contemporary readers.

This is somewhat surprising in that, at first glance, Arnault's poem, organized around the motif of a leaf torn from a branch, appears to be a timeless meditation on human vanity and the fleetingness of life:

De la tige détachée,
Pauvre feuille desséchée,
Où vas-tu? Je n'en sais rien.
L'orage a brisé le chêne
Qui seul était mon soutien.
De son inconstante haleine
Le zéphyr ou l'aquilon
Depuis ce jour me promène
De la forêt à la plaine,
De la montagne au vallon.
Je vais ou le vent me mène,
Sans me plaindre ou m'effrayer:
Je vais où va toute chose,
Où va la feuille de rose
Et la feuille de laurier. ([1802] 1825:168)
[Torn from the stem,
Poor dried leaf,
Where are you going? I do not know.
The storm has smashed the oak
That was my sole support.
With their erratic breathe
The zephyr or the aquilon
Have since that day led me
From forest to plain,
From mountain to valley.
I go where I am led,
Without complaint and without fear:
I go where all things go
Where goes the leaf of the rose
And the leaf of the laurel.]

The juxtaposition of the rose and laurel in the final stanzas of the poem adds to the traditional treatment of the motif of death. To the extent that the rose is associated with love and the laurel with public recognition, the flowers evoke the opposition of private and public, respectively, putting forward in this way the notion that death comes for rich and poor alike. The contemporary deployment of that symbolism, however, suggested a more historical interpretation. The rose was also associated with secrecy and was, of course, the symbol of the Rosicrucian movement, while the laurel was co-opted by Napolean as a crown to associate himself with ancient Greece, thus suggesting the opposition of a mystical secret world (the rose) to an ego-driven public world of "great" men (the laurel), and specifically, of *the* great man of the time.

At the same time, the biography of the poet suggested to contemporary readers an interpretation of the leaf torn from its branch as a metaphor for political exile. Arnault, who established his reputation as a writer with two "republican" dramas: *Lucrèce* (1792) and *Marius á Mintume* (1794), which he wrote while in exile in England, was arrested when he attempted to return to France. He was eventually freed when the Comité declared that poets are by nature cosmopolitans. Arnault was granted various commissions by Napoleon and remained faithful to his patron throughout his life. After the Hundred Days, Arnault lived in exile until 1819. These biographical facts informed an alternative, "political" interpretation of the leaf. As Vol'pert comments, "It is logical that 'The Leaf' was written by Arnault: the French poet was twice subjected to exile and after each period he created a work that would remain in the cultural memory of the time. It seems that fate itself had dictated the theme to Arnault [...] The idea that exile could be a feat of stoicism turned out to be extremely relevant for the period of the [French] Revolution" (Vol'pert 2010:244).[13] Vol'pert here asserts the notion that a poet's biography should indeed be reflected in his verse. This is, in fact, an important aspect of Russian reading practices that endures still today. As the Russian émigré writers Petr Vail and Aleksandr Genis point out, "For the Russian reader, the writer is the creator of a certain way of life—not of a certain literary work. [...] What mattered were the forms of perceiving life created by the writer. These forms could be imitated. They could be filled with one's own content" (1998:64–65).

While Arnault's biography suggests a reading of the leaf as a metaphor for political exile, the poem's title "La feuille" may also refer—unwittingly or not—to the Feuillants or Club de Feuillants, a moderate political organization in Revolutionary France, members of which also referred to themselves as Amis de la Constitution [Friends of the Constitution]. The Decembrists of the Northern Society generally supported the idea of a constitutional monarchy. In any case, "the popularity of this work in Russia," Vol'pert asserts, "was determined by an entire complex of reasons: knowledge of the unusual fate

---

[13] This interpretation was not unique to Russia poets. An unauthorized collection of Arnault's works was published in 1823 under the title *Les loisirs d'un banni* [The leisure activities of an exile], the epigraph of which is a fable by the French poet Etienne Gosse (1773–1834), entitled "Fable XX et dernière. L'arbre exotique," where the connection between the dried leaf and political exile is made very explicit: "Ton écorce n'a plus d'odeur. / Ta feuille, hélas! parait flétrie: / Bel arbre, d'où vient ta langueur? ... / --Je ne suis plus dans ma partie" (Gosse 1818:243; qtd. in Arnault 1823:front matter).

of Arnault, an understanding of the meaning of the allegory ('the mighty oak' is Napoleon), and the innovative verse" (2010:245).[14]

On a textual level, the Russian translations of the poem tend to intensify the motif of exile by playing up the sentimental elements of the poem and by offering subtle cues regarding the poem's political subtext. Vasilii Zhukovsky, the first Russian translator of Arnault's poem, sacrificed semantics for the sake of rhyme and meter, producing an excellent, freestanding work:

Ot druzhnoi vetki otluchennyi
Skazhi, listok uedinennyi,
Kuda letish'? "Ne znaiu sam;
Groza razbila dub rodimyi,
S tekh por po dolam, po goram
Po vole sluchaia nosimyi,
Stremlius', kuda velit mne rok,
Kuda na svete vse stremitsia,
Kuda i list lavrovyi mchitsia
I legkii rozovyi listok." (1818:25)
[Separated from the friendly branch,
Tell me, solitary leaf,
Where are you going? "I don't know;
The storm split the native oak
That was my sole support;
Since then, across valleys and mountains,
I've been carried by the will of chance,
Going where fate commands,
Where goes the laurel leaf
And the light leaf of the rose."]

In line one, Zhukovsky uses the phrase "ot druzhnoi vetki" (from the friendly branch) and in line five, "dub rodimyi," or "native oak." Both modifiers

---

[14] In the introduction to his 1968 collection of translated poetry, *Mastera russkogo stikhotvornogo perevoda*, Etkind discusses Arnault's poem and how it served as a metaphor for political exile. In what may be an example of covert irony, discernable by the "happy few," Etkind comments: "While then, at the beginning of the nineteenth century, 'The Leaf' was read as an allegory for the fate of the political exile, today it appears as simply a good poem, and however perfect a new translation, it would be doomed to oblivion in [our] social and literary life" (1968:15–16). No theme could have been more relevant in late 1960s Russia, however, as Etkind himself, like Daniel', Tertz, Solzhenitsyn, and Brodsky, would be forced into exile.

intensify the sentimental aspects of the poem, and the adjective *rodimyi*, etomylogically linked as it is to *rodina*, or "homeland," makes the theme of exile, or separation from one's homeland, more explicit. Moreover, *rodimyi* itself means both "native" and "dear," providing the semantic support for a more sentimental reading. Other lexical choices introduced by the translator, such as *volia* (will) and *stremlius'* ("move toward" or "aspire to"), were key terms in the nationalist struggles for independence in the Romantic period. The Russian Romantic poet Mikhail Lermontov, who was himself subjected to internal exile for a poem he wrote implicating Russian society and the tsar himself in Pushkin's death, produced a translation of Arnault's poem that is more an adaption. He further explicitates the poem's political allegory by adding "surovaia otchizna," or "severe fatherland," and by strengthening the association of *rodimyi* and *rodina* by using *rodimyi* in its feminine form, *rodimaia*, to modify *vetka* (branch) instead of *dub* (oak). The distinction introduced into his translation between *rodina* (homeland) and *otchizna* (fatherland) underscores the gap between the nation and the state.

The leaf as a metaphor for internal exile does not, however, exhaust the interpretive possibilities of this short lyric. One might venture a meta-literary interpretation of Arnault's poem and its Russian translations based on the fact that *feuille* and *listok* can refer both to the leaf of a plant or tree and to a sheet of paper, suggesting the unpredictable fate of a work of art once it is torn from the author's—or translator's—hand.

The hermeneutic practices developed during the time of the Decembrists mark the beginning of a tradition of evasion that would endure for almost two centuries and that would place Russian literature—and literary translation— at the very center of Russian, then Soviet, opposition. Indeed, the rich and tragic tradition of prison translations in Russia began with the Decembrists Vil'gel'm Kiukhel'beker and Aleksandr Murav'ev[-Apostol], prominent members of the Decembrist movement, who were arrested and sentenced to prison and exile. Kiukhel'beker served time in the prison fortresses of Shlisselburg, Dinaburga, Revel, and Sveaborg, where he spent much of his time studying and translating the historical dramas and tragedies of Shakespeare. During his confinement, Kiukhel'beker came to see "literature, history, the people surrounding him, even the events of his own life […] through the prism of Shakespearean imagery" (Levin 1988:65).

Although Kiukhel'beker's translations of Shakespeare's history plays, among the first in Russia, were not published in his lifetime, they reflected the general turn toward "historical thinking" among the elite in post-Decembrist Russia (Levin 1988:64). The translation and imitation of Shakespeare's plays was at that time a way for progressives in Russia to contemplate notions of monarchical power and the moral right of subjects to oppose that power in light of the failed uprising. While Kiukhel'beker's views on political opposition may have grown more conservative during his incarceration, his fascination with the "popular spirit" [narodnost'] of Shakespeare's plays can be seen as a nod in the direction of a more democratic notion of state power. As Iurii Tynianov put it in his introduction to Kiukhel'beker's historical drama *Prokofii Liapunov*, "The very concept of popular spirit for the Decembrist Kiukhel'beker was democratic" (1938:10). Also evident in his choice of plays for translation is the belief that only extreme immorality should jeopardize a monarch's position, and even then, not the monarchy itself. For example, Kiukhel'beker chose in the end not to translate *Richard II* because that king's virtue made his tragic fate appear as unjust. He much preferred the play *Richard III* insofar as that monarch's profound immorality better justified his ignominious demise. Indeed, in the title of his introduction for a future edition of his translations, Kiukhel'beker placed special emphasis on that play: "A Discussion of Eight Historical Dramas by Shakespeare, in particular, *Richard III*" (Tynianov 1938:16). His translation of Shakespeare's plays in turn greatly influenced his own historical drama, *Prokofii Liapunov*, in which Kiukhel'beker suggested many parallels "between popular movements in the 17th century and the revolutionary movement of the 19th to which he belonged" (21–22).[15]

Even more politically charged in the years immediately following the failed coup was Murav'ev's translation of the New Testament Book of Matthew into modern Russian insofar as the translation of the bible had been thoroughly politicized in early nineteenth-century Russia, much as it had been in many Western European countries during the Reformation. The translation of the bible into the vernacular granted laypeople the right to read and interpret the scriptures on their own. This new readerly authority served as both a metaphor and a metonym for the modern political authority of citizens.

E. N. Tumanik divides the history of bible translation in Russia into three periods, inseparably linked to the politics of the time: 1816–1826, when translation was sponsored by the Russian Bible Soviet; 1826–1856, when translation of the bible into Russian was forbidden in the wake of the failed Decembrist uprising and only isolated individuals engaged in covert translation; and 1856–1876, when translation of the bible was once again allowed, leading to the publication of the first complete Russian translation of the bible in 1876. The Russian Bible Society which was a product of the Pietism that spread throughout the educated classes in the early nineteenth

---

[15] Nevertheless, in his translation approach Kiukhel'beker avoided translating many English-specific titles lest readers confuse the English rulers with Russian ones (Tynianov 1938:16).

century was a progressive movement, not unlike the Reformation in the West, which promoted a personal relationship with God. The link between Pietist beliefs and political practices was not lost on the new tsar, Nicholas I, who immediately shut down the Russian Bible Society. Nevertheless, Murav'ev, who had been active in the Bible Society, continued to work on his own translation while in exile. Moreover, the books that Murav'ev consulted while translating the bible give some indication of his eclectic, progressive spiritual leanings: "the 'famous work' of Arius Montanus, the Vulgate, the Septuagent, the Berlenburg Bible, Luther's translation, the King James Bible, fragments of E. Swedenbourg's translation of the Gospels and the Apocalypse, M. Mendelson's German translation with commentary in Hebrew, among others things" (Tumanik 2008:13). The influence of Protestantism is clear; Murav'ev's writings and translations display what Tumanik refers to as a "Christian liberalism":

> ... bible truths became for A.N. Murav'ev a symbol of the liberation of the individual and the foundation of state power in law. This was the first time he referred to freedom [vol'nost'] as a "heavenly gift" and declared the equality of all social classes before Christian law ("The Gospels were written for all people"). [...] A.N. Murav'ev's translation activity was no doubt an expression of social protest and a symbol of opposition to the virtual outlawing of the broad "circulation" of the Word of God and of translations of the Bible into Russian. (Tumanik 2008:13)

The practice of speaking through translations did not die with the Decembrists—nor did the practice of prison translations—but rather became an enduring tradition for generations of writers and translators who followed them. Lasting well into the Soviet period, this tradition was a defining feature of the Russian intelligentsia.[16]

One of the most prominent inheritors of this tradition was the nineteenth-century writer, publicist, and translator Mikhail Mikhailov, who revered the Decembrists and, like them, expressed his progressive political views largely through translation. Like Kiukhel'beker and Murav'ev, Mikhailov continued to translate after being imprisoned for his radical political views. There, he produced a translation of Aeschylus's *Prometheus Bound*, which he managed to have smuggled out and published

---

[16] For more on the role of translation in Soviet culture, see Baer (2006).

in 1863 under a pseudonym. In that work, Mikhailov "expresses his view on the state of the country, on the bloodthirsty autocracy, on the mass shootings of peasants, on the arrest of revolutionaries, and on his own situation" (Fateev 1969:350), ideas upon which he elaborated in an article entitled "The Execution of Prometheus," which, too, was published under a pseudonym. Mikhailov also translated an excerpt from Thomas Moore's *Irish Melodies*, inspired by the failed Irish Uprising of 1798, which was brutally suppressed by the British. "In his choice of authors for translation and for commentary," P. S. Fateev notes, "Mikhailov followed his principles. Near and dear to him were those writers and journalist who fought against feudal despotism and arbitrary rule, against capitalist oppression, and for a republic, freedom, democracy, and socialism" (1969:230).

In fashioning his life as a translator-activist, he was clearly modeling himself on the example of the Decembrists. Mikhailov, in fact, wrote extensively about the Decembrists, who, in his words, "loved truth and freedom, and struggled and suffered for them, going to their death with a calm and clear expression on their faces and with the conviction that the time would come" (Fateev 1969:226). Found among the possessions of Mikhailov and the other members of his circle upon their arrest were forbidden works of literature by Herzen and Ogarev, and by foreign authors on the revolutions of 1848–1849, as well as portraits of the Decembrists.

The Decembrists' legacy as translators was an enduring one, representing for future generations of Russians the ideals of the Russian *intelligent* and modeling literature—both original and translated—as a complex site of opposition to the state, generating elaborate hermeneutic strategies, on the one hand, and close-knit communities of sophisticated or shrewd readers, on the other. By its very nature, translated literature fostered among generations of progressive-minded Russians bonds of "human solidarity," which stretched far beyond the boundaries of Russia and comforted them with the thought that they were not alone.

2

The Translator as Forger: (Mis)Translating Empire in Lermontov's *Hero of Our Time* and Roziner's *A Certain Finkelmeyer*

Imperialism and translation not only can but also must be connected for they are the basis of the national definition.

Andrew Wachtel (1999:53)

The first major works to introduce postcolonialism to Translation Studies, such as Eric Cheyfitz's *The Poetics of Imperialism: Translation and Colonization from The Tempest to Tarzan* (1991) and Tejaswini Niranjana's *Siting Translation: History, Post-Structuralism, and the Colonial Context* (1992), presented translation as deeply implicated in the colonial project, serving as a vehicle to carry out, justify, and naturalize colonial oppression. Since the appearance of these seminal works, however, scholars have increasingly focused on the ways translators and interpreters from colonized cultures, despite the asymmetrical power relations involved, have nevertheless managed to "talk back to empire," using translation and multilingualism to resist, subvert, and oppose the hegemony of colonial domination (Venuti 1992, Alvarez and Vidal 1996, Bassnett and Trivedi 1999, Tymoczko and Gentzler 2002, Tymoczko 2010, and Asimakoulos and Rogers 2011). As Vincente Rafael argues, "We can think of translation, then, as something other than an instrument of imperial power. As the agency of mediation, it is itself a kind of power productive of other modalities of empowerment that comes with *crossing and double-crossing* differences, linguistic as well as social" (Rafael 2007:242; italics added). The capacity of translators to "cross and double cross," which is nicely captured in Michael Cronin's phrase "the translator as forger of nation and empire" (2006:103), is central to the fictional representations of the translator that I will discuss below.

Translating empire

The Russian empire, "the largest and most diverse territorial empire the world has ever seen" (Hosking 1997:3), is a rich source for the study of translation and national identity. Russia has been a large, multilingual, multiethnic empire since 1552 when Ivan IV conquered the Khanate of Kazan and first assumed the title *tsar*, derived from the Latin *caesar*, meaning "emperor." As Russia continued to annex a huge number of non-Russian-speaking peoples in the South, Peter the Great's policy of forced Westernization led to the creation of a polyglot urban elite. In fact, many members of Russia's elite in the eighteenth and nineteenth centuries spoke French—some as their first language—and many were not ethnically Russian. Nonetheless, imperialist themes in Russian literature were long ignored not only by postcolonial scholars, who favored the overseas theaters of European colonization—Africa, Asia, and the Americas—but also by scholars of the region itself, who tended "to conflate the Russian nation with its empire" (Miner 2001:online; see also Thompson 2000, Lieven 2000, and Etkind 2011).[1] Peter Scotto noted in 1992 that "Russia's literary engagement with the Caucasus has yet to receive an adequate interpretation" (1992:246). Eva Thompson, in *Imperial Knowledge: Russian Literature and Colonialism*, went somewhat further, suggesting a tacit complicity in the Russian imperial project on the part of scholars of Russian literature: "Within the agreed-upon conceptual framework of literary scholarship on Russia," Eva Thompson argues, "Russian colonialism faded from view" (2000:2).

Serious engagement on the part of literary scholars with Russia's imperial identity is relatively recent. The publication of Edward Said's *Orientalism* in 1978, which exposed how Western literatures were deeply complicit in naturalizing a vision of the Orient as underdeveloped and decadent, led Russianists finally to confront the relationship of Russia's literature to the Russian imperial project. As Scotto puts it, "In the light of the work done by Edward Said and other critics of colonial literature, it is no longer tenable to understand Russia's Caucasian literature in a strictly literary-historical sense as a local variant of thematic material adopted from western European models" (1992:247). While Thompson insists that Russian writers were fully complicit in Russia's empire building, other studies, such as Scotto's "Prisoners of the Caucasus: Ideologies of Imperialism in Lermontov's

---

[1] Even following the collapse of the Soviet Union, scholars in postcolonial studies tend to ignore Eastern Europe and Eurasia. As Moore puts it, "How extraordinarily postcolonial the societies of the former Soviet regions are, and [...] how extraordinarily little attention is paid to this fact" (2001:114).

'Bela'" (1992), Susan Layton's *Russian Literature and Empire: Conquest of the Caucasus from Pushkin to Tolstoy* (1994), and more recently Valeria Sobol's "The Uncanny Frontier of Russian Identity: Travel, Ethnography, and Empire in Lermontov's 'Taman'" (2011), present a more nuanced picture. While Layton ascribes complicity to a number of writers, such as Bestuzhev-Marlinsky, who were enormously popular in their time but are largely ignored by scholars today, she singles out several authors who clearly sought in their literary works to expose the violence and hypocrisy of Russia's civilizing mission in the Caucasus, the legacy of which is felt still today in the ongoing conflict in Chechnya. Most illustrative in that regard, according to Layton, is Tolstoy's late story *Hadji Murat*.

Layton's reading of this novel is unique in its focus on acts of translation as central to the anti-imperialist thematics of the work, which, she argues, "blasted Russia's reigning cultural mythology of the civilizing mission, while recuperating violated truths of romantic discourse" (1994:253). By unpacking what she calls the novel's "preoccupation with language's embedment in the structure of imperial power," Layton models a reading of translation as theme in Russian colonialist literature (264). Tolstoy, Layton argues, triangulates language use in the novel by introducing the question of class into his representation of cultural and linguistic difference. Early in the novel, for example, a Russian peasant soldier, Avdeev, has a successful, although almost entirely nonverbal, conversation with some Chechen scouts. That conversation, "comprised of a few words, gestures, tone of voice and a sense of understanding which passes through eye contact" (268), is contrasted to the complex, élite style of Tolstoy's narration. "Sophisticated vocabulary, complicated syntax and *untranslated French* in conversation between aristocratic characters create a verbal texture which is opaque" by comparison not only with Tolstoy's earlier writings but also, more clearly, with Avdeev's talk (270; italics added). Tolstoy's purpose in doing this, Layton conjectures, is to implicate his upper-class readers "in crimes of the imperial Russian state" (271).

Throughout the novel, Tolstoy contrasts the orality of simple people, associating it with honesty and authenticity, to the written idiom of the élite and of the state, which is marked by obscuring layers of mediation and a hint of mendacity.[2] This contrast is brought home in the hollow heroic rhetoric

---

[2] Compare this to earlier depictions of Caucasian tribes, whose orality marked them as primitive and uncivilized. As Scotto puts it, "To the Europeanized Russians who undertook to describe them, the mountain tribes of the Caucasus could only appear 'primitive.' They had no writing system and hence no written literature or history" (1992:248).

of the official army communiqué announcing Andreev's senseless death in battle. Moreover, against the backdrop of a textual world "where dialogue fails," the conspicuous presence of interpreters in the novel is no coincidence. In *Hadji Murat*, Layton claims:

> Very few direct connections are made within the vast cast of dramatis personae. Foreign languages and cultural codes erect barriers to unmediated communication. Interpreters are required, and words are wielded regularly in officialdom to distort reality. In this realm of impeded communication the Caucasian hero finds no Russian other able to understand him properly and complement his self. Nobody is there but Tolstoy to orchestrate the story of the elaborately failed cross-cultural dialogue which in its closing episode degenerates into an exchange of bullets. (281)

Tolstoy's focus on translation also serves to call attention to "the near non-existence of the authentic tribal word in Russian literature prior to *Hadji Murat*" (291).

Following Layton, I will investigate scenes of translation—specifically, scenes of mistranslation—in two Russian novels: one from the early nineteenth century, Mikhail Lermontov's *A Hero of Our Time*, and the other from the late twentieth century, Felix Roziner's *A Certain Finkelmeyer*. But, unlike Tolstoy, who in *Hadji Murat* presented translation as an instrument of imperial domination, I will focus on the subversive potential of (mis)translation as carried out by the translator-forger, who exploits the slipperiness of language and the false equivalence of homonyms not only to expose the precarious foundation of Russia's imperial identity but also to "reshape the terms of hegemony" (Rafael 2007:242).[3] The character of the translator-forger challenges Thompson's contention that "not a single Russian writer of note has questioned the necessity or wisdom of using the nation's resources to subjugate more and more territory for the empire or to hold on to territories that are not Russian, or even Slavic. Not one has questioned the moral ambiguities of colonial violence" (2000:33).

---

[3] For an insightful discussion of the deconstructive potential of homonymy, see Barbara Cassin's "Homonymy and Amphiboly, or Radical Evil in Translation," in which she argues "that homonymy destabilizes language in its very structure" (Apter 2013:25).

Translation effects

One of the ways authors lend metaphorical meaning to foreign words in literary texts is by staging acts of translation. By commenting on the translatability of a word or phrase, or of a language, authors establish, however tentatively, some kind of relationship between the native and foreign cultures. Perhaps unavoidably, translatability assumes a political resonance in works of colonialist literature. To the extent that an imperial identity is founded on transcending linguistic and cultural differences, the translatability of foreign words cannot help but comment on the state of the empire. In thematicizing translatability, authors can support the illusion of an imperial identity, as well as challenge, or even subvert it. In order to understand the various effects produced by the representation of translation in works of Russian imperial fiction, I will present a simple typology of translation effects. I describe these effects below as *total translation, zero translation*, and *mistranslation* before focusing on scenes of mistranslation in the two novels.

If we imagine this typology as a scale, one end of that scale would be represented by what can be referred to as *total translation*, produced when the source utterance is suppressed and the reader is provided only with the target utterance, that is, the translation. In such situations, the reader is given to believe that the translation represents an unproblematic exchange, a perfect—faithful—mapping of the two languages and cultures. This may be accomplished by simply indicating that the speaker's utterance was spoken in the source language, i.e., "he said in French," or by providing a description of the speaker's linguistic ability as in the following passage from Tolstoy's *War and Peace*: "He spoke that refined French in which our grandfathers not only spoke, but also thought, and with the gently modulated, patronizing intonation that was natural to a man of consequence who had grown old in society and at court" (Tolstoy 2007:5).

Total translation typically produces the "effect of equivalence," similar to what Venuti describes as the "effect of transparency" (1992:4), George Lakoff as "total commensurability" (1987:322), and Niranjana as "universal translatability" (1992:55). In his essay "The Effects of Translation," Phillip Lewis describes how this effect is produced in the English translation of Jacques Derrida's essay "Mythologie blanche" [White Mythology] through the elimination of foreign words. "The text of [Derrida's] 'White Mythology' sometimes drops the words in brackets [German source terms]," Lewis notes, "making do with just the English words. One effect of this kind of omission is to reduce the attention paid to translation that is sustained in the original" (2004:265). By removing the source terms, the translator de-problematizes his translation, denying the reader the opportunity to evaluate the translation against the original. In this way, the translator creates an effect, or illusion, of equivalence where there was none in Derrida's original. The effect of equivalence produced in instances of total translation often downplays the specific or denotative message content of the utterance in favor of a broader referent—translatability itself. In this way, representations of total translation contribute to what Niranjana describes as "the absence, lack or repression of an awareness of asymmetry and historicity" in translated encounters (1992:9).

At the other end of the scale of translation effects lies *zero translation*, which describes a situation in which no translation of the source text or utterance is provided, suggesting a problematic or impossible mapping of the two languages and cultures.[4] For example, in Dostoevsky's *Crime and Punishment*, the hero Raskolnikov encapsulates the continental philosophy of social Darwinism, which he condemns, in the following statement: *Crevez, chiens, si vous n'êtes pas contents* ("Die, dogs, if you're not happy").[5] By delivering the statement in French and offering no translation, Dostoevsky suggests the incompatibility of this philosophical position with Russian cultural values: it is untranslatable. Along the same lines, Raskolonikov refuses translation work offered him by his friend Razumikhin. The text for translation is a socially progressive treatise in German entitled "Is Woman a Human Being?"[6] Raskolnikov rejects the

---

[4] Zero translation is often used to describe one of the unusual cases of translation compiled by G. C. Kálmán (1986), specifically case number three, in which a source text has no target text. What I refer to as "total translation" is related to Kálmán's first case, in which a target text has no source text. While this case is often referred to as pseudo-translation, I use total translation to refer also to cases in which the source text is, for whatever reason, unavailable, and so the reader cannot check the accuracy of the target text. In other words, case number one need not always be a ruse. In any case, the effect of withholding the source text is that the reader is unable to verify the accuracy of the target text and so is led to believe the translation is unproblematic, transparent, unworthy of comment.

[5] All translations are my own unless otherwise indicated.

[6] Dostoevsky does not provide the German title of the article. The Russian translation of the title, however, sounds like a parody of an article by Dostoevsky's contemporary G. Z. Eliseev, "Various Opinions on the Question: Are Women People? Ancient and Modern Opinions. Ours is on the Side of Women [Raznye mneniia o tom: zhenshchiny—liudi li?—Mneniia drevnikh, mneniia noveishie.—Nashe predubezhdeniie v pol'zu zhenshchin"], which was published in the journal *Sovremennik* in 1861 (Dostoevskii 1973:371n). Of course, by making the article German, Dostoevsky indexes this progressive debate as foreign. And so, it is interesting that when Raskolnikov, on the road to repentance, begins to read the bible, no mention is made of the fact that this text too is a translation. Fully consonant with Russian cultural values, this text reads "like an original."

offer, telling Razumikhin: "I don't need...translations!" (1999:108). Here, translation serves as a metonym for the corrupting influence of contemporary Western culture (for more on this, see Chapter 3 in this volume), which, Dostoevsky suggests, should not be carried over into Russia.[7] Through this refusal to translate, then, Dostoevsky "show[s] in his major characters the persistence of something he considers 'Russian,' even in those who are most powerfully and corrosively affected by Western European ideas" (Frank 2010:244). In *War and Peace*, Tolstoy suggests the inapplicability of Western medical approaches to Russia by showing the utter failure of Western-trained doctors, "who talked endlessly in French, German and Latin" (1964:II. 776–777; qtd. in Sirotkina 2002:82), to treat his heroine, Natasha Rostova—they could not translate her Russian malady into the language of Western medicine.

Acts of *mistranslation* represent a third category and produce effects quite different from those of either zero or total translation. While mistranslation is related to zero translation insofar as both attest to the complex, problematic nature of cross-cultural communication, acts of mistranslation expose the distorting power of translation and the ignorance and/or deception of the translator. And so, whereas zero translation suggests, as in the above-mentioned example from *Crime and Punishment*, resistance to foreign ways, or cultural untranslatability, mistranslation goes further, one could say, by exposing the "asymmetry and historicity of translation" (Niranjana 1992:9) and so has a deconstructive potential that zero translation lacks.

Much interesting work has been done in exploring representations of mistranslation in the context of émigré literature, specifically in the work of

---

[7] Dostoevsky's relationship to translation was profoundly ambivalent. On the one hand, the author, who appeared in print for the first time as the translator of Honoré de Balzac's *Eugénie Grandet*, "continued to the end of his days to entertain a conviction that Russia would benefit from works of foreign provenance" (Burnett and Lygo 2013:16). At the same time, his participation in the Petrashevsky Circle—which led to his mock execution and subsequent imprisonment and exile—must have made him acutely aware of the politically subversive potential of the translation of Western texts. Mikhail Butashevich-Petrashevsky, the leader of the group, was a translator at the Ministry of Foreign Affairs and kept a large library of "forbidden"—mostly Western—works, which he lent to the members of the circle. Dostoevsky is known to have borrowed several French works on socialist theory from the library (Frank 2010:137, 142). Moreover, Petrashevsky was one of the editors of *The Pocket Dictionary of Foreign Words Which Have Entered the Russian Language*, which promoted democratic and materialist ideas. Petrashevsky coedited the first edition and edited the second, for which he wrote a great many of the articles. For more on Petrashevsky and his circle, see Semevskii (1922), especially Chapter II (*Karmannyi slovar' inostrannykh slov*, 58–83) and Chapter VI (*Biblioteki Petrashevtsev*, 132–165).

Vladimir Nabokov. As Juliette Taylor comments, "throughout his oeuvre, Nabokov's fictional treatment of translation tends to highlight the incommensurability of different languages, and the failure of complete and effective interlingual communication" (2005:266). Nabokov's exiles are often lost in a linguistic maze, led astray by the false equivalence of homophones. Consider, for example, the Russian heroine of Nabokov's short story "Krasavitsa" [The Beauty], translated into English as "Russian Beauty." A Russian émigré living in Berlin, the eponymous heroine's speech is described in the following way:

> She spoke French fluently, pronouncing *les gens* (the servants) as if rhyming with *agence* and splitting *août* (August) in two syllables (*a-ou*). She naively translated the Russian grabezhi (robberies) as *les grabuges* (quarrels) and used some archaic French locutions that had somehow survived in old Russian families, but she rolled her r's most convincingly even though she had never been to France. (Nabokov 1973:4)

Her language, somehow out of sync with her time and place, reflects the general disorientation of the émigré experience.

The effect of mistranslation is amplified when it highlights, as Vincente Rafael puts it, "the sheer lack of connection that threatens the terrifying dissolutions of communicative possibilities" (2005:15). Consider, for example, the mistranslation offered by Pushkin at the beginning of part two of his novel in verse, *Evgenii Onegin*. There, he presents the following "translation," based on the illogical—from a semantic point of view—association of homophones: O rus!, the Latin for countryside, which he attributes to Horace, followed by O Rus'!, the medieval, poetic term for Russia. The translation signals his characters' move from the capital to the countryside while simultaneously lampooning the imperial pretensions of Alexandrine Russia, as exemplified by the imperial capital of St. Petersburg, and mocking the idealization of the countryside in Romantic nationalist discourse.

Colonization as mistranslation: Lermontov's *Hero of Our Time*

The motif of mistranslation is deployed in a sustained way throughout Mikhail Lermontov's *A Hero of Our Time* (1840) as a commentary on Russia's imperial project. The novel has a complex structure consisting of three narrative frames and five stories, and the action takes place in the Caucasus region of the Russian empire. In the first story, "Bela," Maksim Maksimych, a simple Russian soldier who has risen to the rank of junior captain, relates to the story's first person narrator, a would-be writer traveling in the Caucasus, of how Pechorin, the elusive "hero" of the novel, traded a horse for a Tartar princess, who then died of neglect in the Russian fort. While recounting the tale, the narrator tells the readers they might want to skip a few pages to the end of Bela's tale, but then adds: "Only I don't advise you to do this because the passage over the Mountain of the Cross (or, as the scholar Gamba calls it, *le mont St. Christophe*) is worthy of your curiosity" (Lermontov 2004:29).[8] The Russian reader immediately understands that Gamba—a reference to the French consul in Tiflis, Georgia, who published an account of his travels in Russia's colonized periphery—has mistranslated the mountain's Russian name, *krestovaia*, an adjective derived from the Russian word *krest*, meaning "cross," which despite a phonetic similarity, has nothing to do semantically with Gamba's *St. Christophe, or "St. Christopher."* Vladimir Nabokov, who translated the novel with his son Dmitry, apparently felt the mistranslation was so important to the novel's thematics that he translated the Russian verb *nazyvat'*, "to call," as "to mis-call." He also added a footnote, describing Gamba's mistranslation as a "blunder" (Lermontov 1992:179). The effect of the mistranslation is indeed significant insofar as it cues the reader to interpret the passage ironically, putting Gamba's scholarly credentials into question.

Lermontov's treatment of Gamba would have come as no surprise to contemporary Russian readers. Gamba's *Voyage dans la Russie méridionale* was, in Layton's words, "full of disdain for Russia's failure to transform the Caucasus into a viable colony" (1994:79). Moreover, he assigned Russia "to a low, Asian rung on civilization's great ladder" (79), suggesting that Russia was not civilized enough to successfully colonize other peoples. It is difficult, however, to see this scene of mistranslation as merely an act of revenge on the French consul. There is no reliable narrator in Lermontov's novel who might put an end to the irony unleashed by the passage, fixing it firmly on Gamba alone. While on an extratextual level, exposing Gamba's mistranslation may have been a way for Lermontov to assert his superior knowledge of the region—he spent many years in the Caucasus as a soldier—at the same time, he may have been in partial agreement with Gamba's critique. In a preface to the first publication of "Bela" in *Notes of the Fatherland* in 1839, Lermontov offered "a description of the journey past the Mountain of the

---

[8] The original Russian reads: "Только я вам этого не советую, потому что переезд через Крестовую гору (или как называет ее ученый Гамба, le Mont St. Christophe) достоин вашего любопытство" (Lermontov 1959:II. 386.)

Cross and a scholarly gloss on the legend that the cross was placed there by Peter the Great" (Binyon 1992:xv). In other words, Lermontov was aware that the Russian name for the mountain symbolized Russia's imperial conquest of the region. And so, while Gamba may have mistranslated the Russian name for the mountain, suggesting the arrogance of Western Europeans' "imperial knowledge," Peter's celebration of a bloody imperial conquest with a cross says something about the contradictions at the center of Russia's civilizing mission in the Caucasus. In fact, in his narrative poem "Izmail Bey," Lermontov suggests that for the natives of the region, the cross did indeed symbolize Russian colonization: As they are preparing Izmail Bey for burial, "they take his St. George award as the Christian cross of an 'accursed giaour' " (Layton 1994:139). Moreover, the narrator's failure to provide an "original" native name for the mountain only reinforces the ironic theatricality of Lermontov's presentation of the Caucasus as a stage for Russia's élite, with the locals playing only bit parts.[9]

The theme of mistranslation continues into the next paragraph, when the narrator recounts his subsequent travel in the region:

> And so, we were descending Mount Gud into the Chertova Valley. There's a romantic name! You could already see the evil spirit's nest among the inaccessible precipices—but that wasn't true. The name Chertova Valley comes from the word *cherta*—line—not *chert*—devil—for here at one time ran the border with Georgia. (Lermontov 2004:29–30)

Here, the romantic mistranslation of the valley's name obscures the colonial reality of the region by substituting a fictitious spirit for the border of a once independent Georgia. The passage then concludes with the narrator's observation that: "This valley was buried in snow-drifts that reminded me *rather vividly* of Saratov, Tambov, and other dear spots of our fatherland" (Lermontov 2004:30; italics added). Nabokov suggests the narrator's comment regarding Saratov and Tambov should be read ironically as the cities "connote backwood, in-the-sticks provincialism" (Lermontov 1992:179). However, in keeping with the passage as a whole, the irony here more likely involves the notion that a comparison between these Caucasian villages and good old Russian cities is predicated on their being covered

---

[9]   Valeria Sobol makes the point, "In Lermontov's novel the Russian military men—be it the traveling narrator of 'Bela,' the experienced officer Maksim Maksimovich, or Pechorin himself—never directly face danger from the highlanders, while the idle members of Russian high society at the spa of Piatigorsk only fantasize about the Circassians' supposed attacks in broad daylight. Instead, a more authentic danger, at least for the protagonist, typically comes from within, from Russia proper, as it were" (2011:65).

in snow; that is to say, similarity is only achieved through the masking of differences. The effect produced by these banalizing comparisons is similar to the one achieved in Pushkin's travel essay "Journey to Arzrum" (1836), in which the cosmopolitan traveler is denied authentic interaction with the foreign, entering instead, as Monica Greenleaf describes it, a "system of citation from other textual authorities" (Greenleaf 1994:146). "Attempting to escape from Russia and contemporaneity," the Russian characters in *Hero of Our Time*, like Pushkin, "discovered the impossibility of crossing over into another culture, another land, another state of mind; every border crossed evaporates, is not *the* border" (155).

These glaring examples of mistranslation cast some doubt on Valeria Sobol's claim that the Caucasus is presented in Lermontov's novel "as a culturally 'translatable' world that can be described in familiar terms with relative ease" (2011:77). She then gives several examples of translations provided by Maksim Maksimych that reduce Caucasian customs and artifacts to banality through comparison with everyday Russian customs and artifacts. I would read these translations, however, not so much as proof of the "translatability" of the Caucasus but as another example of mistranslation, or at least bad translation, on the part of the Caucasus's imperial overlords. This kind of radically domesticating translation by the simple Maksim Maksimych does indeed, as Sobol suggests, undermine, "to a large degree, the Caucasus's exoticism so avidly sought by the Russian travelers of the Romantic era" (77). But this, I would argue, is less a commentary on the exoticism of the Caucasus than it is a critique of Maksim Maksimovich's banalizing translations, which fail to do justice to the cultural specificity of the region. Scotto alludes to the political implications of Maksim Maksimovich's translations, which stand in for real native voices: "Marginalized as part of the scenery, the [Ossetian] drivers, like their horses and oxen, apparently exist only to facilitate the Russians' travel. *They have no real voices of their own* and emerge from the background only to the degree they are spoken for by Maksim Maksimovich, an old Caucasian hand whose commentary on the journey 'interprets' the Oriental world of the Caucasus for the less experienced traveling narrator" (1992:250; italics mine). Here, Maksim Maksimovich, with his cultural biases, appears as the representative of a tradition "in which the West is authorized to speak for and about the people it considers" (251).

Throughout the novel, Lermontov associates the Russian empire with both figurative and literal acts of mistranslation insofar as all the stories involve some sort of failed or foiled border crossing: Pechorin's native bride, Bela, won for a horse, is taken from her native tribe and eventually wastes away in a Russian fort; the locals in "Taman" engage in smuggling, an activity that, as Sobol points out, "invokes border crossing, both physically and metaphorically" (2011:71–72), and Pechorin's cross-dressing as a Circassian warrior in "Princess Mary" only underscores the absence in the story of true originals—that is, native Circassians. In this sense, the Caucasus and Russia's borderlands are presented in the novel, I would argue, not as easily translatable, but as ultimately resisting translation—as when Bela on her deathbed refuses to convert to Russian Orthodoxy, much to the chagrin of Maxim Maximovich.[10]

That the theme of mistranslation in the novel carries with it oppositional political import is lent further credence by the intertextual references to George Sand's short story "L'Orco," which offers a negative portrayal of the colonization of the Italian city-state of Venice by Austria, which occurred in the late eighteenth century.[11] The liberation of Venice, like the liberation of Greece, became a cause-célèbre among the Romantic writers of the early nineteenth century. André Chénier's poem "Près des bords où Venise est reine de la mer," for example, was well known in Russia and translated by Pushkin. In Lermontov's "Taman," the local, colonized people (the blind boy in "Taman" speaks Ukrainian) are symbolized by an alluring, enigmatic woman who affects an almost supernatural power over the male protagonist, reversing the colonial relationship of master and subject. Similarly, Sand's heroine—despite her repeated lamentation "O servitude! Servitude!"— exerts absolute power over the infatuated Austrian officer Franz. And, despite the squalor of the Russian coastal town of Taman, which suggests Lermontov is parodying Sand's magnificent Venice, Lermontov's first person narrator, Pechorin, is, like Franz, disoriented and befuddled by the almost supernatural "powers" of the ethnically mixed locals: Lermontov's blind boy can speak both in dialect and in standard Russian and travels about on his own along treacherous cliff-side paths, while the captivating heroine is described by the narrator as the water-nymph Undine. Indeed, both authors make a point of mentioning that their male protagonists do not speak or understand the local dialects, which puts them at a distinct disadvantage. (When Franz first encounters the nameless heroine of "L'Orco," she is

---

[10] Mistranslation is also a theme in Lermontov's narrative poem "Izmail Bey." As Layton explains, "When the villagers prepare Izmail-Bey's body for burial, they misread signs of his fourteen-year sojourn in Russia. They take his St. George award as the Christian cross of an 'accursed giaour' and are puzzled by a golden curl in his locket" (1994:139).

[11] The city-state of Venice was colonized by Napoleon in 1797 and then became an Austrian possession under the Treaty of Campo Fornio, which was signed later that year. Venice acquired independence briefly in 1848–1849 and would become a part of the newly created Kingdom of Italy in 1866. Like the cause of Greek independence from the Turks, the colonization of Venice was a popular theme among Romantic writers.

speaking in the Venetian dialect; similarly, when Pechorin first encounters the blind boy, the latter answers him in Ukrainian, considered at the time to be a dialect of Russian.)

The theme of mastery and oppression runs throughout both works. As Priscilla Meyer points out, "By using 'L'Orco' as a subtext, Lermontov draws an implicit parallel between Austria's imperial domination of Venice and Russia's colonization of the Caucasus. Aware, like Franz, of 'all the vices of the government he served,' Lermontov sympathizes with the Caucasians, yet, also like Franz, finds himself in the role of [a] Russian officer attempting to impose an oppressive foreign rule on them" (2008:59). Lermontov, Meyer argues, offers a realist rewriting of Sand's story. Whereas Sand's heroine is believed at first to be a smuggler and then turns out to be a supernatural incarnation of Venetian patriotism, the demonic-seeming local characters in Lermontov's story are revealed in the end to be nothing more than "honest smugglers" (2004:70)—benign forgers who make their living by crossing and double-crossing the various linguistic and political borders meant to contain them.

Mistranslation as political dissent: Roziner's *A Certain Finkelmeyer*

Translation played an important and very visible role within the Soviet empire as reflected in the domestic policy of *druzhba narodov*, or friendship of Soviet peoples, on the one hand, and in the Soviet Union's foreign policy, which sought to establish Moscow as the capital of world communism. This is evident in a 1949 speech by Soviet writer Aleksandr Fadeev, in which he boasts of the large number of American titles translated into Russian and the other languages of the Soviet Union, and of the enormity of their circulation numbers:

> According to data from the All-Union Book Chamber, from 1917–1948, that is, for the entire existence of the new Russia, the works of 206 American writers (I am speaking here only of literature) were translated into Russian and other languages of the Soviet Union. Overall, 2,245 works of American literature were published in a general circulation of 39,709,000 copies. Among them, Jack London's works were published in a print run of 11,164,000, in 29 of the languages of the peoples of the Soviet Union, Upton Sinclair's, in a print run of 2,951,000, in 15 languages, [Ernest] Thompson Seton's, in a print run of 2,268,000, in 21 languages, Mark Twain's in a print run of 3,464,000, in 22 languages,

O'Henry's, in a print run of 1,618,000, Theodore Dreiser's, in a print run of 501,000, James Fenimore Cooper's, in a print run of 452,000, [Erskine] Caldwell's, in a print run of 290,000, Sinclair Lewis's, in a print run of 276,000, Edgar Allen Poe's, in a print run of 204,000, Washington Irving's, in a print run of 276,000, Longfellow's, in a print run of 195,000, Steinbeck's, in a print run of 375,000, Walt Whitman, in a print run of 104,000, of Hemingway's, in a print run of 130,000, and Langston Hughes's, in a print run of 119,000. (Fadeev 2013a:84)

Within the Soviet Union, translation policy had a "civilizing" dimension, providing the indigenous peoples of northern Siberia and the Soviet Far East with a written alphabet and providing all the peoples of the Soviet Union with access to the greatest works of world literature.

While the statistics generated by the Soviet translation project are impressive and the ostensible purpose, noble, the actual practice was often much less so. Many translations were made from an interlinear "trot" (*podstrochnik*), and the selection of texts for translation was based on ideological correctness. As Werner Winter put it, "the use of translation as a tool in political strategy" left a dubious legacy (1964:295). Instead of providing a conduit for truly "foreign" ideas, the translations of what came to be referred to as the Soviet School of Translation exhibited deeply domesticating tendencies, condemning stylistic innovation of any kind, whether the result of a close translation of the source text, referred to as *formalizm*, or of the imposition of the translator's own style onto the target text, referred to as *otsebiatina* ("from oneself").

The official Soviet policy of friendship of peoples was also predicated on a deep-seated Russian linguistic, cultural, and political chauvinism. Very little translation occurred among the "minor" languages of the Soviet Union; most translation took place between the center (Russia) and the periphery (non-Russian peoples). It is only through translation into Russian, the Soviet writer Fadeev proclaimed, that the works of the non-Russian peoples could enter "the cultural fund of the entire Soviet people" (1960:447). Moreover, the reality of censorship in the Soviet Union often cast the translator, in the words of the Soviet-era translator and theorist Vladimir Rossel's, as "a *propagandist* of friendship among the peoples of our country ... an active figure of Soviet literature, to struggle against all manifestations of bourgeois nationalism" (qtd. in Leighton 1991:18). And so, many of these translations from the languages of the various Soviet peoples were of very poor quality, something lampooned by the poet Arsenii Tarkovsky in his poem "The Translator" (Perevodchik), which included the refrain: "Oh, those eastern translators! How you make my head hurt" (*Akh, vostochnye pervodchiki, kak bolit ot vas golova*) (1982:69).

The much-vaunted policy of friendship of Soviet peoples also served to conceal the unsavory realities of life for Russia's non-Russian peoples, especially those living outside the two capitals of Moscow and Leningrad. In Siberia, for example, native peoples enjoyed a significantly lower standard of living than Russians:

> In 1989, only 3 percent of native dwellings had gas, 0.4 percent had water, and 0.1 percent had central heat. Most had no sewage disposal, and their size was half of that of Russian dwellings. The native villages were often destroyed by fiat of the Moscow government, and the natives were forced to move to larger settlements, which made it difficult or impossible for them to provide for themselves. (Thompson 2000:137)

In his novel *A Certain Finkelmeyer* (*Nekto Finkel'meier*), which circulated in the Soviet Union in samizdat in the late 1970s until it was finally published in the West in 1981, and then in 1991 in an English translation, Felix Roziner exposes the contradictions and hypocrisy of the Soviet policy of friendship of peoples through the character of the translator-forger Aaron-Chaim Mendelevich Finkelmeyer. The eponymous hero of the novel, whose name Harriet Murav points out, "is supposed to sound too Jewish" (2005:2401), is unable to find a publishing venue for his original poetry in the Soviet Union and so poses as a translator of a fictional native Siberian poet in order to get his work into print.

Finkelmeyer is patterned in many obvious ways on the poet Joseph Brodsky, whose trial as a social parasite was a cause célèbre for the Soviet intelligentsia in the 1960s. In fact, Finkelmeyer's trial on the same charge contains actual quotations from Brodsky's trial. Roziner, however, refuses to portray Finkelmeyer in a hagiographic light, presenting him instead in comical terms as a complex, thoroughly flawed individual with an extraordinary poetic gift. Roziner eschews the simple dichotomies of Cold War thinking, which divided Soviet cultural production into official and dissident. Indeed, Finkelmeyer is empowered by his ruse. As Murav points out, "Finkel'maier produces his best poetry in the guise of translations of the works of 'Aion Neprigen'" (Murav 2005:2402). In this way, Roziner illustrates how the unique disciplinary regime that regulated artistic production in the Soviet Union "both enabled a specific type of cultural production, and was at the same time fractured by its own products" (Murav 2005:2402). From the point of view of the individual artist, translation is a highly ambivalent site of cultural production, involving the humbling of the individual—in this case, the minority individual—while offering what Murav refers to as "counter-hegemonic possibilities" (2404). Finkelmeyer becomes the very embodiment of the contradictions underpinning the Soviet imperial project, which would collapse only two decades later.

The novel opens when Leonid Nikolsky, an engineer and Moscow intellectual, first discovers Finkelmeyer's poems on a flight to Siberia while paging through the journal *Friendship*, which "specialized in translations from literatures of the non-Russian nationalities" (Roziner 1991:11). Nikolsky notes the abysmal quality of the poetry: "One after the other [the poems] proved to be silly, high-flown bouts of rhetoric coerced into a meter and surrounded with empty, unnecessary rhymes by the cold calculation of their translators. As a poetry lover Nikolsky felt something akin to revulsion" (11). But then he alights on a cluster of five poems in Russian translation authored by a certain Aion Niprigen, described as a poet of the Tongor people of North Siberia. Nikolsky finds the poems to be "magnificent": "they had a primordial feeling about them, a feeling of the world's perfection, overlaid by a mother-of-pearl reflection of the North and suffused with an inexplicable, all but ineffable yearning" (11–12). He even finds a similarity to Dante. These poems, it turns out later, were actually written by Finkelmeyer. The reference to Dante here is significant for a number of reasons. First, it sets up an opposition of the state-sponsored ephemera that made up the bulk of the journal's contents to the "eternal" works of the canon of World literature. But Dante is also significant in Russia as a poet-exile, a popular topos for Russian, then Soviet writers. As John M. Kopper notes, Dante "became a critical fulcrum on which the nation's intelligentsia balanced its arguments about culture" (1994:25). He was also seen as being thoroughly connected to the politics of his time. As Aleksandr Veselovsky puts it, Dante "became in turn a heretic, a revolutionary, and the fervent defender of a unified Italy—in each instance according to the requirements of the time" (qtd. in Kopper 1994:25); in other words, he was a literary survivor.

From the very start, the novel exposes the contradictions and absurdities of the official Soviet policy of friendship of peoples for, while Finkelmeyer's editor in Moscow encourages him to bring back a "native poet" (Roziner 1991:83) from Siberia, Finkelmeyer himself is unable to attend university or to publish under his own name because he is a Jew. Similarly, his lover Danuta is a Lithuanian who is exiled to Siberia. Nikolsky, an ethnic Russian, is little concerned with the fate of Russia's ethnic minorities, commenting rather nonchalantly that "he had heard some vague reports about nationalities being shuffled about, but he hadn't remembered which ones they were" (Roziner 1991:212). The brutal reality was that "the deportations from Latvia, Lithuania, and Estonia that took place at that time [1939–1941] destroyed some 20 percent of these small nations' citizens" (Thompson 2000:134). The Soviet policy of friendship of peoples did not, it seems, extend equally to all the peoples of the

Soviet Union, and Finkelmeyer's adventures expose the brutal realty behind what Terry Martin (2001) refers to as the "affirmative action empire."

It turns out that while on official business in Siberia—having been forced to take a job in the Ministry of Fisheries—Finkelmeyer met Danil Manakin, a cultural representative of a small ethnic people, the Tongors. Finkelmeyer, who had published a collection of military verse—he had been named the regimental poet while serving in the army—under the Russified pseudonym A. Yefimov, concocts the scheme to publish his poems as translations of Tongor originals; he finds Manakin to be the perfect dupe to pose as the first poet of the Tongor people. The premise of Roziner's novel is not entirely absurd if one considers the case of Dzhambul Dzhabaev, a Kazazh folk bard who became a factory of "pseudotranslations" when a number of Russian translators were tasked with creating translations of non-existent Kazakh originals (Toury 1995:44).[12] Or, consider the experience of the prose writer Sergei Dovlatov while on a trip to the Kalmyk city of Elista, where he was greeted by a local poet who presented the Russian writer with what he said was an interlinear translation of one of his poems, asking Dovlatov to provide a poetic Russian translation. It turned out, however, there was no original (Friedberg 1997:179).

The scheme is successful at first and Manakin is offered a contract for an entire volume of "translated" verse. Finkelmeyer, however, grows uncomfortable with the arrangement and so consults his mentor, referred to throughout the novel as the Master, an avant-garde poet in the 1920s who turned to literary translation from the French when he was no longer permitted to publish his own original work. As a translator, the Master is adept at "elevating" the interlinear translations he is given:

> All the Master had to do was make a twist here, a turn there, and suddenly the poem would work. The poets he thus rendered into Russian wrote articles about problems of translation, naively admitting that the Russian version surpassed the original and thanking him for guiding their "mountain streams into the ocean of Russian poetry." (Roziner 1991:83)

The Master tries to convince Finkelmeyer to continue using Manakin as his "double," explaining that:

> Manakin has given you the chance of a lifetime. No Finkelmeyer could publish these poems. No Ivanov for that matter. They're too removed

---

[12] Of course, with representations of pseudo-translations—as opposed to pseudo-translations themselves—the mystification is exposed, or, in Gideon Toury's words, "the veil has been lifted" (1995:40).

from reality—asocial, idealistic, pantheistic. That's what any editor would tell you in his rejection note. But poets from national minority groups have a certain leeway. They don't need to satisfy rigorous socialist standards. So long live Danil Manakin! (86)

Once he explains to Finkelmeyer what he must already have known—that because of the content of his poems and because he was a Jew, he could never publish his work in the Soviet Union—Finkelmeyer agrees to continue as Manakin's translator. Finkelmeyer finally acknowledges, not without irony, that there are many ways to live as a poet under the Soviet regime, "the most honorable being translation" (182).

Nikolsky, in turn, encourages Manakin to remain in his arrangement with Finkelmeyer by posing as an official in the realm of culture and aping official Soviet-ese: " 'The cultural front is important now,' said Manakin slowly and clearly. 'We are a small minority. The party says we need national forms of socialist culture to … so we can …' " At this point Nikolsky prompts him, " ' … take your place in the multinational socialist state, isn't that it? [...] Well, if that's what the Party says, then of course it's important' " (73). Nikolsky, entertaining himself at the expense of Manakin and Soviet literary policy, encourages the Tongor "poet" to continue the ruse for the sake of the Party.

Their arrangement, according to which they split all royalties, falls apart, however, when Finkelmeyer is brought up on the charge of "social parasitism" for having quit his job with the Ministry of Fisheries so as to devote himself entirely to writing poetry. He planned to live off the advance from the volume of translations, half of which Manakin had already transferred into his bank account. Manakin, too, was dissatisfied, tired of playing Finkelmeyer's double, especially now that he was celebrated throughout the USSR as "the first Tongor poet" (171). In a gesture of independence, he decides to discard his pseudonym Aion Neprigen, which means "good fortune" in Tongor, in favor of his real name. He also employs the hack poet Prebylov to "modify" Finkelmeyer's "translations" in order to distance himself from the poet. However, when Manakin is unable to produce the originals, it becomes clear to the court that the translations are Finkelmeyer's original work. As a consequence, Manakin is stripped of his post as cultural representation of the Tongor people and sent back to Siberia. There, in a plot twist reminiscent of Nabokov's *Lolita*, he tracks down his "double," who is now serving a four-year sentence with compulsory labor and shoots him. A very drunk Manakin, whom the local Russians refer to as "walrus-face," underscoring once again the social reality behind official Soviet ethnic policy, freezes to death in a Siberian snowstorm.

Through this picaresque romp through late Soviet culture, *A Certain Finkelmeyer* exposes the cultural and economic inequalities—and the violence—that characterized the Soviet empire, offering, on the one hand, a tribute to those translator-forgers who learned to survive in the regulated textual economy of the Soviet Union, and, on the other, a lament for the lives and talent that were squandered.

Conclusion

As a hero, the translator-forger is, of course, an ambivalent figure. The form of resistance he practices is fraught with moral and other contradictions. Within the interstices of languages, the translator-forger learns to get by—he "passes"— mischievously exploiting the gap between ideology and reality, words and their meanings, and what Murav describes as a text-centered and an author-centered model of literary production. Offering few solutions, he exposes, along his precarious way, "the complex heteronomy that inheres in all of our constructed solidarities" (Bermann 2005:3). What Rafael describes as the "risk of mistranslation," which leaves one "unrecognized as the bearer of messages and the author of one's own speech" (2005:15), is for the translator-forger an opportunity, a chance for survival, an enabling, productive ruse.

why it is he should have forgotten the Latin indefinite pronoun *aliquis*. He eventually admits to Freud that he is worried his lover may be pregnant. His hope that she was not, Freud concludes, contradicted the desire for progeny expressed in Dido's curse, which, Freud suggests, caused him to forget the word *aliquis*, which the gentleman associated with liquid and so with his lover's period. The act of forgetting is symptomatic, Freud concludes, serving both to conceal and reveal the unresolvable predicament of the speaker, the double bind in which he finds himself. Freud then traces the cause of the lapsus to the young man's identity as a Jew, tying the parapraxis directly to the young man's ambivalence over his lover's pregnancy.

Lev Tolstoy in *War and Peace* uses parapraxis involving foreign words as a literary device to highlight the importance of forgetting in modern nation-building, continually reminding the readers of his generation of all their Frenchified forebears had to forget following Napoleon's invasion of Russia in order to become Russian. Several scholars (Uspensky 1973, Grutman 2002, and Beck 2007) and translators (see Remnick 2005) have convincingly argued that the multilingualism in the novel serves a deeper artistic purpose than merely to create a "reality effect," i.e., to portray French-speakers speaking French. Richard Pevear, for example, insists that "Tolstoy used French for a reason, or for several reasons: to give the tone of the period; to play on the ironies of a French-speaking Russian aristocracy suddenly finding itself thrown into war with France; to suggest a certain frivolity and uprootedness in characters like Prince Vassily and the witty Bilibin" (Remnick 2005:109). The text's complex multilingualism, then, eschews a simple "us" versus "them" opposition by relativizing foreignness, exposing it as historically and culturally contingent—an essentially modernist perspective.[1] As Orlando Figes points out:

> Tolstoy was no Russian nationalist. He understood that foreign imports were integral elements of Russia's literary language and high culture, and wrote with irony about the futile efforts of the aristocracy to rid themselves of these. For example, in the scene [in *War and Peace*] in Julie's circle where they decide to ban the use of French and impose a fine on those who make a slip, he makes them use a German loan-word (*shtraf*) for "a fine" and (as if to underscore the irony) repeats it several times. (2007:online)

---

[1] As Emily Apter sees it, "Pevear implies that the Untranslatable performs a metafunction in the novel, tormenting its would-be translator with the impossibility of the task at hand; demonstrating, with a certain realism, how language-savvy aristocratic society lives in a world in which blunted comprehension and linguistic subterfuge are the norm" (2013:17).

It is interesting to note that among the English translators of this novel who make mention of the problem of foreign words in the source text—not all of them do—only one, Pevear, notes the presence of foreign languages other than French ("There are passages in German as well" (2007:xi)), and the fact that the Russian of some of the novel's artistocratic characters is itself "gallicized" (2007:xi). Figes also mentions, "There are entire paragraphs in French (including all but seven words of the book's opening paragraph) and many sentences where the Russian and the French are all mixed up, sometimes with several other languages, as in the first chapters of the book, where the guests at Anna Pavlovna's soirée also speak in German, English, and Italian" (2007:online). This complicates the experience of the foreign presented in the source text, suggesting not a binary opposition of Russian and French, of native and foreign, but rather a more slippery opposition between nationalism and cosmopolitanism.

A cursory look at the novel's opening paragraph, in which "the entire novel is laid out for anyone's inspection" (Conroy 2007:10), suggests the sophisticated ways in which Tolstoy complicates and relativizes the very concept of "foreignness" through the use of foreign words and code switching. Because the novel's opening sentences are in French, the novel's first Russian word—*pomest'ia* [estates]—appears in Cyrillic letters as a culture-specific foreign term. Russian here is the figure set against the ground of French. In that same sentence, Tolstoy uses the Italian spelling of Napoleon's surname, which prepares the reader for Anna Sherer's subsequent description of the French emperor as "an upstart Corsican." In other words, she calls the very Frenchness of the French emperor into question.[2] The next Russian phrase to appear in the text is *moi vernyi rab* [my loyal slave], which stands next to the more egalitarian French appelation *mon ami* [my friend], setting up a subtle contrast between Russia's autocratic system of government and the institution of serfdom and the egalitarian ideals of the French Revolution.

The second paragraph then shifts to Russian. The Russian reader, however, would immediately be struck by the fact that Anna Pavlovna's surname is not of Russian origin. It is German. Her court title, *freilina*, is also a borrowing from German, as were most of the Russian court titles at the time. But, for our purposes, the subsequent mention of the flu, using the new French borrowing *grippe*, but written in Cyrillic, is more significant insofar

---

[2]   It should also be noted that the French names are used for the cities of Genoa and Lucca, which, while the unmarked norm in French speech and so more or less obligatory for Tolstoy here, nonetheless underscores France's dominion over the Italian cities. (In English translation, the Italian names are used, reflecting the English norm.)

as it underscores the relative nature of the foreign. This word was in the process of being assimilated into Russian, as evidenced by its Russian spelling—the French words used previously were written in Latin letters. At the time of the novel's publication, the word *gripp* would have been used by Russians without any thought given to its non-Russian origins. By then, the assimilation of the "foreign" word into the Russian language was complete. In this way, Tolstoy underscores the dynamic, shifting nature of the foreign over time, and reminds his readers of all they have forgotten.

While the use of foreign words in Tolstoy's *War and Peace* has received a good deal of scholarly attention, I would like to examine two lesser-studied examples of the phenomenon. In the short stories discussed below, Fyodor Dostoevsky's "Peasant Marei" and Fasil Iskander's "Pshada," I will analyze the phenomenon of *parapraxis* involving foreign words—among other symptomatic behaviors—to highlight the ultimate failure of these works to repress the otherness at the core of Russia's national/imperial identity.

Forgetting the empire in Dostoevsky's "Peasant Marei"

Dostoevsky's quasi-autobiographical text "Peasant Marei," inspired by an incident that occurred during the author's incarceration in a Siberian prison camp, exposes the various acts of repression necessary to enable the author's "re-discovery" of the Russian folk. Indeed, the short story appears to invite a psychoanalytic interpretation insofar as it features such phenomena as recovered memory and audio hallucinations. Moreover, the incident that spontaneously "returns" from the narrator's memory is from his adolescence and is set in a forest, a site which, according to Jung, represents the unconscious itself. And the story has indeed inspired a number of psychoanalytic interpretations (Kanzer 1947, Erlich 1981, and Rice 1989), which see the literary text as largely symptomatic of neuroses, the roots of which are found in the author's psycho-sexual biography. Erlich, for example, argues that "Peasant Marei" represents a screen memory, which simultaneously expresses and represses Dostoevsky's "submerged homosexual wishes," the product of sexual abuse as a child.

In focusing on Dostoevsky's personal psychology, however, these scholars largely ignore what might be called the political or ideological unconscious of the text, which is rather surprising when we look at the story within the context of its original publication, as one of a series of entries in Dostoevsky's *Diary of a Writer* dealing with the question of Russian national identity. And so, I will offer a reading of "Peasant Marei" that addresses the political—not libidinal—forces that destabilize the interpretive unity of a text that was meant to narrate the author's "discovery" of the Russian folk, as embodied in Marei. By addressing the text's political unconscious, as revealed through acts of *parapraxis* involving foreign words, I hope to provide some insight into what Ashis Nandy refers to as "the psychological biography of the modern nation-state" (1994:ix).[3]

The text, which was published in 1876 in Dostoevsky's regular column *Diary of a Writer* under the title "Peasant Marei" ("Muzhik Marei"), is a short work with a fairly complex structure. It is constructed as a multiple frame narrative. The outermost frame refers back to the two essays preceding it in *The Diary*, both dedicated to the Russian folk: "On the Subject that We Are All Good Fellows. Resemblance between Russian Society and Marshal MacMahon" and "On the Love of the People. The Necessary Contract with the People" (1985a:198, 202). The next frame describes the author's experience in a Siberian prison camp in the 1850s when a fellow-convict, a Pole, who, like Dostoevsky himself, is appalled by the behavior of the Russian peasants with whom they are forced to reside, addresses the following comment in French to the author: "Je hais ces brigands" [I hate these brigands]. This incident then causes the author to remember a long-forgotten incident from his childhood—his encounter with the peasant Marei. The memory opens with a description of Dostoevsky as a ten-year-old boy playing in the woods near his family's modest country estate. While deep within the woods, he hears the cry: "A wolf's running!"[4] Terrified, he runs out of the woods and straight into the arms of the peasant Marei, a gentle peasant who is plowing a rocky meadow. The following exchange takes place:

> "A wolf's running!"—I shouted, quite out of breath.
>
> He raised his head and impulsively looked around, for an instant almost believing my words. "Where's the wolf?"
>
> "Shouted...Someone had just shouted: 'A wolf's running!'"—I lisped.

---

[3] Erlich does touch on the political context of the essay, noting that "Peasant Marei" appeared in Dostoevsky's regular column, *Diary of a Writer*, which had initially appeared in the conservative journal *The Contemporary* (Sovremennik) but in 1876 was being published independently by the author, "follow[ing] immediately upon a descriptive entry, 'On the Love of the People,' which insists upon the inner beauty of the Russian people, buried like diamonds 'under impassable alluvial filth'" (1981:385).

[4] Unless otherwise indicated, all translations of this story are taken from "Peasant Marei" in *Diary of a Writer*. trans. Boris Brasol. Salt Lake City: Gibbs M. Smith: 205–210.

"What's the matter with you?—What wolf?—This appeared to you in a dream! Look! How can a wolf be here!"—he muttered, trying to enhearten me. (1985a:208)

Marei places his finger, covered in earth, to the boy's quivering lips and smiles at him with "a long motherly smile" (208). At this moment, Dostoevsky realizes that there was no wolf and that the whole thing was an auditory "hallucination." He then admits to having such hallucinations before—and not only about wolves. Marei then blesses him and sends him on his way: "'All right, go! And I shall be keeping thee in sight! Be sure I shall not surrender thee to the wolf!'—he added with the same motherly smile.—'Well, Christ be with thee. Now, go!'" (209). Marei watches the boy as he leaves, nodding every time he turns around to look at him.

In order to put forward his vision of the Russian folk as authentic and unmediated, Dostoevsky insists that the memories he relates "rose up on their own, I rarely called them forth by an act of will" [*vstavali sami, ia redko vyzyval ikh po svoei vole*] (Dostoevskii 1981:8, 47; translation mine). He emphasizes the involuntary nature of the memory again later in the text, when he writes:

> And very soon I also forgot about Marei… And suddenly now—twenty years later, in Siberia—I was recalling that meeting, so distinctly, in every minute detail. This means that it had hidden in my soul imperceptibly, of its own accord, without any effort of my will [*sama soboi i bez voli moei*], and then it came to my mind at the needed time: that tender, motherly smile of a poor peasant serf, his crosses, the shaking of his head. (Dostoevsky 1985a:209)

Dostoevsky seeks here to present the memory as directly transferred, without alteration, from the time of his original meeting with Marei, protected in his soul from distortion.

Dostoevsky himself admits elsewhere, however, that memory is not entirely reliable, that it is subject to correction. As he writes early on in the story before recounting the tale of Marei: "I used to analyze these impressions, adding new touches to things long ago outlived, and—what is more important—I used to correct [*popravial*], continually correct them" (1985a:207). And so, while Dostoevsky claims that these memories "made it possible for me to survive in prison," James Rice notes that, "Survival of course can depend as much upon the suppression of memories as their recovery, or their transformation" (1989:255).

That Dostoevsky's memory of Marei may have been "transformed"—
and for political or ideological reasons—is perhaps most evident when
one compares the author's treatment of the Polish inmate M—cki in his
semiautobiographical *Notes from the House of the Dead* (1862) with his
later treatment of the Pole in "Peasant Marei." The general details contained
in the short story's second frame were first recounted in the prison novel.
The comment "Je hais ces brigands," in fact, appears twice in part two
of the novel, once in chapter seven and again in chapter eight, which is
entitled *Tovarishchi* [Companions]. Both times, it is spoken by the Polish
convict M—cki. In the first instance, M—cki utters the statement in
order to explain why he refused to take part in a prison rebellion with
the other prisoners, testifying to his estrangement from his compatriots.
In the following chapter, *Companions*, M—cki receives a much gentler
treatment by the author. The narrator mentions that he often spoke in
French with M—cki, for which they earned, for reasons unknown to
them, the epithet "the medics." French is presented here as a we-code, to
use Gumperz's (1982) term, distinguishing the narrator and M—cki from
the other prisoners. The narrator then goes on to note that M—cki was
deeply embittered: "As he recalled this, he would grit his teeth and attempt
to avert his gaze" (Dostoevsky 1985b:334). The only time M—cki becomes
animated is when he remembers his beloved mother in Poland. While
Dostoevsky presents M—cki's bitterness and resentment as unattractive, he
also exhibits compassion for the man, understanding that his personality
was adversely affected by the cruelty of (Russian) prison life and a longing
for his homeland. In fact, he describes M—cki as "a man of strong character
and excellent breeding" (1985b:323). These Polish convicts, the narrator
explains, were "suffering from a kind of moral and mental sickness; they
were bitter, irritable, mistrustful. *This was understandable:* they had a very
hard time in the prison and their situation was far worse than ours. They
were far from their own country" (324; italics added). He then goes on to
note that while the Poles could see nothing in the Russian convicts but
brutality, "this, too, was perfectly understandable: they had been compelled
to take this point of view by force of circumstance, by fate" (324).

Interestingly, the despotic Major of the prison, who has taken a special
dislike to M—cki, describes the Poles as *brigands* (*razboiniki*) before
M—cki uses the term in reference to the Russian convicts. When the
Major uses the Russian word *razboiniki*, the Polish convict Z—cki, who
understood very little Russian and thought they were being asked about
their prison status, replies: "We're not brigands, we're political offenders"
(326). That comment makes clear that the Poles were not common
criminals but were most likely involved in political resistance to Russian

imperial rule in Poland, something which would become unmentionable when the story is retold in "Peasant Marei." Moreover, the term *brigand* was often used by Russians to describe the colonized tribal peoples of the Transcaucasus region and Central Asia. As Madhavan K. Palat observes, Russia's international conflicts with Central Asian khans "were universally and successfully described in both colonial and modern historiography as slavery and *brigandage*" (1989:122; italics mine), terms that served as justification for Russian colonial rule. At the same time, the Polish prisoner's declaration of his status as a political prisoner may be an oblique reference to Dostoevsky's own status as a political prisoner; he was imprisoned for his participation in the radical Petrashevsky Circle, but because this was unmentionable in print, Dostoevsky makes his first person narrator into a wife murderer. (In fact, as a convicted criminal, Dostoevsky was unable to use his real name when publishing *Notes*.) In *Notes*, then, the Pole functions as a kind of stand-in for Dostoevsky. And so, when M—cki utters the statement "Je hais ces brigands" in *Notes*, he is repeating, albeit in French, an insult that had first been directed at the Poles by the Major, underscoring the colonial implications of the term, whereas in "Peasant Marei," no mention is made of the Russian Major's insult.

Overall, the representation of the Pole M—cki in *Notes* is far more complex and nuanced than in "Peasant Marei." Dostoevsky's narrator is in fact touched by M—cki's devotion to his mother and acknowledges the Pole to be one of his best friends in the prison, although with the caveat that, in his opinion, the Pole could never fully open himself up to another person. M—cki's fate, moreover, is a relatively happy one. He is released from prison thanks to a petition from his beloved mother, and he settles in the nearby village where he lives a contented life.

In the 1875 reedition of *Notes*, however, just a year before the publication of "Peasant Marei," Dostoevsky removed chapter eight altogether and with it his ambivalent and compassionate treatment of the Pole, suggesting, as Rice argues, "that consciously or unconsciously the author sought to clean the slate, so to speak, before presenting the public with his revised account" (1989:253). And indeed, the Pole appears in the "Peasant Marei" in a much less flattering light. All the mitigating circumstances that might have elicited compassion on the part of the Russian reader are removed. In fact, in "Peasant Marei," the Pole seems to include Dostoevsky in his remark about the brutish Russian peasants: "He looked at me gloomily, his eyes flashing; his lips began to tremble: '*Je hais ces brigands!*'—he told me in a low voice, grinding his teeth, and passed by" (1985a:206). Here, the Pole's French appears as a they-code, representing the cosmopolitan Pole's alienation from the uneducated prisoners—and from Dostoevsky.

Whereas in *Notes* the use of French suggests a solidarity between the two educated prisoners, in *The Diary* that solidarity is downplayed, and the Pole's exclamation "Je hais ces brigands" highlights the foreignness of the speaker and his beliefs, drawing a metonymic association with the ironic use of French in the opening line of the essay: "However, all these *professions de foi* is a bore, must make weary reading. Therefore, I will relate an anecdote" (1985a:205). In the context of the newspaper essay, the use of French suggests the insincerity of such patriotic professions and inaugurates a series of anti-French, or rather, anti-cosmopolitan jabs.

For example, in his recounting of the incident in "Peasant Marei," Dostoevsky notes, "I recalled the month of August in our village: a dry and clear day, though somewhat chilly and windy; the summer was coming to an end, and soon I should have to go to Moscow, again to be wearied all winter over French lessons" (207; italics added). As Iza Erlich comments, "Like a day residue in a dream, the French in the memory of the Pole, 'Je hais ces brigands!' finds its counterpart in the memory of hateful French lessons" (1981:383). Moreover, while in the woods, the young Dostoevsky occupies himself with beating frogs with a switch—another even more antagonistic reference to French culture. (The Russian term *lgeediashchie*, or *"frog-eater,"* was a derogatory reference to the French.)

Finally, the remark "Je hais ces brigands" returns in the final lines of the text when Dostoevsky offers his most negative appraisal of Polish culture, one that is dripping with sarcasm or, as Rice describes it, a "condescending (Russian Slavophile) lament" (Rice 1989:253): "That same evening I met M—tzki [sic] once more. The unfortunate! Perhaps he could not have had reminiscences about any Mareis, and he could not have viewed these men differently than 'Je hais ces brigands!' Yes, the Poles in those days had endured more than we! (Dostoevsky 1985a:210)!" The implication here is that M—cki could have no such memories of Polish peasants because Polish peasants did not possess the spiritual virtues of the Russian Peasant Marei. Moreover, alienated from the Polish folk, the French-Speaking Pole is unable to see the Russian folk as anything but brigands. Dostoevsky's association of the Pole with French culture presents him as cynical, elitist, and cosmopolitan; in doing so, Dostoevsky tacitly invokes the opposition between (French) *civilization* and (German) *Kultur*, which animated much of Russian nationalist discourse at the time.

This opposition was a product of the Romantic reinterpretation of civilization in negative terms, as summarized by John Stuart Mill in his essay on Coleridge: "loss of independence, the creation of artificial wants, monotony, narrow mechanical understanding, inequality and hopeless poverty" (qtd. in Williams 1983:58). As Coleridge himself wrote, "*Civilization* is itself but a mixed good, if not far more a corrupting influence, the hectic of disease, not the bloom of health, and a nation so distinguished more fitly to be called a varnished than a polished people, where this civilization is not grounded in *cultivation*, in the harmonious development of those qualities and faculties that characterize our humanity" (qtd. in Williams 1983: 59; italics added). Culture, with its origins in agriculture, came to represent the "genuine" mores and beliefs of the folk, unmediated by class and other hierarchies associated with civilization.

While Rice does an excellent job in tracing the transformations of the character of Marei in Dostoevsky's work, which, of course, raises doubts about the historical authenticity of the event and the reliability of Dostoevsky's memory, he has little to say about why Dostoevsky should have so drastically altered his view of the Pole. There is, however, a rather straightforward political explanation of Dostoevsky's treatment of M—cki: the Polish Uprisings of 1863–1864, which took place between the writing of *The Notes* (1860) and "Peasant Marei" (1876). The intelligentsia's reaction to the Polish uprising was largely split along political lines, with liberals generally supporting the Poles' struggle for independence and conservatives condemning it—until the massacre of sleeping Russian soldiers in their barracks. After that, even the liberal Nikolai Nekrasov condemned the Poles and praised the violent suppression of the insurrection by the Russian general Count Mikhail Murav'ev.[5] Popular opinion was, however, on the side of the conservatives throughout. Moreover, "the pressure exerted by France and England on behalf of [Poland's] claims only succeeded in whipping up Russian nationalism to a fever pitch" (Frank 2010:360). The problem of Poland, a nation seeking the right to self-determination, placed in stark relief the contractions inherent in Russia's identity as an imperial nation. As Geoffrey Hosking notes, "The debacle was not only disastrous for Poland, but led to a decisive souring of the reform efforts of Alexander II" (1997:33).

Dostoevsky was deeply involved in the debates over Poland and published an essay on the topic by his coeditor Nikolai Strakhov in his journal *Time* (*Vremia*), which led to the closing of the journal. Ironically, Joseph Frank points out, Strakhov's article, "although intended as a public avowal in favor of the Russian cause, was written in such tortuous and elusive terms that it could be misread as a justification of the desperate

---

[5] Even the liberal-minded Nekrasov advocated for the brutal repression of the Polish uprising following the murder of the Russian soldiers. Kornei Chukovsky dedicated an entire monograph, titled *Poet i palach* [Poet and Executioner], in an attempt to understand the apparent "hypocrisy" of Nekrasov: "How could a revolutionary poet praise the bloody pacification of Poland and advocate for new atrocities?" (1922:3).

Polish revolt" (Frank 2010:360). The article was an expression of many of Dostoevsky's own views on Poland, as he himself described them in a letter to Ivan Turgenev:

> The idea of the article was as follows: that the Poles despise us as barbarians to such a degree, are so boastful to us of their "European" civilization, that one can scarcely foresee for a long time any moral peace (the only durable kind!) with us. But, as the exposition of the article was not understood, it was interpreted as follows: that we affirmed, of ourselves, that the Poles have a civilization so superior to ours, and we are so inferior, that obviously they are right and we are wrong. (Qtd. in Frank 2010:360)

Note here the distinctly negative inflection Dostoevsky lends to the word civilization (*tsivilizatsiia*), associating it with inequality and overrefinement.

But fitting Russia into the mold of *Kultur* as outlined by the German Romantics requires the repression, or forgetting, of at least two things: first, Russia's imperial identity, and second, the fact that Dostoevsky's vision of the Russian folk is itself borrowed, a translation, if you will, of a German Romantic concept. Both efforts at repression are revealed/concealed in the course of Dostoevsky's narrative in acts of parapraxis. The repression of Russia's imperial identity is accomplished, largely, by demonizing the Pole M—cki, projecting an oppressive imperial identity onto him, thus transforming him from a victim of Russian imperial domination into a victimizer, a representative of French cultural hegemony and elitist civilization. Dostoevsky continually invokes the positive rhetoric of national liberation: the memories "rose up on their own" and not "at his will." But as a parapraxis, Dostoevsky here makes an unwitting reference to the Polish uprising, when the Poles, in defense of their right to national self-determination, *rose up* to express their national *will*. Indeed, the Polish Uprising of 1863 is referred to as *Pol'skoe vosstanie 1863 goda*, with *vosstanie* and *vstavali* formed from the same root; no such expressions appear in *Notes from the House of the Dead*. Moreover, the rhetoric of national liberation fit the Polish situation far better than it did Russia's—for in Poland, the nation was rising up against an imperial overlord whereas in Russia uprisings were carried out by Russians themselves against the state or the nobility. And so, while Dostoevsky may have succeeded in projecting a negative imperial identity onto the hapless Pole, his invocation of the rhetoric of Romantic nationalism betrays a deep-seated ambivalence over the Polish struggle for liberation and Russia's role as colonial master.

The incompatibility of these two visions of the folk—as violent threat to the social order and as idealized embodiment of the national spirit—is underscored by a second parapraxis in the text. The Russian word for "wolf," *volk*, is a homograph, and a close homophone, of the German word for "the folk," *Volk*. It is interesting, then, that the hallucinated *volk* (wolf) leads Dostoevsky to his discovery of the true Russian *Volk*, in a person who embodies the idealized folk of German Romanticism. The signifying chain established by this play of homographs both enables and deconstructs the transformation that occurs in Dostoevsky's heart when he is able to see his brutal and threatening compatriots with new eyes, as gentle and deeply spiritual creatures. This connection of *volk* and *Volk* is made elsewhere in Dostoevsky's writings, where he describes the Russian folk as wolves: "… about the common folk—wolf" (qtd. in Rice 1989:254).

The inseparability of the ideal of the *Volk* with the threat of violence represented by the *volk* is reiterated when, immediately after being comforted by Marei, Dostoevsky sees his dog, named Volchok. "Of course, with Volchok," Dostoevsky states, "I felt quite safe" (1985a:209). The threat (*volk*) is transformed again into something comforting (Volchok). Textually, the threat that Russian peasants will exercise their will and rise up is transformed into comforting memories of loyal servants (Marei and Volchok), who rise up on their own (*po svoei vole*) to comfort their master—like the memory of Marei, Dostoevsky's dog "suddenly appears." This resolution, however, achieved through the false logic of phonetic association—false in the sense that there is no semantic basis for the association of *volk* and *Volk*—permanently conjoins these two mutually exclusive visions of the folk: as violent threat and spiritual ideal. As a site of repression, volk/Volk both reveals and conceals the threat posed by the people's will (*volia*) that Russia's educated elite faced from both outside (the Poles) and inside (the Russian peasants) Russia proper.

At the same time, the German origin of *Volk* underscores the mediated nature of Dostoevsky's "spontaneous" memory of the true Russian folk, that is, his indebtedness to German Romanticism. Here, Dostoevsky reveals/ conceals what scholars have referred to as the double bind of nationalism: the fact that every modern nation claims its *sui generis* individuality, but it does so according to a general (borrowed) model or template. As Derek Offord explains, "[The Russian intelligentsia's] search for *narodnost'*, the distinctive character of their own people […] may on the broadest level be seen as part of that general European search for ethnicity, the concept of *Volkstum* advanced by the eighteenth-century German thinker Herder, which was so pronounced in the first half of the nineteenth century" (1999:25). Dostoevsky attempts to get himself out of that double bind by claiming a special historical destiny for Russia, which was to serve "in the midst of humankind as its all-unifying, all-reconciling and all-regenerating element" (Dostoevsky 1985a:940). But, in this, too, he was borrowing a claim

Schiller had made almost a century before for Germany: "The day of the German is the harvest of time as a whole" (Dowling 1982:18). And so, by associating *volk* (wolf) and *Volk* (the folk), Dostoevsky exposes the foreign origins of his archetypal Russian, Marei. In the very act of discovering the "true" Russian folk, Dostoevsky reveals those origins—like his memories—to be mediated, borrowed, and imagined.

The reliance of Russian nationalists on German Romanticism to imagine the Russian nation cannot be underestimated. German Romantic nationalism provided Russians not only with an alternative to French *civilization*, which had become especially problematic following the Napoleonic Wars, but also with the discursive means to revalue Russia's underdevelopment as something positive (*Kultur*). As Wayne Dowler comments: "The confusion of philosophy with history and the fascination with cosmic second guessing were traits shared with the Germans by many Slavs, and Schiller's optimism could be and was easily adapted to Russian needs by the simple expedient of substituting Russia for Germany" (Dowler 1982:18). Moreover, Dostoevsky knew German very well and was well-acquainted with German Romantic literature. And so, one could say that Dostoevsky's attempt to contrast hegemonic French cosmopolitanism to a native Russian folk culture misfires when he inadvertently reveals the borrowed origins of that folk culture in German Romantic thought.[6]

Just as Strakhov's elusive prose had left his supposed condemnation of the Poles open to an antithetical reading as a defense of the Polish nationalist struggle, so, too, Dostoevsky's effusive prose turns his story of discovering the *true* Russian folk into a testament to the imagined, thoroughly mediated nature of his vision and to the fictive origins of modern national identity in general.

Forgetting the nation in Iskander's *Pshada*

In "Pshada," Iskander deconstructs Romantic nationalism from the other side, questioning one man's investment in Soviet (imperial) identity following the collapse of that empire. If Dostoevsky must repress Russia's imperial identity in order to imagine the Russian nation, Iskander's hero must forget

---

[6] In Pushkin's short story "Pikovaia dama," the heroine finds herself caught between a grandmother who represents French enlightenment culture—she sits in a Voltaire armchair—and a suitor, Hermann, who embodies German Romantic thought. Hermann's insistence on reading the grandmother's salon anecdote as a German fantastic tale ultimately drives him insane.

his nation in order to become a Soviet citizen. In both situations, however, an act of parapraxis exposes the impossibility of achieving a coherent identity for individuals caught between nation and empire. In both works, the Romantic nation appears ultimately as mythic, imagined, and forever out of reach.

In 1993, two years after the collapse of the Soviet empire, Fazil Iskander's novella *Pshada* appeared in the Russian journal *Znamia*. Iskander was in many ways an imperial success story. Born in Abkhazia, a region located in the northwest corner of the Republic of Georgia, Iskander attended university in Moscow where he continues to live today. Set against the backdrop of the dissolution of the Soviet empire and the Abkhazian struggle for independence, *Pshada* explores the complex relationship between national—in this case Abkhazian—and imperial identities. The hero of the novella is a retired general in the Soviet army who, like Iskander and his most famous literary character, Sandro, is a native Abkhazian from Chegem. Throughout his oeuvre, Iskander "plays extensively with the conceptual category of the Soviet nation subsumed beneath the imperial gaze" (Condee 2009:41). However, as N. N. Shneidman notes, this novella differs significantly from Iskander's other Abkhazian prose not only because it is a straightforward third-person narrative but also because "there is no humour, hyperbole, or fantasy in the story" (1995:77). In addition, the novella's commentary on imperial identity is far darker than in his Sandro tales. After the fall of the Soviet Union, Iskander seems to be posing a very painful question: "Was it worth it?"

The novella opens with the recollection of a brutal incident from the Second World War. The general, then a colonel, is facing two German soldiers who have killed his beloved Abkhazian aide-de-camp. Now captive, the Germans plead for mercy, but the colonel is unmoved and summarily executes the two men. This memory is only the first in a string of memories from the war, all involving encounters with fellow Abkhazians. A beneficiary and protector of the Soviet empire, the general recalls confronting Abkhazians who were collaborating with the Nazis, seduced by the promise of an independent Abkhazia following the war. The general's loyalty to the Soviet Union, it appears, does not waver. However, interwoven with these war memories are thoughts of "the lost world of his childhood in Abhazia" (Laird 1999:22), which constitute a kind of nationalist counter-narrative.

The juxtaposition of the general's nostalgic reminiscences of Abkhazia and his brutal memories of war points to cracks in the ideal of a Soviet imperial identity. Moreover, the general speaks Russian with an accent and "has suffered professionally because of it" (Haber 2003:66), while he has almost entirely forgotten the Abkhazian language. Like Nabokov's émigrés, he is permanently dislocated between two languages and two identities, unable to fully inhabit the one or to return to the other. Moreover, the empire that made him a general and that he defended throughout his career is crumbling around him. As a result, Haber points out, "he feels lost, rootless, and without an identity" (2003:66). In the final pages of the story, the general recalls his childhood in Abkhazia and in particular the happy time he spent in the village of Pshada, which, in the general's memory, is a place "where peace always reigns" (Shneidman 1995:77). However, the general cannot remember the meaning of the village's name, which is "shelter." He wracks his brain until he is suddenly stopped by a severe pain in his chest and dies of a massive heart attack, "a lonely death among strangers" (1995:77). Like Iskander himself, the general is an imperial success story, rising from the periphery of empire (Abkhazia) to the very center (Moscow). However, he is unable to survive the collapse of the imperial myth that gave his life significance and made him a success; he dies not the death of a Soviet hero, but that of a stranger.

Read in the light of Freud's concept of everyday psychopathology, the general's inability to recall the meaning of the word *pshada* points to a repression insofar as the Abkhazian word echoes the Russian word *poshchada*, or "mercy," mentioned twice in the opening paragraph in reference to the vivid scene of execution that would come to haunt the general. The incident involves captive German soldiers, one of whom holds his hands behind his head "as if asking for mercy" (*prosia poshchadi*) (Iskander' 1993:3). The general, however, shows the soldier no mercy and shoots him in the back of the head—precisely where his hands were clasped together. This traumatic incident, associated in his memory with the Russian word for mercy, appears to block his recollection of the meaning of the Abkhazian world for shelter. In this way, the Abkhazian word for shelter is transformed into a site of conflict through a metonymic association with the general's merciless execution of the German soldiers. His ambivalence over the act is manifested as a failure of translation and of the promise of universal translatability and friendship of peoples.

In a discussion of psychoanalysis and translation, Lawrence Venuti describes as the fundamental dream of the translator "that a translation will restore the foreign text in its entirety, in its materiality, without loss or gain, that the translation will establish such a similarity to the foreign text as to overcome the irreducible differences between languages and cultures" (2002:221). By analogy, I would argue, the colonialist dreams that empire, too, can overcome the irreducible differences between languages and cultures. In Iskander's novella, however, the general's (mis)translation of *pshada*, produced here by a false phonetic resemblance (*pshada/poshchada*), disrupts both dreams, revealing that "the signifying chain created by the translator doesn't translate any dream embodied in the foreign text, but rather replaces it with the translator's own unconscious desire" (Venuti 2002:221). Rather than overcoming differences between languages and cultures, the (mis) translation represents the return of the repressed: the general's awareness of the irreducible difference between his imperial Soviet and his national Abkhazian identity, and, on a more profound level, between political identities and a common humanity.

In an interesting symmetry, Freud's ambitious young Jew worries that his minority ethnicity might stand in the way of his career, while Iskander's ambitious old Abkhazian wonders if he was wrong to have sacrificed his minority ethnicity for the sake of a career in the Soviet army. The general's subconscious, it would seem, is literally denying his conscious shelter (*pshada*): there is no escape from Soviet history. And with the fall of the Soviet empire, how can he now justify his actions? This tale of (mis)translation then, by providing "a perceptive elaboration of the relationship between different nationalities in the allegedly happy family of Soviet nations" (Shneidman 1995:77), underscores not only the incommensurability of an ethnic identity and an imperial Soviet one, particularly for non-Russian citizens of the USSR, but also the imagined, mythic nature of national identities en gros. Indeed, the failure of translation in Iskander's "Pshada" lays bare, as Nancy Condee' puts it, "the foundations of, among other things, our own existing incoherence with respect to so-called national culture" (2009:42).

Mourning the nation

The association of nation with childhood both in Dostoevsky's "Peasant Marei" and in Iskander's "Pshada" reveals Romantic nationalism to be an essentially melancholic structure, fully present only at some distant, elusive origin, only partially recovered—resurrected—through memory. The failure of memory in both these stories underscores the shaky ontological status of the modern nation, which is reflected in modernist theories as a preoccupation with acts of remembering, specifically, the act of mourning. As Benedict Anderson puts it in *Imagined Communities*:

> No more arresting emblems of the modern culture of nationalism exist than cenotaph and tombs of Unknown Soldiers. The public ceremonial reverence accorded these monuments precisely *because* they are either deliberately empty or no one knows who lies inside them, has no true precedents in earlier times. [...] Yet void as these tombs are

of identifiable mortal remains or immortal souls, they are nonetheless saturated with ghostly *national* imaginings. (1991:9)

Vincente Rafael in his study of nationalism and translation in the Philippines also sees mourning as central to enabling the modern nationalist project: "The call to mourn the dead is an oblique acknowledgment that the nation is founded on what it cannot comprehend, much less incorporate. But, it is also a means for disavowing this fact. Put differently, the substitution of the 'sacrificial dead' for the intractable complications of history and technology is a way of remembering to forget the essential strangeness of national origins" (2005:xvi).[7] Unwittingly perhaps, both Dostoevsky and Iskander, by highlighting acts of *parapraxis*, or mistranslation, present the nation as a site of repression, of remembering/forgetting, and of mourning lost origin(al)s, lending credence to Venuti's claim that "Translation lies deeply repressed in the cultural identities that are constructed by academic, religious, and political institutions" (1999:2).

---

[7]   The notion that translation may represent a similar kind of substitution, that is, a way of remembering to forget the essential strangeness of origins *tout court*, is suggested by the discourse of mourning that has surrounded it since at least the Romantic Age: translation as sacrifice, as that which is lost.

4

Refiguring Translation: Translator-Heroines in Russian Women's Writing

How have the sites of translation theory been implicitly gendered and how can this theory be transformed?

Sherry Simon (1996:2)

Scholars in the field of Translation Studies have long noted a distinct gender inflection in the way translation is discussed and represented in Western cultures (Simon 1996, Von Flotow 1997, Chamberlain 2000, and Santaemilia and Von Flotow 2011). "Translators and women," writes Sherry Simon, "have historically been the weaker figures in their respective hierarchies: translators are handmaidens to authors, women inferior to men. [...] Whether affirmed or denounced, the femininity of translation is a persistent historical trope" (1996:1). In her now seminal essay "Gender and the Metaphorics of Translation," Lori Chamberlain argues that this gendering of translation is represented perhaps best in the eighteenth-century tag *les belles infidèles*—or beautiful cheats, which is gendered feminine:

> For les *belles infidèles*, fidelity is defined by an implicit contract between translation (as woman) and original (as husband, father, or author). However, the infamous "double standard" operates here as it might have in traditional marriages: the "unfaithful" wife/translation is publicly tried for crimes the husband/original is by law incapable of committing. Such an attitude betrays real anxiety about the problem of paternity and translation; it mimics the partilineal kinship system where paternity— not maternity—legitimizes an offspring. (2000:315)

Until only recently, translation scholars have tended to generalize the relationship of gender and translation across cultures based on data culled almost exclusively from the modern West. And, while Geert Hofstede contends that "Masculine/Feminine, or tough versus tender," is a universal dimension of culture—he refers to "the duality of female versus male [as] nature's number two law (after the duality of life and death)" (1998:11)—this duality is constructed differently across cultures. So, too, are translation and the related concepts of originality and imitation, a point brought home by recent studies of translation traditions in Asia and Africa.[1]

Scholars dealing with translation in cultures outside the West have long recognized the methodological danger of, to quote Harish Trivedi, "subscrib[ing] implicitly and unquestioningly to the assumption that the Western concepts of the 'original' and the 'translation' are universal" (2006:107). In many non-Western cultures, and in minor cultures both inside and outside the West, a markedly different valuation of translation and of the more general concept of imitation persists. As Judy Wakabayashi notes:

> Western/capitalist notions of "ownership" of the text and copyright— deriving partly from the fixedness and authoritativeness imparted by printing (unlike, for example, the impermanence of the palm-leaf manuscripts long used in India and South-East Asia)—are linked to "reverence for the written word and a highly developed sense that language expresses the thoughts of individuals" (Cummings 2005:196). This differs from traditional notions in South and South-East Asia, where public/private boundaries have been less sharply delineated, multiple retellings made authorship (often anonymous) of little interest, and there was "creative disrespect" (Jedamski 2005:213) for the original. (2011:27)

These notions of authorship are clearly linked to broader notions of personal identity and subjectivity to the extent that originality in modern Western cultures "serves as the guarantor of subjectivity" (Gutbrodt 2003:13). In Asian cultures, however, as Eva Richter and Bailin Song note:

> The very Western concept of personal identity rests on the foundation of the idea of a "person" as distinct from the generic "man." Its related construct is the "self," a conscious, thinking, reflexive and autonomous entity—individual, distinct from others, but sharing common characteristics with them. This construct is an integral part of Western and particularly of American philosophy and literature, but it has long roots in Western philosophy since the Greeks. (2005:91)

---

[1] Chamberlain's reading, while popular, has not gone unchallenged. For an alternative reading of the gendered metaphorics of translation in Florio, see Goldberg (1997).

This, Richter and Song go on to argue, complicates the translation of Western notions of "identity" and "subjectivity" into Chinese "where 'self' has different connotations and where individualism is frequently seen as negative" (2005). Such deep cultural differences regarding subjectivity and authorship, then, can be expected to produce a gendered metaphorics of translation that is quite different from that in the West.

While many scholars trace the privileging of (male) originality over (female) imitation to Western Platonic philosophies, especially as they were reflected in Romantic notions of individual genius, few question the cultural relativity, or the Western bias, of those philosophical assumptions. Doing so would raise the question of how the representation of gender and translation might differ in a culture that is not so thoroughly influenced by Platonism and positivism, and by the Romantic cult of originality, that is, in a culture like Russia that, "privileges social totality and neglects or subordinates the human individual" (Boym 1995:140). Moreover, in cultures constructed within a Western developmental model as underdeveloped and/or belated, the question posed is not whether or not to translate—translation was a fact of life and perceived as a necessary means of "catching up"—but rather *how* to translate.

Further complicating these issues is the fact that Russia itself was often imagined vis-à-vis the West in distinctly gendered terms. Some writers and thinkers, like Fyodor Dostoevsky, celebrate the "feminine" qualities of humility and empathy, which they saw as distinguishing Russians from their soulless counterparts in the West (see Chapter 3). Others, like the philosopher Nicolas Berdyaev and the writer Vasily Rozanov, critiqued the "feminine" qualities of Russian culture, which Berdyaev associated with passivity and blind submission to authority, leading him to condemn Russia's "eternal womanliness," or *vechnoe babe*. Rozanov argued that the asceticism of Russian Orthdox culture had deprived Russian men of virility, turning them into what he called "spiritual homosexuals."[2]

In this chapter, I will explore how the gendering of translation in Russian culture is shaped not only by the gendering of the nation but also by the Russian critique of Romantic authorship and its cult of originality. I will attempt to map the cultural construction—and more specifically, the gendering—of translation and translators in modern Russian culture,

---

[2] For more on the gendered identity of modern Russian, See the section "Gender and National Identity" in Barta (2001): 89–162, as well as Costlow, Sandler, and Vowles (1992), Chester and Forrester (1996), and Goscilo and Lanoux (2006). Of particular interest in the last collection is Zaitseva's discussion of gendered language in Chapter One, "National, Cultural, and Gender Identity in the Russian Language" (2006:30–54).

revealing these representations to be thoroughly intertwined with notions of Russian national identity, an identity that was in many ways born in translation. In particular, I will examine the work of three female authors who in their work re-signify the relationship between translation, gender, and Russianness, suggesting an alternative to the reigning Western metaphorics of translation. Striking in these works is the absence of the popular Western opposition of male author to female translator. Rather, male and female translators are often juxtaposed in a way that constructs the female translator as a representative of traditional Russian spiritual values, an embodiment of the Russian critique of Western values, and a rejection of the Platonic opposition of an ideal original to an imperfect translation or copy.

Women translators in Russia

Before exploring the gendered representations of translation and translators by Russian women writers, it might be useful to situate women in Russian translation history. For a variety of cultural and political reasons, Russian women have engaged actively in translation work since the eighteenth century, although none has received the kind of praise reserved for Vasilii Zhukovsky. First of all, there was a real need for translators. Following Peter the Great's turn to the West, the translation of Western works, both scientific and literary, acquired enormous importance. As Wendy Rosslyn notes, fully one third of the books published by the Russian Academy of Sciences in the eighteenth century were translations (Rosslyn 2000:13). Second, the fact that most upper-class Russian women were well-versed in foreign languages, specifically, in the prestige languages of Western Europe (as opposed to the ancient languages), made them qualified to translate. Third, frequent government pleas for translators cast translation as a civic duty, service to the state and nation, thus making women translators less vulnerable to the charge of personal ambition than women writers, who for the most part had to "apologize for writing" (Harussi 1989:40). Fourth, translation was seen as educational, contributing to the development, or *Bildung*, of the individual and the nation. As Zhukovsky put it: "Translation is for a language what travel is for the education of the mind" (Zhukovskii 1985:82). And finally, for the women themselves, translation provided a creative literary outlet at a time when original writing was not generally considered "a respectable long-term profession [for women], comparable with, say, a position at court" (Kelly 2009:42), providing them access to, among other things, "the celestial world of poetry" (Dolack 2011:39). This helps to explain why "the number of translations by women in the eighteenth century far exceeded women's original compositions" (Rosslyn 2000:4).

The fact that Catherine II and her close friend Princess Ekaterina Dashkova, the first president of the Russian Academy of Sciences, engaged in translation work themselves and encouraged it must have lent status and acceptability to such work, in particular, for women. As Rosslyn notes, "The first translation to be published by a Russian woman, Ekaterina Dashkova, appeared in print at the beginning of Catherine II's reign in 1763 and from then onwards upper-class women contributed to the translation project, and translated not only in 'women's' subject areas but also more widely" (2000:1). In 1798, the empress provided not only an example to follow but also material support to translators when she created the Society for the Promotion of the Translation of Foreign Books into Russian, which placed ads for translators in newspapers and paid translators for their work. The general promotion of translation at this time certainly benefited women as much if not more so than men as there were fewer other opportunities available for women to enter the literary field. As Rosslyn points out, "by 1826 S. V. Russov was able to list thirty-four women who had translated into Russian" (2000:3), which is undoubtedly an underestimation as many women were believed to have published translations anonymously.

The relationship of the literary representations of women translators discussed below to the historical reality of women translators in Russia is, of course, not one of simple reflection. As Sergey Tyulenev insists, there is no evidence that Russian women translators practiced translation in a way that was fundamentally different from that of Russian men. "While there were translating women," Tyulenev points out, "in Russian history there has never been such a thing as women's translation as a separate social and professional (sub)system" (2011:79). The representations discussed below, however, present clearly gendered representations of translators that provide, if not an accurate historical depiction of women translators, then an insight into Russians' ambivalent relationship to the (Western) Romantic model of Authorship.

Translation as a male problem: Dostoevsky's *Crime and Punishment*

Fyodor Dostoevsky was one of the first Russian writers to develop the theme of translation in any serious way in Russian literature and to lend it clearly gendered connotations. For the novelist, who first appeared in print as the translator of Balzac's *Eugénie Grandet*, in a heavily Russified version, the question was not whether or not to translate but rather *how* to translate foreign works without compromising one's national identity, that is, how to reconcile the national and the foreign, *svoi* and *chuzhoi*, in translation. This was a running concern throughout his oeuvre. Dostoevsky's contribution to the gendered metaphorics of translation, in particular, is, perhaps, in the way he posits translation as a distinctly male dilemma insofar as it problematizes "a traditionally masculine privileging of the autonomy, self-sufficiency and independence of the individual" (Shread 2011:52).

This is a central—if not *the* central—theme of his psychological detective novel *Crime and Punishment*. In this novel, the protagonist, Raskolnikov—whose name is formed from the Russian world *raskol*, or "schism"—is torn between contemporary Western philosophy and the "Eastern" spiritual truths of Russian traditional culture. On an allegorical level, the two opposing sides of that philosophical schism are represented in gendered terms by the character Razumikhin, on the one hand, whose name derives from the grammatically masculine noun *razum*, meaning "reason," and Sonia, the virtuous prostitute, on the other, whose full name, Sofiia, grammatically feminine, means "holy wisdom."[3] Discussion of translation, then, appears in the novel within an already clearly gendered symbolic landscape.

In Part 2, Chapter 2 of the novel, Razumikhin, who "knew three European languages fairly well," proposes that Raskolnikov help him with a translation of a progressive philosophical treatise from German about the status of women in contemporary society, which Razumikhin describes derisively in the following way: "In my opinion, it's the most blatant fake. Is woman a human being or not a human being? That sort of thing. Well, naturally, you prove triumphantly that she's a human being" (Dostoevsky 1999:107). Razumikhin is here parodying an actual review by G. Z. Eliseev that appeared in 1861 in the journal *Sovremennik*, entitled "Various Opinions as to Whether Women Are People."[4] The choice of a progressive German text here is a realistic touch that reflects the enormous role played by translation in the radical Russian

---

[3]   The association of the feminine with Eastern spirituality in Dostoevsky's writing is evident elsewhere when male characters embodying this spirituality are often described as having feminine attributes. For example, of the detective Porfiry Petrovich, Dostoevsky writes: "All he had to do was place the palm of his hand on his cheek and tilt his head to one side, and he would have looked completely like a woman" (1999:340).

[4]   With his choice of text, Dostoevsky alludes to the enormous role played by translation among the members of Russia's political left in the nineteenth century. In fact, Mikhail Petrashevsky, the leader of a radical study group, participation in which would lead to Dostoevsky's arrest and exile, was a translator at the Russian Foreign Ministry and kept a library of "forbidden" books which members of the circle were free to borrow. Petrashevsky was also involved in the publication of the *Pocket Dictionary of Foreign*

left. In terms of the gendered metaphorics of translation, men are presented here as the translators and women as the translated.

Within the spiritual/intellectual opposition organizing the novel, it is clearly ironic that Razumikhin is offered the treatise to translate by a publisher named Kheruvimov, a name derived from the Russian for "cherubim," whose only concern appears to be turning a profit. Declaring, "And, boy, does his stuff sell!" (107), Razumikhin explains how he will expand the text and affix "the most lavish title you've ever seen, half a page long" in order to make the most money possible. He goes on to suggest that he and Raskolnikov translate some of the "duller scandals" (107) from Rousseau's *Confessions*. Kheruvimov's peddling of Western pulp is a damming portrayal of the spiritual vacuity of contemporary Russian culture, which was so enraptured by the latest political and literary developments in Western Europe. Raskolnikov, however, wants none of it. He indignantly returns the three-rouble advance, telling his friend: "I don't need … translations" (108).

The gesture is a highly ambivalent one. On the one hand, Raskolnikov's defiant rejection of the translation work can be read as an expression of his excessive pride, his investment in being original, which leads him to murder the pawnbroker and her sister. Moreover, Razumikhin is one of the most positively-portrayed characters in the novel and will later become the husband of Raskolnikov's beloved sister, Dunia, and so cannot be read here as a moral seducer. In rejecting the translations ("I don't need translations!"), then, Raskolnikov is rejecting the help of a sincere friend, echoing a statement made shortly before: "But now it's clear to me, I don't need anything. Nothing at all, do you hear? No services. No help … I myself … I am alone … Very well, then! Let me be!" (107). Raskolnikov's rejection of Razumikhin's kind offer appears as an act of hubris—a refusal of what Michael Cronin describes as an "ethics of dependency" (2003:40).

On the other hand, Raskolnikov's refusal can be seen as a critique of Kheruvimov's crude capitalism, according to which profit is the main if not

Words [*Karmannyi slovar' inostrannykh slov*, 1845 and 1846], which was a kind or primer on progressive Western political and social thought, or, as Harriet Murav describes it, "a radical philosophical tract in the form of a dictionary" (1994:54). Moreover, almost all of the "democratic" poets (*poety-demokraty*) of the 1860s translated Western literary works on social and political themes, such as the poetry of Heinrich Heine and the abolitionist poetry of Henry Wadsworth Longfellow. For more on Petrashevsky and the members of his circle, see Semevskii (1922). For more on the "democratic" poets Russian poets of the 1860s, see Egolin (1969). Dostoevsky may have also been alluding here to his famous English contemporary, Mary Jane Evans, better known as George Elliot, who, in addition to novel writing, translated progressive philosophical texts from German into English.

sole consideration in choosing works for translation and, as Razumkhin puts is, scandal sells. Razumikhin also implies that Kheruvimov is a materialist: "He does a little publishing—natural science, stuff like that" (107). Raskolnikov's rejection of the amorality of the marketplace, one could say, suggests the possibility of his future redemption. His refusal to translate this text, however, cannot be taken as a rejection of Western progressive views *en gros*, for we know that Raskolnikov developed the idea that there were individuals who were above the law from his reading of Western philosophy. The rejection of translation might then reflect a need to deny or repress the foreign origin of his "original" ideas.

Razumikhin's approach to translation, on the other hand, suggests that he can engage in translation work without being contaminated. His willingness to alter the original texts for his own purposes, for example, indicates a skeptical relationship to Western culture—he does not treat these works as sacred—as well as a high degree of agency as a translator. Razumikhin, in other words, is able to translate without being translated, while Raskolnikov is, as Razumikhin suggests later in the novel, a bad translation, adopting Western views uncritically and then carrying them to their most extreme conclusion. Dostoevsky's representation of translation, then, is a sophisticated, nuanced one, which cannot be neatly pigeonholed on either side of the Slavophile/Westernizer opposition.

The mention of Rousseau's *Confessions* here is not insignificant insofar as Rousseau's version of Romanticism (especially as presented in his *Confessions*) symbolized what Dostoevsky critiqued as the individualism and narcissism of Western culture. "Dostoevsky's reaction to Rousseau," notes Robin Feuer Miller, "spanned the length of his writing career. Most often, Dostoevsky chose to polemicize with and parody the 'Jean-Jacques' of the *Confessions—The Insulted and Injured, Notes from Underground, The Idiot*, and *A Raw Youth* all contain both parody and polemic directed at Rousseau" (1984:78). The reference to Rousseau in a conversation about translation may also allude to *The Social Contract* in which Rousseau presents his concept of "young" or "immature" nations, situating Russia on the developmental margins of European culture. When Tsar Peter the Great forcibly "westernized" the Russian administrative structures and the culture of the upper classes and subjected his "young" nation to laws, he displayed, in Rousseau's judgment, only "a genius for imitation" [le génie imitatif]— "he did not have true genius, the kind that creates and makes everything out of nothing" (1997:73). Razumikhin's off-handed reference to Rousseau, therefore, could be said to model the kind of relationship to the foreign that Dostoevsky promotes throughout the novel and would later elaborate on in his 1880 speech at the Pushkin monument—how to take in the foreign without being taken over by it; to translate without being translated; and to be original without being an individualist.[5] This was, Joseph Frank argues, a central theme in Dostoevsky's post-exile writing:

> Dostoevsky was passionately persuaded (and he accepted his own experience as irrefutable evidence of its truth) that the instinctive sentiments and loyalties of Russians would always break through in some way, no matter how impenetrable might seem to be the overlay of Western European culture in the makeup of their personalities. Referring to his years in *katorga*, he adds: "I learned ... that I had always been a Russian at heart. One may be mistaken in ideas, but it is impossible to be mistaken with one's heart." (Frank 2010:244)

As a trope, translation in *Crime and Punishment*, understood as the problem of being original in a culture of belated modernity like Russia, where even the desire to be original was already a borrowing, is presented as an essentially male problem and can be understood within the context of the novel's broader theme of copying or imitation. This theme is reflected in references to a "gang of counterfeiters" (1999:157) and later when Porfiry Petrovich exclaims that Nikolai, in his false confession, "wasn't using his own words" (338). The charge of imitation is made most forcefully and consistently, however, by Razumikhin, directing it at Raskolnikov:

> I tell you, you're all, every one of you, a bunch of big talkers and swaggerers! The minute something goes a little bit wrong, you start brooding on it like a mother hen! And you're *plagiarists* at that. There's nothing *original* or independent in you! [...] I wouldn't trust any of you! The first think you always concentrate on is how to avoid resembling a human being! [...] If you weren't a fool, a common garden-variety all-around fool—if you were an *authentic original instead of some translation from a foreign language* ... Well, you see, Rodia, I admit you're a clever guy, all right, but still you're a fool! (162; italics added)

Here, Dostoevsky exploits the meaning of Raskolnikov's first name, Rodion—Razumikhin uses the diminutive form Rodia as a sign of their friendship. The name is formed from the Russian root *rod-*, which is

---

5 Later, Raskolnikov will encapsulate the Western philosophy of social Darwinism in the French statement: "Crevez, chiens, si vous n'etes pas contents" [Die, dogs, if you are not happy]. The remark appears only in French, suggesting the incompatibility, or untranslatability, of these Western ideas with traditional Russian values.

associated with birth and family ties, as in the words *roditeli* (parents) and *rodina* (homeland, native land). His name resonates in these scenes as a call to the wayward intellectual to return to his native culture. Later, Razumikhin will again instruct Raskolnikov on how to be a Russian original: "We don't even know how to talk nonsense intelligently, though! If you're going to give me big nonsense, better make it your own big nonsense, and I'll kiss you for it. Talk nonsense in your own way. That's almost better than talking sense in somebody else's. In the first case you're a man; in the second just a parrot! [...] We'd rather live off other people's ideas—that's what we're used to! Not so?" (194).

Dostoevsky's critique of the Romantic (Western) cult of originality does not, however, entail a critique of originality per se. In the notion of "nonsense," or "holy foolishness," Dostoevsky asserts a Russian form of originality rather than deconstructing the concept of originality itself.[6] By suggesting that Raskolnikov's problem is not that he wants to be original, but that he tries to do so according to Western models, Dostoevsky in fact reasserts national difference. What was somewhat inchoate in *Crime and Punishment*, Dostoevsky's first great post-exile novel, would be given its most eloquent and cogent expression in the author's 1880 speech at the opening of the Pushkin monument, only a year before his death. There, Dostoevsky asserts that Russians' ability to take in foreign influences without being overtaken by them—like Razumikhin, to translate without being translated—is the essence of Russia's national genius, which, he claims, will allow Russia to speak the last word to the world.[7] In this way, Dostoevsky attempts to recuperate originality as a masculine privilege, as embodied in the work of Russia's "universal man" Aleksandr Pushkin.

In the sections that follow, I will analyze the attempts of three Russian women writers to rethink the gendered metaphorics of translation and, by extension, to deconstruct rather than recuperate the tenets of Romantic authorship, presenting an alternative view of translation that does not see it

---

[6] In *Crime and Punishment*, Raskolnikov is humbled through the influence of the virtuous prostitute, Sonia Marmeladova, a version of the holy fool. She reads the Bible with Raskolnikov, a gesture of submission to holy wisdom (the meaning of her name). Dostoevsky, however, makes no allusion to the fact that Sonia's Bible is a translated text, a somewhat surprising fact given the novel's thematization of translation. Moreover, the translation of the bible into modern Russia was ongoing during the time Dostoevsky was writing *Crime and Punishment* and was fraught with political implications. Work on a modern Russian translation of the Bible sponsored by the Russian Bible Society was halted in 1826, following the failed Decembrist Revolt; it was permitted to continue only in 1858 under the more progressive tsar Alexander II. The first complete edition of the Bible in modern Russian finally appeared in 1876.

[7] For a discussion of the imperial implications of this vision, see Wachtel (1999).

as a threat to individual autonomy but rather as a celebration of what Michael Cronin has described as the "ethical value of dependency" (2003:40). The female writers discussed below level a very Russian critique of Romantic authorship, offering in its place a subjectivity that does not eschew translation but instead sees it as an acknowledgment and affirmation of "our multiple dependencies and the connectedness underlying the consoling fictions of absolute autonomy" (Cronin 2003:40). The works will be presented not chronologically but according to the profundity of their critiques of Romantic authorship, with the most radical text, Nadezhda Kvoshchinskaia's *Boarding School Girl*, discussed last.

Translation as service: Aleksandra Marinina's *Stylist*

In the mid-1990s, one of the best-selling authors in post-Soviet Russia was Aleksandra Marinina, whose novels featured the female detective Nastia Kamenskaia, who, in addition to her full-time job with the Moscow police department, translates detective novels from three languages. Other fictional female translators appeared at this time, such as Vera Saltykova, a translator from English and French who becomes embroiled in a crime arising from the former Soviet bloc nation of Czechoslovakia, in Polina Dashkova's 2002 detective novel *No One Will Cry* [*Nikto ne zaplachit*, 2002], and Dasha Valieva, a Russian teacher of French who serves as an ad hoc interpreter during a murder investigation in Paris, in Darya Dontsova's 2003 "ironic detective novel" *Hard-boiled Heirs* [*Krutye naslednichki*, 2003]. I will focus here on Marinina's novel, *The Stylist* [*Stilist*, 2005], however, because it provides the most sustained and complex engagement with the theme of (gendered) translation.

The heroine of Marinina's best-selling novels represents a rather unique image of the Russian woman. As Rosalind Marsh notes, "Kamenskaia undoubtedly constituted an interesting new type of Russian heroine in the 1990s, and some western critics have perceived her as a 'feminist' to some extent (mainly because she spends her time engaged in rational thought, sending her male colleagues off to do the routine police legwork, while her supportive partner shops and cooks for her)" (Marsh 2011:411). At the same time, she expresses deep-seated resistance to the post-Soviet influx of (Western) capitalist practices and values. Although she could be making big bucks in one of the new private enterprises cropping up throughout the country, she chooses to remain in her position as an analyst at the police department; in other words, she chooses service to society over material gain.

In *The Stylist*, an investigation of a serial murder of young boys leads Kamenskaia to the home of a former lover, Vladimir Solov'ev, a one-time professor of Asian languages and literatures, who has amassed some wealth since the fall of the Soviet Union as a translator of Japanese popular fiction. From their first encounter, Marinina makes clear that Kamenskaia and Solov'ev are on different sides of the ethical divide that ran through the center of early post-Soviet society, as when Solov'ev expresses surprise that with her law degree Kamenskaia works for the police and then asks her how much she makes. She responds: "You know my love of order. I could never have worked for an office that makes big money through illegal means. But by legal means, after taxes, I don't make a lot of money" (Marinina 2002:31). Solov'ev, however, has joined the ranks of the New Russians, whose ostentatious lifestyle made them an object of ridicule and scorn for the average Russian. As Kamenskaia approaches his housing complex for the first time, she writes: "Who lives in these expensive homes? New Russians, of course. They're too expensive for the 'old' Russians. But the New Russians who move into these spacious brick homes more often than not leave their parents in their apartments in the city" (13). From the start, Kamenskaia presents the New Russians' lifestyle as a threat to traditional Russian values—it breaks up Russian families.

Moreover, Marinina makes it clear that Kamenskaia feels no envy for her former lover. Although he lives in the lap of luxury, Solov'ev is a broken man. His wife was killed in a car crash, and his only son, who lives in the Moscow apartment, is living a life of utter dissipation and no longer speaks with his father. Solov'ev has been crippled in an attack, which he suspects his son may have had something to do with, and is confined to a wheelchair. Despite his wealth, Solov'ev feels "very vulnerable" (180) and is subject to periodic panic attacks. So compromised is his masculinity in Kamenskaia's eyes that she wonders, betraying a gender-based understanding of homosexuality, whether he might not be the homosexual murderer she is looking for. And so, while his work as a translator supports his New Russian lifestyle, it also provides him with a needed refuge: "Only when he was working did he feel autonomous and independent, and most importantly, unnoticeable" (28).

If Solov'ev's New Russian lifestyle is presented as a betrayal of traditional Russian values, his translation of Japanese pulp fiction is presented as a betrayal of his class. As a professor of Asian languages and literatures, Solov'ev had been a model representative of the *intelligentsia*:

He was a recognized expert in his field. There was no doubt about that. Just take a look at his bookshelves, with his own works on Chinese literature, Japanese philology, as well as number of novels and stories with the words "Translated by V. A. Solov'ev" on the title page. He was an outstanding philologist who worked with two of the most complex languages, Chinese and Japanese. (6)

Now he translates popular Japanese thrillers and detective novels—translated pulp fiction did indeed flood the post-Soviet market, but most of the works were translated from Western European languages, especially English, not Asian. And, while Kamenskaia feels that Solov'ev is basically honest, she suspects that something is amiss with the translation series that has brought him his wealth.

The key to understanding the moral taint Kamenskaia senses in Solov'ev's lucrative translation practice is his employer, the most successful publishing company in post-Soviet Russia, Shere Khan, named for the tiger in Rudyard Kipling's *Jungle Book*. The owners, described as "typical New Russians," purchase the poorly written novels of a Japanese writer and employ Solov'ev, the stylist referred to in the novel's title, to rewrite them in a Russian literary style that Kamanskaia herself finds captivating: "It's no surprise, she thought, that the books in this series sell so well. They're really well written. And the language is simply marvelous—light, elegant phrasing, no heaviness, not the least roughness" (267). She cannot put the novels down. But, Solov'ev does more than add style to the Japanese works; he is instructed to radically domesticate them in order to reach the largest possible readership. The publisher's business strategy is described in the following way:

He was able to spot the kernel that would make these books widely read. That kernel was *"Europeanization."* The only things purely Asian in these books were the names and the many exotic elements that adorned these works. The plot unrolls basically in Europe and America, and most of the characters are not of Asian descent. In the homeland of these authors, however, such prose was not popular and there was little interest from publishers. *In Japan and China they honor and cultivate traditional literature*, which is of little interest to the undemanding contemporary reader raised in the countries of European civilization. (16; italics added)

European "civilization" here has, of course, a distinctly ironic ring, and the Russian translator is situated between East and West. The opposition of Europe and Asia here contrasts a culture of novelty, with its undemanding readers, to a traditional culture, in which literature is honored. This New Russian enterprise, the narrator suggests, participates in the hegemony of Western culture by exoticizing and erasing from these novels the elements of true Asianness, which Russian thinkers for almost two centuries have argued distinguish Russia from the narcissistic West—a point driven home in the title of the company, which references Kipling's *Jungle Book*, a major source of Western stereotypes of the Orient. It is perhaps no coincidence, then, that Marinina names her translator Vladimir Solov'ev, the name of the nineteenth-century Russian philosopher, theologian, poet, and literary critic who denounced Western positivism in favor of intuitive experience. Central to his thinking was the Russian Slavophile notion of *sobornost'*, or "perfect integration," "unity." His essays were hugely influential in the debates over Russia's position between East and West at the turn of the nineteenth century, and so the reference inscribes Marinina's novel, which appeared at the turn of the twentieth century, within a traditional Russian discourse on national identity that preferences Eastern spirituality over Western materialism.

Although Solov'ev is in the end not found guilty of any crime, Marinina calls into question the morality of his translation project by juxtaposing the novel's two plotlines, or criminal investigations, the one involving the serial murder of young boys and the other, the attack on Solov'ev. When Kamenskaia stands next to the original suspect in the murders, she remarks that she has the same feeling as when she read one of the novels translated by Solov'ev, *The Blade* (*Klinok*) (168). She later realizes that she has seen the suspect before and then realizes that she has also seen the language of *The Blade* before—in Solov'ev's own writings. In this way, through this double act of recognition, she uncovers Solov'ev's role in the money-making publishing concern and concludes that the attack was organized by his employers to keep Solov'ev under their control and on their payroll. Without his inimitable style, the novels would never sell. Solov'ev himself recognizes a certain moral ambiguity in his approach, which he describes in the following way:

> When Solov'ev was shown the manuscript of the Japanese author at Share Khan publishing, he was horrified. It was an illiterate text, filled with "he said," "she approached," "he left," "she took." He forced himself to read the manuscript to the end, and only then did he realize that underneath this hopeless linguistic babble, there was something captivating hiding with dizzying twists. But it would have to be rewritten all over again. And in such a way that no one would doubt the author was Japanese, and not an American or a Russian. A book written about Japanese life by a Russian author isn't worth much. Everyone knew that. (365)

Solov'ev's crime, according to the logic of Marinina's novel, is that he tried to "pass," not as a homosexual but as a translator, when he was something closer to an author. In surreptitiously "Europeanizing" these Asian texts, he participated in the commodification of foreign cultures in a way that hopelessly problematized any notion of authenticity. The Russian *intelligent's* decision to involve himself with a New Russian publishing venture is presented as a capitulation to the West in at least two ways. First, the translations support—through the domesticating approach—the hegemony of Western cultural values; and second, Sovol'ev translates primarily for the sake of personal aggrandizement, whereas the modest Kamenskaia translates—faithfully, one can imagine—for a "little extra money." These two clearly gendered approaches to translation symbolize the moral and economic inequities of Post-Soviet society:

> [Kamenskaia] couldn't understand how a person who knows three languages could live in such a large, comfortable home, while a person who knows five languages, and who, by the way, contributes to society with her difficult, dirty but essential work, is forced by her income to live in a tiny, crowded apartment with a combined toilet and bath. She didn't doubt for a moment that her former lover was an honest man. He wasn't a crook or a swindler. And his money was clean, honestly earned. *But there's something that's just not right about how our society is organized today. And the result of this is the difference that exists between Nastia and Solov'ev, a difference that, strictly speaking, shouldn't be.* (64; italics added)

In *The Stylist*, Marinina inscribes her translators—Nastia and Solov'ev—within a broad set of post-Soviet anxieties related to questions of property ownership, the survival of "high literature," the hegemony of Western culture, and the nature of Russian identity in a post-Soviet world. Nastia and Solov'ev are metonymically associated with opposing value systems. As a New Russian translator, Solov'ev is tainted with the un-Russian qualities of narcissism, wealth, and capitulation to Western cultural values. As a part-time translator and full-time police detective, Nastia displays modesty, fidelity, and service to the community. This gendered tale of translation in post-Soviet Russia recognizes the necessity of translation in Russian culture but cautions against the covert infiltration of Western values into Russia through the Trojan horse of commodification and globalization.[8] What

---

[8] It is an interesting historical coincidence that Marinina's *Stilist* appeared in the same year as Boris Akunin's first detective novel. Akunin, the pseudonym of Grigorii Chkhartishvili, turned to fiction writing after a very respected career as a translator of Japanese literature—like Marinina's Solov'ev!—and as the editor of the journal *Inostrannaia Literatura* (Foreign Literature). Akunin would soon replace Marinina as Russia's best-selling author of detection fiction.

becomes clear by the end of *The Stylist* is that Marinina is lending Solov'ev's criminal translations a broader metaphorical meaning, using them to refer "not only to the transfer of specific texts into European languages, but to all the practices whose aim was to compact and reduce an alien reality into the terms imposed by a triumphant Western culture" (Simon 2000:11). By contrast, Kamenskaia's modest translations represent an ethical compromise similar to the one proposed by Dostoevsky's Razumikhin—how to translate without being translated. But, whereas the female characters in *Crime and Punishment* appear to be untroubled by the problem of translation or foreign influence, making translation into an exclusively male dilemma, Marinina's contribution to the gendered metaphorics of translation in Russia is to gender that ethical compromise as female.

Translation as transformation: Nina Gabrielyan's *Master of the Grass*

One of the most interesting literary treatments of women and translation is found in Nina Gabrielyan's novella *Master of the Grass* (*Khoziain travy* 2001). Gabrielyan was born in Armenia and now lives in Moscow, where she writes poetry and prose in Russian. She is also a well-respected painter and translator, who has published many translations of Aremenian poetry into Russian. Coordinator of the "Women and Creativity" program under the Independent Women's Forum, Gabrielyan is deeply concerned with women's issues, which represent a central theme in her writing.

The novella *Master of the Grass* features a successful translator of modern French poetry, Pavel, who takes in a homeless young painter, Polina, whose timidity and naiveté attract the older man; he becomes her first lover and mentor. The gendered metaphorics of translation is elaborated in this novella through the themes of mastery versus submission, originality versus imitation, and rationality versus intuition and sensuality. Beset by bizarre, ominous dreams, Polina produces avant-garde paintings of insects, associating her with a world of sensuality, instinct, primal urges, and opaque symbolism. When she refuses sugar in her coffee, she tells Pavel, "I try not to have sweet things. I'm too sensual. I have to watch it" (36), and when Pavel decides to buy one of her paintings, he is presented with a choice between a painting titled "Psyche" and one titled "Civilization." He chooses "Psyche." At one point, Pavel reads the descriptions Polina has written of her dreams: "She seemed not to know the difference between colour and sound. The dreams were probably too strange to ever be published. So I suggested that she should have a go at translating" (52). From the start, then, translation is presented as a kind of compromise between the subconscious and the conscious realms, between intuition and reason, between the highly individualistic and the communal (read: publishable). Moreover, both Pavel and Polina are described not as mere imitators but as having distinctive styles: "She thought I had a distinctive style of translating, particularly my epithets… " (42); "you could tell her [Polina's] style anywhere" (57).

Initially, Pavel sees translation as the perfect opportunity for him, as "a promising poet and translator, an editor for a prestigious publishing house" (30), to assert his power over Polina, who at first dutifully submits her translations for his approval, which pleases him: "They were happy days. I enjoyed tutoring her. She turned out to be a very able pupil, picking up everything straightaway. If I smiled at a particularly apt turn of phrase, she would break into an answering smile. If I frowned, *she would obediently copy that too*" (52; italics added). But, when she decides to enter a translation contest for the best translation of a poem by the Romanian-born French poet Countess Anna de Noailles, she works on the translation by herself, refusing to let Pavel help her in any way: "I was already anticipating the pleasure of working together. How she would show me her first timid attempts, and I would comment on them, when suddenly I came up against resistance" (53). That resistance—Polina's assertion of her creative agency as a translator— renders Pavel impotent and leads him to violence:

> "How's the translation going?" I asked and felt her body stiffen. "Alright," she replied. "Wouldn't you like to show it to me?" "Afterwards." "After what?" "After the contest." Her face went tight and I saw the same obtusely stubborn expression again. "Kiss me," said the stupid face. I kissed it. Then again and again. But my body remained indifferent. "Never mind, that sometimes happens," she whispered. I crawled away from her, devastated. The stupid face stared at me, and the tendrils round it bristled, ginger and unpleasantly soft. "Kiss me," the stupid face whispered, "kiss me, kiss me." The red lamp shone, lighting up the impudent, ginger face. But I didn't want to kiss it. I wanted it to stop being stupid and rejecting me. So I hit it with my elbow. I did it cleverly to seem like an accident, but the face still looked frightened and began to push me away. It grew two arms at the side, and they pushed me away, these frail arms. Just then the limpid part of my body came to life and I thrust it into her. I wedged her into the sofa, flattened her, smashed her—no distance between us, none at all. (54–55)

Despite the violence, Polina eventually completes her translation of the poem "L'Image" [The Image], the first stanza of which Pavel recalls in the story:

Pauvre faune, qui va mourir,
Reflètes-moi dans tes prunelles.
Et fais danser mon souvenir
Entre les ombres éternelles.
[Poor faun, about to die,
Reflect me in your eyes
And make the memory of me
Dance amid eternal shadows.]

The choice of both poet and poem here is highly significant for a number of reasons. First, the author of the poem is a woman while all the other poets mentioned thus far in the story have been men: Verlaine, Malarmé, and Valery. The poet's sex, as well as the poem's theme of female empowerment, seem to inspire identification between the poet and the translator; the fact that de Naoilles, like the author Gabrielyan and her protagonist Polina, was also a serious artist suggests additional lines of identification. Second, de Noailles's poetry is, if not conventionally feminist, deeply concerned with issues of women's power. The Russian poet Marina Tsvetaeva, incidentally, was a great admirer of de Noailles and translated her novel *The New Hope* (*La Nouvelle Espérance*, 1903) into Russian in 1916 as *Novoe upovanie* (Karlinsky 1986:54). This novel opens with an empowering epigraph from Nietzsche's *Thus Spoke Zarathustra*: "O my soul, I gave you the right to say Nay like the storm, and to say Yes as the open heaven says Yea." (The word *soul* in the original German, in the French translation used by de Noailles, and in Tsvetaeva's Russian translation is gendered feminine.) "This epigraph," Catherine Perry suggests, "indicates Noailles' will to assert her own views; though invoking Nietzsche's authority, she implicitly appropriates it to affirm her own authority and independence from the norms of traditional morality" (2003:97).

It should be noted here, insofar as it relates to Polina in *Master of the Grass*, that the heroine in *La Nouvelle Espérance* also faces death at the novel's end. De Noailles's fascination with death, in particular the death of her female characters, certainly complicates any straightforward interpretation of her novels as advocating female empowerment. There is, however, a feminist reading of the novel, according to which "the proximity of the heroine to death represents the preliminary stage for the birth of the writer, who emerges from, or is empowered by, writing her own death in a creative act of self-reflexivity" (Perry 2003:355 n77). Death, in that reading, is an allegory for the heroine's creative birth.

Death and empowerment are also prominent themes in the poem by de Noailles that Polina undertakes to translate. The poem is structured around two clearly gendered images—that of the dying (male) faun and that of the (female) lyric subject—which reflect in interesting ways Polina's own ambivalence over her growing autonomy. The dying faun, symbolizing passivity, submission, and death, contrasts sharply with the powerful, confident voice of the female poet who commands the faun to proclaim her immortality in the hereafter. The lyric subject invokes a pagan image of female power rooted in a profound sensuality. As Perry explains, "The accentuation of the speaker's body in Noailles's poem would then exemplify the notion that poetry has now returned to a pagan celebration of life and of the senses, and specifically, that the strongly Neoplatonic 'image' of the beloved in previous male poetry has now acquired substance as well as its own subjectivity through the power of speech" (2003:100). Especially relevant to the theme of translation is Noailles's inversion of the traditional gendered associations of reflection and mirroring: "In a reversal of conventional imagery, the female subject, instead of accepting to be a mirror, or an object, reflecting the forms that men have invested in her, asks the 'faun' to reflect her in its eyes. Although she may put herself forward as an object of desire, it is nonetheless she who manipulates the images that she sends" (2003:101).

The translation of this poem proves particularly empowering for Polina, especially when she receives preliminary word that she has won the translation prize for her work. Her new-found empowerment, however, is short-lived. Threatened by her growing independence, Pavel exploits his connections in the Writers Union to see that the award is not given to Polina, but to "old B." She is devasted by the news, and Pavel, motivated perhaps by guilt, begins to physically abuse her. She eventually becomes pregnant but is uninterested in having Pavel's son. She has an illegal abortion, which is botched, and she dies. No longer in control of her image, she becomes in death the dying faun.

The whole experience sends Pavel on a spiritual journey, which, as with Raskolnikov, involves humiliation of the (male) ego self:

Suddenly a blue gap appeared in the wall with a shining white church in the middle. I walked up to the church. Inside the white was a red and yellow light. It quivered with tongues of flame from the candles, and looked down at me from the walls with a hundred grieving eyes. Quiet chanting came from all sides. "Lord have mercy, Lord have mercy." "Lord have mercy," I whispered and immediately a gold-sleeved arm turned in my direction, swinging something on a long chain that enveloped me in a cloud of fragrance. "Lord have mercy, Lord have mercy," voices sang around me, the voices of grey old women, dressed in grey. "Lord have mercy," they sang, and the candles flickered, hundreds of candles. "Lord have mercy," I whispered. "Lord have mercy." And everything quivered and intermingled, and I swam in a stream of gold, melting into the crowd of worshippers. "Lord have mercy!" (Gabrielyan 2004:73–74)

Surrounded by women, Pavel loses himself, dissolving into the crowd. Beginning in childhood, long before he meets Polina, Pavel has had a narcissistic relationship with his image in the mirror. That narcissistic mirroring continues throughout the story: the names of the main characters—Pavel and Polina—are, in fact, distorted reflections (Paul/ Paulina), and in order to stoke his sexual desire, Pavel insists that he and Polina make love before a mirror. The fact that the boy he sees in the mirror is typically associated with the color pink may suggest that he represents feminine qualities that Pavel feels he must repress.

Pavel projects the feminine qualities of passivity and submission onto Polina and then further distances himself from them through acts of physical violence. Moreover, Gabrielyan historicizes Pavel's masculine dilemma by suggesting that passivity was a mode of survival in the Soviet Union for Russian men: "I had already learnt that obedience was the most effective form of resistance" (10); "my method of resistance was to comply" (15). The fact that Pavel forces Polina to make love with him before a mirror suggests perhaps an impossible longing on his part to integrate those two aspects of his identity, which he refers to elsewhere as his workday self and his nighttime self. His religious epiphany in the closing paragraph of the story would appear then to represent his abandonment of a patriarchal masculine identity based on ego-driven mastery, something alluded to in the novella's title, in favor of a more humble sense of communal identity— he is surrounded in the church by old women.

The theme of humility and its relationship to mastery is raised by Polina in an earlier conversation with Pavel:

"Insects ruled the earth for millions of years, until we arrived on the scene, built our stupid houses and proclaimed ourselves masters of the earth. Compared to them we're just newborn babes, perhaps still unborn. Who knows, perhaps," she gave a puzzled look at her hand still circling the cup, "perhaps we don't even exist at all. I sometimes even think," her voice dropped to a whisper, "that we are just a product of their imagination and when they wake up we'll disappear. With all our houses, and factories and flights into space." (37)

As in Marinina's *Stylist*, translation in *Master of the Grass* is presented not within the opposition of translation to original writing but rather within the opposition of female translation/authorship to male. Gabrielyan's female translator assumes a more intuitive approach to the selection and translation of texts, which is starkly opposed to the ego-driven translations of her abusive lover. Moreover, Polina's solidarity or identification with Anna de Nouailles is set against Pavel's obsession with mastery, which Gabrielyan reveals in various philosophical digressions to be a chimera.

Gabrielyan offers distinctly gendered views on imitation. For Pavel, imitation is symbolized by the mirror, which becomes for him a narcissistic dead end and a necessary erotic prop. Gabrielyan's female characters, on the other hand, express suspicion of the perfect resemblance of mirrors; they celebrate instead the creative potential of transformation. In Gabrielyan's "The Lilac Dressing Gown," for example, the female narrator states: "The passion for transformation may have been my greatest passion of all" (qtd. in Marsh 2011:84). As Rosalind Marsh explains:

> Gabrielyan gives a fuller explanation of what she means by "transformation" in her "essay" "Dom v metekhskom pereulke" ("The House in Metekhi Lane") through the monologue of the female narrator who tells a male artist that, in her view, ordinary mirrors "distort the essence of things" because they seem to suggest that the viewer is simultaneously both separate and distinct and split into two. What is needed, she argues, is a "special mirror" [...] "capable of endless transitions and transformations, which means that you are immortal." (2011:430)[9]

Translation, one might say, is just such a mirror.

While ostensibly Polina's story ends in tragedy, the reference to de Nouailles's work offers an alternative interpretation:

> A feminist reading of *La Nouvelle Espérance* would indicate that the proximity of the heroine to death represents the preliminary stage for the birth of the writer, who emerges from, or is empowered by, writing her own death in a creative act of self-reflexivity; this act would enable her to remove herself from her obsessive attachment to the man she believes she loves, thereby to gain her autonomy. (Perry 2003:355)

---

[9] Khvoshchinskaya expresses a similar notion in her short story "At the Photographer's Studio: A Sketch," from the collection *Al'bom—Grupy i portrety* [Album: Groups and Portraits, 1875] about a photography studio in a Russian provincial town. The women of the town exploit the opportunity presented by photography to transform themselves, having their photos taken while dressed in all kinds of exotic costumes. The male narrator, however, is deeply troubled by the phenomenon. She also plays with the idea of originality and imitation in the 1864 short story "Staryi portret—Novyi original" [Old Portrait—New Original].

The notion of translation as an alternative (female) form of authorship, one that recognizes the polyglossia and intertextuality inherent in all writing, was central to Gabrielyan's creative oeuvre, in which "everything is connected, everything is alive, the past and the future transcend the boundaries of time and merge into the present to live within the poet" (Trofimova and Goff 1994:190). Ethnically Armenian, she received a degree in French translation from Moscow State Institute of Foreign Languages, after which she published both original writing and translations. In 1994 she would become editor of the Russian feminist journal *Preobrazhenie*, meaning "transformation."

The idea that all artistic production, including translation, involves transformation was central to Gabrielyan's philosophy.[10] As she stated in a recent interview: "The world has many faces, many borders; every person sees it in her own way. It is impossible to see the world objectively. In my view, the objective world is a world in which no one lives. It is important for the writer, the artist, to acquire a face, it is important to have one's own style. But I feel no affinity for the artistic quest for originality [*original'nichanie*]" (2013:online). This rejection of the cult of originality is reflected throughout her oeuvre. Her poetry collection *Trostnikovaia dudka* (The Reed Pipe), for example, contains both original poetry and translations of classical and contemporary Armenian poets. Although she wrote in Russian, the voices of her Armenian ancestors "are constantly speaking to her and influencing her life and work" (Trofimova and Goff 1994:190), making all her "original" work into a kind of translation, while her translations are closely related to her original writing: "Just as the translations bear the mark of her original style, so too, the very selection of these poems, which continue themes and motifs prevalent in her own work, asserts her worldview" (Trofimova and Goff 1994, 190). Only in *Master of the Grass*, however, does Gabrielyan so clearly gender this vision of translation as a kind of polyglossic authorship that, by rejecting the quest for mastery and originality, transforms rather than reflects and liberates rather than confines.

Translation as emancipation:
Khvoshchinskaya's *The Boarding School Girl*

An even more radical transvaluing of Romantic authorship was offered by a contemporary of Dostoevsky, Nadezhda Kvoshchinskaya, in her novella *The Boarding School Girl* (*Pansionerka*), which appeared in 1861, only a few

---

[10] This also applies to the visual arts as Gabrielyan is also, like her character Polina, an accomplished painter.

years before the publication of *Crime and Punishment*. Khvoshchinskaya published her novel under a male pseudonym, V. Krestovsky, during an especially turbulent time in Russian history when the "woman question" was at the front and center of public debate.[11] Born in the provincial city of Riazan, Khvoshchinskaya made life in the provinces and the education of women into a major theme of her fiction, which, according to M. S. Goriachkina, was "closely tied to the work of democratic authors, who were raised under the direct influence of Chernyshevsky, Nekrasov, and Shchedrin" (1963:3). Khvoshchinkaya had two younger sisters, Sofia and Praskovia, who also wrote fiction, and, like Khvoshinskaya, published under male pseudonyms—Iv. Vesen'ev and S. Zimarov, respectively. The sisters were very close and were known in their time as the "Russian Brontës" (Solomon 1999:261). In addition to her fiction, Nadezhda, who possessed a firm command of French, Italian, and Latin (1999: 262), translated works by George Sand. Incidentally, Khvoshchinskaya and her sister Sofia were avid painters, an interest they share with the heroine of Khvoshinskaia's story "The Boarding School Girl"—and with Gabrielyan and her heroine, Polina.

Khvoshchinskaya's novel presents the intellectual and spiritual coming of age of a 15-year-old Russian girl, Lolenka, in the fictional provincial city of N. under the unofficial tutelage of an internal exile, Veretitsyn. A parodic rewriting of the Adam and Eve myth and its take on women and knowledge, the novel stages most of the encounters between Lolenka and Veretitsyn in the garden of Lolenka's family home, near the apple tree. There, Veretitsyn, who is now reduced to working, significantly, as a copy clerk, criticizes Lolenka's education, which appears to be based entirely on the soulless memorization of facts and figures. Under Veretitsyn's influence, Lolenka soon loses interest in memorization and seeks a deeper form of learning. A central moment in her "not-so-sentimental education," as Karen Rosneck puts it, occurs when Veretitsyn lends her a translation of Shakespeare's *Romeo and Juliet* in French. The work, which she devours in secret, also serves to stoke the flames of Lolenka's youthful passion for her mentor, who is, Khvoshchinskaya makes clear, "all too human"—he misquotes the German title of a work and mistakes a poem by Dmitriev for one by Kheraskov.

Although the fact that Lolenka has access only to a French (probably prose) translation of Shakespeare would seem to contribute to the representation of the provinces as a place of "bad" imitations, that French translation nonetheless precipitates a profound rethinking on Lolenka's

---

[11] For a general overview of the "woman question" in Russia and its relationship to Western feminism, see Wood (2009) and Rosenholm (1996).

part of what education and knowledge are in a moment of epiphany that takes place in the garden:

> Once, after dinner, at a time when everyone in her house was napping, when, as far as she could tell, even her neighbor was usually sleeping, Lolenka remembered his book, *Romeo and Juliet*, and ran back to get it. She didn't want to read from the beginning, and some parts in the middle didn't quite interest her, but she'd suddenly remembered scenes that, it seemed had to be reread. She searched for them impatiently, started to read hurriedly, and it seemed strange to her that the language and style that had been so difficult before could now be understood without any trouble. *Somehow they had been translated in her mind, in her heart, not into words, but into a sensation clearer and fuller than words.* When Lolenka rasied her head from the book, the branches of the linden tree darkening overhead frightened her. She didn't dare look at the window and suddenly ran out of the garden. (101; italics added)

After this epiphanic moment, it is impossible for Lolenka to go on living in the intellectually stifling milieu of the provinces. The use of the word "translated" in this passage is crucial, juxtaposing a holistic female vision of translation (sense for sense) to a legalistic male vision (word for word). Her flight from the garden represents on a symbolic level her rejection of traditional views of women and education, which construe knowledge not only as corrupting for women but also as setting off a chain of corruption (snake-Eve-Adam). It also functions, Jehanne Gheith argues, as a rejection of "the great man narrative" as nonsense (2004:172). In Russian culture, in the opposition of rationality/feeling, feeling is generally weighted far more favorably than in the West; in fact, Russia's soulfulness is often juxtaposed to what the philosopher Nicolas Berdyaev referred to as "the Western cult of cold-blooded justice" (Berdyaev 1962:87).

While the French translation of Shakespeare might seem a rather unlikely vehicle for Lolenka's enlightenment—after all, both hero and heroine die tragically—its thematics celebrate modern notions of romantic love, and the two lovers appear as equals. In the classroom, when Lolenka is asked about some war, she consults her copy of *Romeo and Juliet*: "Lolenka looked into *Romeo and Juliet* as if consulting a textbook and found there, almost on the first page, something about the absurdity and evil of the sin of bloodshed. Next to her, her classmate Olenka Belyaeva was answering the question and *reciting the names of great men*" (Khvoshchinskaya 2000:76; italics added). *Romeo and Juliet* appears in this scene to represent an alternative to the masculinist history of great men and great deeds recited obediently by Olenka. Lolenka asks herself: "What great men? They're villains!" (76).

Those in authority, however, put Shakespeare's play to another use, highlighting the superficiality of women's education and exposing its true aim—obedience. This notion of Shakespeare as canonical male author is brought home when Pelageya Semyonovna, a friend of Lolenka's mother, asks Lolenka to read to them in French—an absurd request insofar as neither of the women knows French and the text is a translation, thus making Lolenka's knowledge of French into a hollow signifier of cultural capital. Lolenka objects to the pointlessness of the task and, moreover, she has already thrown the translation over the fence, indignant over Veretitsyn's unreturned affection. She ends up reading them a passage from her French grammar book, a symbol of the kind of rote memorization of rules she has come to despise:

> Lolenka's throat tightened, her ears burned with fury and anguish. Right then, right then, she would've run away somewhere but didn't have the strength! She didn't want to cry but scream, tear out her hair ...
>
> "Don't upset your mother," Pelageya Semyonovna told her in a whisper. "Well, that's some character you've got! You'd better break that habit, my angel, break it—tone yourself down! You'll have to live with your husband and his family.... Don't get caught within reach of your husband—you'll gain nothing. It's easy to accept from your papa and mama, but from your husband... oh, that's really difficult! I know ... Read just three little lines, my beauty."
>
> Lolenka started to read her French grammar book aloud; tears fell on the book thick and fast. Pelageya Semyonovna shook her head in the direction of the kitchen, amused by the foreign words.
>
> "Look at her go, so smart!" she said. "Well, that'll be enough, my beauty; we've been entertained. Just submit, you have to submit," she added in a whisper. "But now you and I are off to the garden, the little garden green, we're off to walk away sadness and misery." (115)

Soon after this episode, Lolenka runs away to live with an unmarried aunt in St. Petersburg.

Eight years later, she bumps into Veretitsyn at the Hermitage museum where they are both copying works of the old masters. It turns out that Lolenka has become sufficiently accomplished as a painter to sell her copies; she also works as a translator from three languages. Interestingly, the paintings mentioned in the novel are not themselves originals; the Hermitage owns only copies of these works, so Lolenka is in fact copying copies of the old masters. In any case, Veretitsyn appears even more dispirited and broken in St. Petersburg than he had been in N., while Lolenka is thoroughly content with her new life; she is, in the narrator's words, "adept, bold, self-assured" (125). If earlier in the novel Lolenka's fascination with *Romeo and Juliet* implied her affection for Veretitsyn, then Vertitsyn's glance at Domenichino's painting of *Cupid* in the Hermitage suggests that he has now developed romantic feelings for her. The tables now are turned.

As in *Crime and Punishment*, translation and imitation per se are not gendered in the *Boarding School Girl*. Rather, the novel presents the characters' *relationships* to translation and imitation as gendered, that is, there appear to be masculine and feminine modes of translation/imitation. For Veretitsyn, as for Raskolnikov, translation and imitation frustrate his driving desire to be original. In fact, in Chapter IV, Khvoshchinskaya associates (male) translation with mediocrity and mediation:

> At home, Veretitsyn found among his bundles a multivolume, two-columned *French edition of Shakespeare's works*, with a small, poor illustration at the heading of each play. The volumes were somewhat decrepit, a monument of years gone by, which had somehow survived into a much later, busier, more troubled time. Those volumes—acquired with a student's savings, the beginning of a library, the first realization of a cherished dream—more than anything else reminded him of all the failures, all the useless expenditures of life, all his unrealizable, joyful hopes. Somehow they expressed more clearly than anything that it all had died. Yellowed, marked along the margins with fingernail and pencil, with pages of inserted notes and *attempts at translation*, they seemed like a legacy from the dead, while the owner, alive, looked at them without recognizing his altered handwriting, without recognizing his own soul in those notes. (44; italics mine)

In this passage, the French translations of Shakespeare are associated with layers of mediation and alienation, whereas Lolenka lives contentedly "in the present," as she says, not alone but within a close circle of artist-friends. Despite her decision not to marry, Lolenka nevertheless displays, to use Hofstede's terms, more social orientation, a feminine quality, whereas Veretitsyn displays more ego orientation. Moreover, if Kheruvimov's marketing of cheap, scandalous translations in *Crime and Punishment* expresses a traditional Russian suspicion of capitalist enterprise, Lolenka's ability to sell her artistic copies and translations is positively portrayed insofar as it allows her to further her education—she sells a copy of a Greuze painting in order to buy tickets to the opera—and to contribute to the maintenance of her aunt's modest household. In other words, participation in the market does not threaten her sense of self or compromise her morals.

Despite the fact that some contemporary critics interpreted the ending of *Boarding School Girl* as tragic—Lolenka is unmarried and childless—

with the critic Victor Ostrogorsky declaring Lolenka to be an "egotist," most readers of the time found Lolenka to be "a positive model of the new woman" (Gheith 2004:175). Lolenka's embrace of imitation frees her from the tyranny of romantic, ego-driven desires and the bondage of societal expectations of woman. She rejects the useless self-sacrifice of women in unhappy marriages and expresses absolutely no regret over her life's choices. As she puts it, "I say to everyone: Do as I have done, free yourselves, all who have hands and a strong will! Live alone—here's life—work, knowledge, and freedom ... " (Khvoshchinskaya 2000:135). In contrast to the fate of Veretitsyn's former love Sofia—who has sacrificed her own happiness in a loveless marriage to a bureaucrat—Lolenka's independent life in St. Petersburg is presented clearly as the better alternative. Free from the Romantic need to be "original," which plagued Veretitsyn throughout his life, Lolenka overcomes the curse of Eve, creating for herself a thoroughly fulfilling life in translation.

Conclusion

The texts discussed above outline a perhaps uniquely Russian gendered metaphorics of translation in which the hierarchized binary opposition of original writing to translation is not simply inverted; it is deconstructed, giving us a glimpse into a world where textual production and authorship are not defined by originality, and translation becomes an alternative form of authorship. In many ways, these works foreshadow recent Western revisionist histories of the Renaissance, which have sought to revalorize the work of women translators (Goldberg 1997, Kronitiris 1997, Hayes 2009, White 2011, Uman 2012, and Goodrich 2014). In a cultural context before the advent of Romanticism and the construction of translation as the defining other of original writing, the very terms of the literary polysystem must be reimagined by the modern scholar in order to do justice to the role of translation. In such a reimagining, "the key question for authorial agency and authenticity, therefore, shifts from originality to selective assimilation" (Felch 2011:159).

Russia's belated entry onto the European cultural scene led it to take a critical stance toward many of the tenets of Romanticism, which defined Russian culture as imitative and underdeveloped, and promoted individualism, which was seen as antithetical to Russian traditional values. The women writers discussed above took advantage of this Russian critique to rethink the aesthetic and ethical possibilities available to women within a culture of imitation.

5

Imitatio: Translation and the Making of Soviet Subjects

The polarized nature of resistance, where attention is focused on opposing the force of a defined and more powerful opponent, is an unnecessarily limited view of translational activism.

Maria Tymoczko (2010:viii)

Beginning unofficially in the late 1920s and more officially in the 1930s with the creation of the Soviet Writers Union, writers whose original work did not align with the narrowing dictates of approved literature were given translation work to do. This occurred typically with authors who had developed their literary style and thematic preoccupations in the prerevolutionary Silver Age or in the tumultuous aesthetic environment of the early postrevolutionary period. Poets and prose writers affected by this policy included Mikhail Kuzmin, Anna Akhmatova, Osip Mandel'shtam, Mikhail Bulgakov, Marina Tsvetaeva, Boris Pasternak, and Nikolai Zabolotsky, to name but a few. Daniele Monticelli has referred to this phenomenon, as it was replayed in communist Estonia, as de-authorization. As Monticelli explains, "Deauthorization, which can be understood in [Jacques] Rancière's terms as a redistribution of planes and roles, of ways of doing and making and of their legitimation in the literary field, follows [...] a pattern that makes explicit the hierarchical conception of writing activity and *authorial* agency of the Soviet regime" (2013). Evgeny Dobrenko makes a similar point, when he claims that, "the birth of a multinational literature in the USSR" was predicated on "the death of the author" (2011).

While I largely agree with Monticelli and Dobrenko and will elaborate on their arguments in this chapter, I would suggest a slight but nonetheless important Foucauldian revision by renaming the phenomenon *re*authorization in order to acknowledge its productive side.[1] That is, while predicated on the death of a certain kind of Romantic author-centered model of literary production—authorship with a capital "a"—this reauthorization enabled other, more text-centered models of literary production—small "a" authorship—to emerge, which offered a variety of material and creative opportunities to men and women of letters.[2] The term reauthorization also underscores the fact that the practice was not designed to punish, or rather not only to punish, but also to remake and transform these prerevolutionary authors into Soviet subjects. Consider, for example, the short obituary for the poet and writer Mikhail Kuzmin that appeared in the newspaper *Pravda* in 1937 following the author's death, which occurred, miraculously, from natural causes. The obituary lists Kuzmin's only occupation as translator, making no mention of his work as a poet and prose writer—in fact, Kuzmin had been unable to publish any original work since 1927 (Malmstad and Bogomolov 1999:358). While it is tempting to see the obituary as a simple act of censorship, erasing any mention of Kuzmin's original literary output, I suggest it be read alongside the brief obituary that appeared in the newspaper *Literary Leningrad*, in which Kuzmin's surname is misspelled, with a soft sign, transforming his noble name into one of peasant origin (358). As a translator and a commoner, the decadent, aristocratic author of Russia's first gay novel is remade into a Soviet cultural worker.

Or, consider the remarks made by the Soviet writer and administrator Aleksandr Fadeev in 1947 when asked by a Western journalist whether Boris Pasternak was a popular writer in the Soviet Union. Fadeev responded:

> Pasternak was never popular in the USSR with the common reader due to his *extreme individualism* and the formal complexity of his verse, which is difficult to understand. Only two of his works—"1905" and "Lieutenant Schmidt"—had a broad social impact and were written in a simpler way. Unfortunately, he did not continue along that path. Today Pasternak is translating the dramas of Shakespeare; he is famous in Russia *as a translator* of Shakespeare. (Fadeev 2013b:85; italics mine)

---

[1]   In reconceptualizing power in this way, I am following Richard Burt, who advocates for a new approach to censorship, moving away from a model based on *removal* and *replacement*, which defines censorship as a "strictly repressive activity," in favor of "a more complex and nuanced model of censorship involving *dispersal* and *displacement*" (1998:17).

[2]   Murav (2005) describes Soviet culture as characterized by the juxtaposition of author-centered and text-centered models of literary production, which offered opportunities for Felix Roziner's hero, Finkelmeyer, to survive and in some ways prosper under conditions of repression (See Chapter 2).

Even more illustrative of the transformative potential of translation is the case of Nikolai Zabolotsky, who while in internal exile for his original writings undertook a translation of the medieval *Slovo o polku Igoreve* [The Lay of Igor's Campaign]. As we know from his correspondence with friends and family, the translation not only saved him mentally during that time but also reconciled him with his homeland. At the end of one letter in which he describes the beauty and complexity of the *Slovo*, he exclaims: "You read this tale and count your good fortune to be a Russian!" (Zabolotsky 1994: 222) Translation also worked to reconcile the authorities with suspect individuals. Zabolotsky's translation, for example, earned him the right to return to Moscow. Or, consider the case of Tatyana Gnedich, who translated Byron's *Don Juan* while incarcerated. She began the translation in a holding cell, having memorized two of the cantos. When the commandant of the prison saw the final translation, written in her tiny script on stationary headed with Evidence of the Accused, he supposedly declared: "For this you should be awarded the Stalin Prize!" (Etkind 2012:18).

Efim Etkind presents the revalorization of translation under the Soviets in rather cynical terms:

> Poetry translation was always better paid in the USSR—this was material support for an activity that the party leadership saw as useful. The point is that in order to promote the unity of the multi-national Soviet Union it was necessary to constantly create the illusion of fraternity among the constitutive republics and ethnic groups; [...] the government spared no resources to erect this façade, which was meant to hide the rather unsightly reality. (1997:39)

Elsewhere, however, in that same introductory article, Etkind acknowledges the magnificent achievements in poetic translation that occurred under the Soviets (1997:45–46)—correlating the greatest translations with the worst periods of repression. Moreover, regardless of the regime's intentions, many of the relationships formed between translators and their poets were deep and abiding. Pasternak, for example, had great admiration for the poetry of the Georgian poet Titzian Tabidze, which he expressed in letters to Tabidze's widow. Zabolotsky not only formed relationships with the individual poets he translated but also thoroughly bought into the ideal of "friendship of peoples." As his son Nikita explains:

> As he became more and more deeply involved in translation work, [Zabolotsky] did not regard it as a burden or as merely a way of earning money. Translating poetry did not seem to him a mundane literary

craft. On the contrary, he always felt that it was full of high social ideals. Familiarizing the Russian reader with poetry of the other peoples of the USSR and of other countries seemed to him to be an important educational endeavor, and a serious contribution to the strengthening of friendship and collaboration between nations, to their mutual cultural enrichment. (1994:253)

Reconceptualizing state-sponsored translation as reauthorization, therefore, focuses our attention not only on the repressive state apparatus, to use Adorno's term, that enacted and enforced this policy, but on the various ideological means distributed throughout Soviet culture that made it a productive practice. For if, as Maria Zemskova states, for many Russians in the Stalinist period, "'escape into translation' became the only possible answer to the question of *how to be a writer*" (Zemskova 2013:186), it was a viable solution because the regime was committed to improving the status of translators, granting them full "literary citizenship" in the 1930s when they were accepted into the Writers Union with all the rights and privileges of writers (204). In other words, at precisely the time when writers were being relegated to translation work, translation was coming to occupy an increasingly central position in the Soviet literary polysystem. Consider, for example, the three translations of Shakespeare's *Hamlet* that appeared between 1937 and 1940, which Anna Akhmatova declared a "feast of Russian culture" (Chukovskaya 2002:81), or the awarding of the Stalin Prize to Mikhail Lozinsky in 1944 for his translation of the *Divine Comedy*, which Akhmatova described as "the greatest feat [*podvig*] of his life" (2013:98).

Finally, to the extent that de-authorization implies that Romantic authorship, based on originality and inspiration, is the only legitimate form, then reauthorship may allow us to better see and understand the ways in which Stalinist culture was in fact promoting an alternative model of authorship, one in which translation—that is, authorship conceived in terms of craftsmanship (*masterstvo*) and labor—became not only a highly visible practice, a techne of empire, to use Vincente Rafael's term, but also a metaphor for literary production in the Age of Stalin, when original writing had become a problem.[3] My point is that translation should not be seen in simplistic terms as merely punishment or as its corollary, a site of resistance.

---

[3] The seeds for that rethinking of literary production had, of course, been sewn, paradoxically enough, by the Formalists who sought to de-romanticize the study of literature, focusing on how texts were made.

Rather, I hope to show how thoroughly translation was implicated in the project of remaking Soviet citizens. So implicated, in fact, that it might be considered the most Soviet of the arts, at least in the Stalinist period.

A culture of *Imitatio*

In the *Soviet Novel*, Katerina Clark compares the socialist realist novelist to a medieval icon painter:

> In some ways the most definitive characteristic of Socialist Realism is not the mode of writing it envisages but its radical reconception of the role of the writer. After 1932 (at least) the Stalinist writer was no longer the creator of original texts; he became the teller of tales already prefigured in Party lore. Consequently, his function is rather like that of the chroniclers of the Middle Ages, as described by Walter Benjamin." (1984:159)

In her more recent work *Moscow: The Fourth Rome* (2011), Clark documents the fascination among members of Soviet Union's creative intelligentsia with the Western Renaissance (98–99, 108–111, 318–324). While it is common in popular culture to draw a stark distinction between the Middle Ages and the Renaissance, many scholars today reject the idea that Medieval Scholasticism simply ended with the rise of Humanism. In fact, Medieval and early Renaissance cultures had much in common; both were governed by an aesthetics and ethos of *imitatio*.

Let me begin by briefly outlining some of the defining features of imitatio as a model of literary production. First, it was hierarchical. As Thomas Greene notes in *The Light in Troy*, his brilliant study of imitation in early Renaissance Italy and France, authorship in these cultures was heavily influenced by medieval conceptions. According to Greene:

> The author (*auctor, actor, autor*) at a medieval university was a writer whose work had commanded respect for so many centuries as to have become an authority (*autorità*), to be read as an authentic source of knowledge. The term *autorità* and its cognates imply that unflawed capacity for patriarchal communication and instruction through time which few if any medieval men perceived as problematized by history. The faith in authoritative continuity, both verbal and doctrinal, clearly rested on the belief in God as the ground and goal, alpha and omega, of human language. (1982:12)

In this hierarchical system, only the classical writers were considered authors with a capital A, those endowed with true cultural authority. As Anthony Grafton puts it, the most powerful knowledge at this time "is contained in authoritative texts: the Bible; the philosophical, historical, and literary works of the Greeks and Romans; and a few modern works of unusually high authority" (1992:2). This canon, moreover, was largely fixed. Within such a literary economy, the contemporary author interpreted, translated, and disseminated the work of the great Authors of the past, as described by Roland Barthes in his essay "The Death of the Author":

> In ethnographic societies the responsibility for a narrative is never assumed by a person but by a mediator, shaman or relator whose performance—the mastery of the narrative code—may possibly be admired but never his "genius." The author is a modern figure, a product of our society insofar as, emerging from the Middle Ages with English empiricism, French rationalism and the personal faith of the Reformation, it discovered the prestige of the individual, of, as it is more nobly put, the "human person." It is thus logical that in literature it should be this positivism, the epitome and culmination of the capitalist ideology, which has attached the greatest importance to the "person" of the author. (1992:115)[4]

Susan Stewart makes a similar point in *Crimes of Representation*, when she writes, "Before the development of concepts of original genius and intellectual property, all thoughts were potentially held in common, all thoughts were appropriable by readers, and it was those who disseminated ideas who reaped any rewards or punishments by such ideas" (1994:12). To make this point, Anthony Grafton quotes the title of an old German song: Die Gedanken sind frei, "Thoughts are free" (1992:14). Within a culture of imitatio, then, there was no sharp distinction between writing and translation, as true Authorship belonged only to the ancients. As Wendy Wall notes, "the opposition between original and secondary or imitative works is a categorical opposition largely absent in the Renaissance; the notion of original writing became valorized only later" (1993:337).

Second, it was conservative insofar as authors were not judged on their thematic and aesthetic innovation. The emphasis on adherence to dogma discouraged such experimentation, which was in turn reflected

---

[4]   Although Barthes and other postmodern thinker/theorists championed text-centered models of literary production with their concepts of the death of the author, iterativity, and the simulacrum, they were unable to abandon the author-centered model, becoming themselves academic stars.

in reading practices that centered around the rereading and study of classic texts, producing what Mikhail Gasparov describes as a culture of *perechtenia*, or rereading, as opposed to modern cultures of *pervochtenia*, or first-time reading (Gasparov 1997:463). Third, imitatio had an ethical dimension; it indexed a way of life and was deeply implicated in the making of Renaissance subjects, insofar as acts of imitation symbolically reenacted the subject's submission to cultural authority. This was exemplified in the Renaissance practice of the copybook, in which people collected edifying quotations. Often overshadowed by Stephen Greenblatt's more modern notion of self-fashioning, the copybook, Mary Thomas Crane contends, was central to the construction of the humanist subject: "The student learned to gather what was already framed as a saying, it framed his character, and he, in turn, reframed it in his own writing as a sign that he had received the prescribed education" (Crane 1993:8).[5] Moreover, as Wendy Wall notes "humanistic education encouraged translation and imitation as important modes of discursive learning" (1993:337).

And so, not only was translation, along with other forms of imitation, not denigrated in the Renaissance as unoriginal, it enjoyed special status as an exemplary ethical practice. The French Renaissance translator Jacques Peletier du Mans described translation as "the truest form of imitation" (qtd. in Hermans 1985:104)—as expressed in the metaphor of "following in another's footsteps." As Theo Hermans explains, " 'Following' in this context implies not only dependence in the logical and chronological sense (the translated text being derived from the source text), but also a relation of stronger versus weaker, of free versus confined, of owner or master versus servant or slave. *To translate is to accept willful confinement and restriction of one's liberty of movement in order to follow in someone else's tracks*" (1985:109; italics mine). While to the modern ear submission may have a negative ring, in cultures of imitation, submission to the great Authors of the past was of the highest ethical and moral value, as evident in Thomas à Kempis's *The Imitation of Christ*.

Looking at translation not through the lens of Romantic authorship has been especially productive in reevaluating the contribution of translators in early modern Europe, and of women translators, in particular, who for so long had been ignored or undervalued within a literary polysystem that

---

[5] Crane's work serves to balance the emphasis on self-fashioning in Greenblatt's work, which highlights the power of the middle-class individual, freed from the constraints of medieval castes, to create his own destiny.

celebrates original, secular writing (see Goldberg 1997, Kronitiris 1997, Hayes 2009, White 2011, Uman 2012, and Goodrich 2014). When "the key question for authorial agency and authenticity [...] shifts from originality to selective assimilation" (Felch 2011:159), translation is no longer seen as an absence of authorship or as a secondary form of authorship. Scholars now focus on the variety of authorial possibilities offered by translation. As Jaime Goodrich puts it, "Translators, editors, and others working in the space of religious translation cultivated a rich variety of possible authorial poses" (2014:27). In the spirit of that research, I will attempt to read Stalinist culture as a culture of imitation in order to better understand the place of translation within that culture's literary polysystem.

So, to what extent can Stalinist Russia be considered a culture of imitation? First, I would note the hierarchical and conservative nature of literary production. Insofar as literary production in Stalinist Russia was based on the emulation of exemplars, or models, artistic production was characterized by an extreme traditionalism. As Evgeny Dobrenko explains in *The Making of the State Reader*: "Artistic creativity was minimized and the prognosticatory and anticipatory function of art died out since there was nothing for a new form to be born from within the Soviet framework of quasi-traditionalism, which preserved automatism of traditional reception" (1997:22). The guiding principle was imitation. In *The Soviet Novel*, Clark repeatedly compares literary production under Stalin to premodern modes of artistic production, equating it with medieval icon painting and chronicle writing. In such a society, Clark and Dobrenko point out, the ones who could "generate new authoritative texts" were "essentially only Stalin or someone privileged to be delegated by him to perform that function" (2007:xiv). The Marxist–Leninist canon was largely fixed, and contemporary writers were expected to cite the canonical authors to lend their own works authority.

Translation, therefore, can be considered an exemplary form of literary production within such a system insofar as a translation stands in a hierarchical relationship to the original, just as the apprentice stands in a hierarchical relationship to the master. Indeed, the concept of *masterstvo* [mastery, or master craftsmanship], which would become closely associated with translation throughout the Soviet period, was meant to distinguish it—and artistic production, in general—from "original" writing, understood as the product of genius and inspiration.[6] The

---

[6] Indeed, it is a historical irony that the construction of translation as craft allowed translators and scholars to use terms developed by the formalists. Consider, for example, the chapter titled "Priemy" [Devices] in the 1930 *Iskusstvo perevoda*, coauthored by Kornei Chukovskii and Andrei Fedorov. This was a key formalist concept.

conceit that translation was a "craft" made it less suspect than original writing and replayed the narrative of submission to a higher authority. It also fit well into the metaphorics of official Soviet rhetoric of the time, which focused on the "building" of a new society. In this way, translation came to epitomize artistic production in the Stalinist period, which was conceived not in theoretical treatises and manifestoes but rather in the elevation of specific texts as exemplary, which, again, implied the model of apprenticeship to a master, or in this case, masters, and promoted an aesthetic conservatism (see Clark 1984:3). Consider, for example, Pavel' Antokol'skii's rejection of theory in an article titled "The Black Bread of Craftsmanship," which appeared in a 1963 issue of the journal *Masterstvo Perevoda*: "In the field of literary translation, there can be no inventions, no problems that fall to us from the moon. The questions that concern us, our debates, misunderstandings, reticences are essentially the inheritance we have received from many generations of Russian translators" (1963:5).

While some scholars in Translation Studies have suggested that stylistic conservatism is a universal feature of translated texts, it was undeniably a defining trait of the Soviet School of Translation. As Maria Khotimsky notes, "the Soviet school approach to translation exhibited an 'excessive reliance on poetic tradition,' that is, on imitation of the great stylists of the past" (2011:93). In support of her contention, she offers the following piece of advice given to young translators by Samuil Marshak:

> Without exaggerating, one can compare translators to people employed in a hazardous industry. Constantly having to deal with a different language, some translators inadvertently absorb the structure of the foreign speech. And if the workers at hazardous factories get milk as an antidote, translators too need their own antitoxin. They will find it if they read and reread such writers as Pushkin, Herzen, Turgenev, Leo Tolstoy, Chekhov, Gorky, and by listening to people in places where one can hear pure Russian speech." (Qtd. in Khotimsky 2011:93)

The ultimate goal of such hierarchization and conservatism was to de-individualize authorship, and this is one of the things that distinguishes Stalinist culture from premodern cultures of imitation. Those cultures did not know Romantic authorship, while Stalinist culture had to purge itself of it. The centrality of de-individualization in Stalinist culture is reflected in two phenomena that emerged in the 1930s: the promotion of "bardic authorship" and the focus on the self-sacrifice of translators. Taken together, these phenomena attest to a radical re-thinking of Romantic authorship.

Bardic poetry and the de-individualization of authorship

The promotion of bardic authorship, as represented by the works of traditional Central Asian bards, represents a model of artistic production that is based more on the principle of imitation than on the principle of originality, and as such, serves both to downplay the author's role and to elevate the role of the translator. The promotion and publication of the works of the Kazakh bard Dzhambul Dzhabaev (1846–1945) and of the Bashkir bard and rebel Salavat Iulaev (1754–1800), among others, began in earnest in the latter half of the 1930s as the Soviet ideal of internationalism was made to accommodate more traditional forms of nationalism, as evidenced in "a series of festivals of different nationalities, held in Moscow from the spring of 1936 until the war" (Brooks 2000:96).

A key event in the Soviet promotion of bardic authorship was the 1938 collection of Russian translations of Dzhambul's folk poetry, which appeared in a richly decorated edition in a circulation of 10,000. In the introduction, Dzhambul explains the essence of his bardic voice: "I could only sing truthfully about myself and my people [*narod*]. When I sang about my people, I was also singing about myself. When I sang about myself, I was at the same time singing about my people" (Karataev 1938:7). The author of the introduction, M. Karataev, reiterates the idea that bardic authorship represents the seamless union of bard and people: "The folk quality of Dzhambul's songs derives from the fact that they truly and sincerely express the thoughts and moods of his people" (10).[7]

A more interesting case of bardic authorship is that of the Bashkir bard and rebel Salavat Iulaev to the extent that the dubious provenance of his works underscores the invented nature of bardic authorship in the Soviet Union. The originality of Iulaev's "literary works," which were republished in the late 1930s as part of a general effort to promote bardic authorship as a model of artistic production, is problematic in two respects. First, there are no reliable originals. Bashkir at the time was not a written language, so any poems Iulaev may have authored in the modern sense of the term, that is, produced in a fixed written form, would have been written in either Arabic or Turkic, the literary languages of the time, complicating

---

[7] This is very close to Dostoevsky's description of Pushkin in his mature phase becoming one with the Russian folk: "Pushkin loved the people precisely in this manner, in a way required by the people; nor did he guess how the people should be loved; he did not prepare himself therefor; he did not learn how to act: *suddenly he himself became the people*. He bowed to the people's truth: he recognized it as his own truth" (Dostoevsky 1985a:940–941; italics added).

his identity as a Bashkir folk hero. What scholars refer to as his folkloric output, on the other hand, was oral, passed down from bard to bard. Leaving aside the whole question of the authenticity of the inscriptions of these oral forms, they were highly stylized and formulaic. As the scholar M. Kh. Idel'baev notes, the folk forms used by Bashkir *seseny*, or bards, are largely fixed and celebrate cultural continuity over creative invention: "Folkloric works of the Turkic peoples, such as the Bashkirs, over the course of centuries have been stable in terms of form. Authors did not strive after variety in verse form; rather, they were concerned over the accessibility of the content and the ease with which the text could be memorized and recited" (2004b:344).

If there is little place for originality in form, a cursory glance at Iulaev's poems reveals little original content; they are mostly stylized paeans to the beauty of nature, as exemplified in one of his most widely cited poems, "Moi Ural." Iulaev covers traditional themes and inserts almost no distinguishing personal traits. In this way, bardic authorship blurs the line between the individual and the collective. Indeed, so de-individualized is the lyric voice of these bardic poets, many have conjectured that there were no originals and that the works exist only in Russian translations, which are invariably rhymed and metered.[8]

The kind of de-individualization represented by bardic authorship was wonderfully described by the critic Lev Ozerov in a review of a collection of anonymous folk songs, *Songs of Nameless Singers*, published in the journal *Masterstvo Perevoda* under the title "Song—the Soul of the People." Ozerov writes, "In reading the book *Songs of Nameless Singers* (trans. N. Grebnev), we enter the realm of folk poetry, where there is not one without all or all without one. We come into contact with wisdom that is not the invention of a single individual. An individual can sharpen, clarify or beautify it, but authorship remains with the folk" (Ozerov 1963:202–203). While the songs are anonymous and the authorial voice de-individualized, the translator—Naum Grebnev—is named, underscoring the fact that translation and anonymous works of folk culture represented in the Stalinist period two sides of the same coin, that of de-individualized writing, which enhanced the visibility of translators at the expense of original authors. And so, Samuil Marshak was able to scold Soviet critics for failing to recognize Grebnev's poetic achievement precisely because this was a form of authorship that was already, to use the Derridean

---

[8]   For more on the role of Dzhambul in Soviet literature, see Witt (2011) and Bogdanov, Nikolozi, and Murashov (2013).

term, under erasure: "Who among our critics appreciated, for example, the merit of Naum Grebnev's poetic work—*Songs of Nameless Singers* and *Songs of Past Times*? Grebnev did not only wonderfully translate these folk songs, he searched for them himself, like for a treasure" (Marshak [1962] 1990:213). Note here the emphasis on Grebnev's role in finding and disseminating these anonymous works, activities stressed by Barthes in his description of premodern authorship. Like authorship of socialist realist texts, translation "provides some sort of medium, however reduced, for discussion and even self-expression" (Clark 1984:24).

Translation and the de-individualization of authorship

While Iulaev and Dzhambul were born into bardic authorship and so were always already de-individualized, what was to be done with original writers in Soviet Russia? How could they be purged of their Romantic individualism, their egoistic drive to assert their own style or form and in so doing alienate themselves from the collective? For the de-individualization of artistic forms, say, in icon painting, is predicated on the de-individualization of the icon painter, who is typically nameless and whose work is not characterized by a high degree of stylistic or thematic innovation. Moreover, as Clark argues, "a corollary of the Soviet novelist's status as mere teller of tales is his lack of autonomy over his own texts," making translators again into exemplars of literary production in the age of Stalin insofar as the ownership of translated texts, which is quite murky in most legal systems, was especially so in the Soviet one.

One way to understand translation's role in the de-individualization of authorship and the making of Soviet subjects is to inscribe it within what Clark describes as the opposition of elemental forces to consciousness that structures socialist realist literature. The transformation of a character's elemental forces into consciousness is typically achieved as the result of some ritual passage involving an act of self-sacrifice. "When the hero sheds his individualistic self at the moment of passage," Clark writes, "he dies as an individual and is reborn as a function of the collective" (1984:178).

The struggle between elemental and conscious forces animated much of the translation discourse of the time, specifically the rhetoric surrounding the Soviet School of Translation, which was typically defined not in positive terms but rather as a struggle against formalism, read as individual style, on the one hand, and against *bukvalizm*, a literal approach that betrays the style of the source author, on the other. And so, entry into the Soviet School of Translation was constructed as a rite of passage through which a writer or translator is de-individualized, that is, purged of what Ivan Kashkin referred to as "the harmful influence of bourgeois attitudes toward art," followed by symbolic submission—to the norms of literary Russian (Kashkin 1955:121).

As Pavel' Antokol'skii, Mutar Auezov, and Maksm Ryl'skii stated at the Second Congress of Soviet Writers: "The translator should struggle for his mother tongue, in the practice of translation he should struggle for the purity and richness of his mother tongue and for socialist realism" (1955:41).The transformation of writers into translators, then, not only ritually performs the triumph of consciousness over elemental forces, it is a privileged site for doing so. To the extent that, as Clark argues, "the climax of the social realist novel ritually re-enacts the climax of history in communism" (Clark 1984:10), every successful Soviet School translation could be said to reenact the overcoming of individualism, on the personal level, and of linguistic and cultural differences, on the social level, anticipating and precipitating the ultimate triumph of communism worldwide.

The terms of this struggle in the context of translation were already set by Kornei Chukovsky in his 1930 work *Iskusstvo perevoda*, which he coauthored with Andrei Fedorov. In the opening two chapters, Chukovsky reprises his critique of Konstantin Bal'mont's translations of Walt Whitman from a 1906 review article that had appeared in the Symbolist journal *Vesy* under the rather innocuous title "Russkaia Whitmaniana." Reflecting the increasingly politically charged atmosphere of Soviet culture at the time—a period described by Sheila Fitzpatrick (1974) as the Soviet Union's cultural revolution—and more specifically, the desire to rid Soviet literature of the Western diseases of individualism and egotism, Chukovsky reworked his comments from the 1906 review into chapter two of *Iskusstvo perevoda*, which he provocatively titled "The Translator as Enemy." In this chapter, he viciously condemns Bal'mont for imposing his personality and Art Moderne style onto that of the US poet, whom Chukovsky refers to, significantly, as the American bard. Chukovsky goes on to describe Bal'mont's translation in terms of moral corruption—with Bal'mont foisting his decadent baroque style on the plain and straightforward Whitman. The following extract provides a good example of Chukovsky's charged political rhetoric:

> Perevod prevratilsia v bor'bu perevodchika s perevodimym poetom. Inache i byt' ne moglo, ibo, v sushchnosti, Bal'mont nenavidit amerikanskogo barda, ne pozvoliet emy byt' takim, kak on est', staraetsia vsiacheski ispravit' ego, naviazyvaet emu svoi bal'montizymy, svoi vyruchnyi smil' modern, kotoryi Uitman byl tak nenavisten. (Chukovskii and Fedorov 1930:14)

[The translation turned into a struggle between the translator and the translated poet. It could not have been otherwise, as, essentially, Bal'mont hates the American bard; he does not allow him to be what he is; he tries in every way possible to correct him; he foists upon him his Bal'montisms, his recovered style moderne, which was so loathesome to Whitman]

In chapter one, entitled *Litso perevodchika* [The Face of the Translator], Chukovsky makes similar remarks about Bal'mont's translations of the English poet Shelley. Having a personality, *lichnost'*, that is too pronounced, Bal'mont is unable, Chukovsky argues, to render the individual style of another poet: "And as his talent is devil-may-care, or, to tell the truth, foppish, so Shelley becomes in his translations a fop" [A tak kak talent u nego zalikhvatskii, pravdu skazat' fatovatyi, to i Shelli stal u nego fatovat.] This unholy union of two incompatible poetic styles and, we might add, world views, produced monstrosities, described famously by Chukovsky as *Shel'mont*. Bal'mont, Chukovsky alleges, commits the sin of *otsebiatina*—a Russian term that translates literally as 'from oneself'—which Chukovsky uses to describe the imposition of the translator's individual style onto that of the source text author. The term is interesting insofar as it describes this phenomenon not in terms of inaccuracy or unfaithfulness, but as a sin of pride or egotism, which would become a running motif in translation discourse throughout the Soviet period.

Chukovsky would rework this material again for his single-volume work *Vysokoe Iskusstvo* [A High Art], re-titling the relevant chapter "The Translator's Self-portrait," in which he sharpens the charge of individualism. It is perhaps no coincidence that Chukovsky raises the status of translation by adding the adjective "vysokoe" while strengthening his critique of individualism in translators, as if to make clear that conferring this new status on translation was not to be seen as an affirmation of Romantic authorship and original genius. The price of this elevation was self-sacrifice.

In an article titled "Translating Whitman, Mistranslating Bal'mont," Rachel Polonsky convincingly demonstrates that Chukovsky's characterization of Bal'mont's translations is somewhat exaggerated and unfair (Polonsky 1997). We cannot rule out the fact that Chukovsky's attack on Bal'mont may have served the purpose of distancing himself from another decadent author, Oscar Wilde, whom Chukovsky had championed in prerevolutionary Russia. In fact, in the introduction to the twelve-volume complete Russian works of Wilde that Chukovsky translated, he famously declared the British writer to be "our very own Russian writer" [samyi rodnoi Russkii pisatel] (Chukovskii 1912:xxxiii). But, it also reflects the more general project of reconceptualizing authorship, presenting translation as the site of the ritual purging of individualism. By opening his how-to book with a critique of Bal'mont, Chukovsky does not describe how to *do* translations so much as he describes how to *be* a translator, underscoring the fact that translation in Soviet Russia was always about more than the transfer of texts across languages or about the maintenance of empire and the promulgation of communist internationalism. It was at a very fundamental level about the making of Soviet subjects, which, in turn, supports Clark's contention that the "age-old conflict between the individual and society" was in Soviet culture encoded in biographical terms (1984:16).

Chukovsky's *othering* of Bal'mont involved transforming a metonymic association between Bal'mont's decadent literary style and his translation approach into a metaphoric association: to translate in such a way is decadent, corrupting, turning bards into fops. Chukovsky's critique would set the tone for the moralizing rhetoric that would come to characterize the Soviet School of Translation. Consider, for example, Ivan Kashkin's 1951 discussion of "formalist" translators that appeared in *Literaturnaia Gazeta*: "Their translations interchangeably demonstrated bourgeois mercantile indifference toward the quality of translation and mirrored bourgeois-decadent disintegration (*raspad*), which manifested itself in the corruption of the national language" (qtd. in Witt 2016). It is interesting to note that Chukovsky would include a discussion of Tatyana Gnedich's translation of Byron's *Don Juan* in the 1964 reedition of *Vysokoe Isskustvo* as a positive exemplar of the Soviet School approach. The selfless heroism of Gnedich's translation, done in part from memory and while incarcerated, is presented by Chukovsky as the polar opposite of Bal'mont's corrupting translations of Whitman and Shelley, creating a morally charged opposition of self-sacrificing martyr to self-aggrandizing hedonist.

And so, as is obvious from the examples given above, the charge of formalism leveled against translators in the Soviet period was not so much a critique of a translator's style or translation approach as it was a critique of his or her character. Attacks on translators who sought to impose their individual aesthetic concerns onto source text authors were common throughout much of Soviet history—and could be heard from cultural figures from across the political spectrum. Consider the critique by Arsenii Tarkovsky, poet, translator, and father of the film director, of the younger generation of Soviet translators: "Also entering the literary scene are young poets who are not devoid of talent, but neither are they devoid of an exaggerated passion for self-promotion. Translation demands modesty, the ability to retreat into the background, leaving the stage to the author of the original. Translations no longer resemble the original; today they more often resemble the original work of the translator" (Tarkovskii 2013:120). Or, consider the remarks of the Soviet critic Mikhail Alekseev, who described Pasternak's literary career as "the tragedy of a poet aspiring to be a translator." He then went on to advise Pasternak to practice "discipline and *complete subjugation* to the original author" (qtd. in Khotimsky 2011:120).

If we understand the critiques of *otsebiatina* and *bukvalizm* as working toward the same goal of de-individualizing authorship, then this may in the end be the defining trait of the so-called Soviet School of Translation. And so, the term "free", which is often used to describe the Soviet School approach, is something of a misnomer insofar as the practice of translation was in fact highly constrained. The good Soviet translator was meant to be, not unlike the folk bard, de-individualized, a voice of his time, reflecting the reigning stylistic norms. But if *otsebiatina* brings attention to the translator, *bukvalizm* brings attention to the translation, that is, it reminds the reader that the text is a translation and implies limits to translatability, which was anathema in Soviet culture of the time. A seamless translation, then, represented a victory for the Russian language, as expressed by Nikolai Liubimov in an essay entitled "Translation—an Art" [Perevod—Iskusstvo]: "First and foremost is the awareness, which has entered our flesh and blood, that the Russian language can defeat any difficulty, that it is capable of overcoming everything, of expressing everything, that it has no limits. Without this awareness, without this love for our native language, the translator risks surrending when faced with difficulties. Worse yet, he risks falling captive to a foreign tongue" (1963:233–234).

Susanna Witt (2016) has rightly pointed out that it is difficult to define what exactly constituted the much-vaunted Soviet School of Translation. The tenets of the school were vaguely expressed, and typically in negative terms, that is, what the school was not. Moreover, what tenets were articulated changed over time in reaction to political and cultural shifts. As with socialist realist novels, the tenets of the Soviet School were not elaborated in theoretical theses so much as they were defined by exemplars, authoritative models, reinforcing a model of literary production based on *masterstvo* (see Clark 1984:3). As the Belarussian translator Iurii Gavchuk put it, "The Soviet school of translation knows wonderful models [obraztsy] of this high art. There are people to learn from. The road is clear and wide" (1963:353). As a discursive site for the symbolic de-individualization of writers and authorship, the Soviet School was not so much a school in the sense of a group of like-minded practitioners as it was a school in the primary sense of the term: it was where individuals learned how to be exemplary Soviet cultural workers.

This de-individualization was achieved through ritualized acts of self-sacrifice and *smirenie*, just as it was in socialist realist novels and in the biographies of nineteenth-century Russian radicals. The religious aspects of this discourse were made explicit by Etkind who described Gnedich's translation as "a voluntary cross" [dobrovol'nyi krest] and Gnedich herself as "a holy fool" [*urodliva*]. So central was this concept of de-individualization that a seemingly innocuous remark made by Etkind in the preface to his 1968 anthology *Mastera stikhotvornogo perevoda* could produce a firestorm and lead to Etkind's eventual exile (Etkind 1978). Etkind had suggested that Soviet writers used their translations of classic authors, such as Shakespeare and Goethe, to address their own literary concerns during periods of political repression when they were unable to publish their own work, thus undermining the core tenet of the Soviet School—that Soviet translations be de-individualized, selfless.

Conclusion

The construction of translation as a vehicle for the symbolic remaking of Romantic writers into Soviet cultural workers helps us to understand the discourse surrounding the retranslations of classic works of World Literature that appeared in the late 1930s and 1940s, a discourse shared by members of both Soviet officialdom and the increasingly oppositional intelligentsia. This common discourse of heroic self-sacrifice and martyrdom inherited from the nineteenth-century radical intelligentsia challenges the notion that "the parties—the 'regime' versus the intellectuals—could in any circumstances be autonomous and free systems" (Clark 1984:7).

Liberating translation in the USSR from a discourse of punishment may allow us, then, to see how thoroughly translation was implicated in the making of Soviet subjects and in reimagining authorship outside the prism of Romanticism. It was in many ways a privileged discursive site at which many of the tensions of Stalinist culture were negotiated and to some extent resolved—specifically, the tension between the individual and society, between cosmopolitan internationalism and ethnic nationalism, or, as Andrei Sinyavsky put is, between universal compassion and xenophobia (1988:261). But also, it served to resolve the tensions between official Soviet culture and the culture of an increasingly oppositional intelligentsia, for the image of the translator as selfless martyr had broad appeal and deep roots in Russian culture, stretching back at least to the prison translations of the Decembrists Vil'gel'm Kiukhel'beker and Aleksandr Murav'ev. In fact, the phenomenon of prison translations, which reached its apotheosis as a result of the Stalinist purges and came to occupy a central place in intelligentsia folklore, underscores the productive side of submission within a culture of imitation.

6

Reading Wilde in Moscow, or *Le plus ça change*: Translations of Western Gay Literature in Post-Soviet Russia

Far from being a straightforward or naïve act of linguistic transfer, translation typically rewrites the web of discourses, codes and conventions of the literary text in keeping with the conflictual and "intensely social nature" of its cultural histories.

Samah Selim (2010:330)

Azar Nafisi's *Reading Lolita in Tehran* was widely praised in the US press. The story of a group of Iranian female students in Tehran who are transformed through their reading of canonical works of US literature lent support to popular Western beliefs about the workings of art and culture. It suggested that the canon of Western literature is somehow inscribed with basic humanist and democratic values, such as freedom of thought and expression and attendant notions of individual agency, and that these values can travel easily throughout the world, transcending differences of language and culture. True, many of the women Nafisi describes have their own, one could say, culture-specific interpretations of the characters and plots, but overall, the women learn, as Jacki Lyden puts it, to "think for themselves because James and Fitzgerald and Nabokov sing out against authoritarianism and repression" (Nafisi 2003:book jacket). Susan Sontag describes the book as "a stirring account of the pleasures and deepening of consciousness that result from an encounter with great literature and with an inspired teacher" (Nafisi 2003:book jacket). And, as one anonymous reviewer wrote on Amazon.com: "*Reading Lolita in Tehran* is a moving testament to the power of art and its ability to change and improve people's lives" (online). The reading group itself models in private the workings of a democratic civil society or, to use Habermas's term, a bourgeois public sphere, characterized by the free exchange of knowledge and opinions outside official government channels—the women meet in the teacher's home and eschew traditional female dress along with the traditional teacher-student hierarchy. The reviewer for *The Smithsonian* described the novel as "a kind of secret garden into which [these women] escaped beyond the mullahs' control. In fiction, the students were free to meditate upon their individuality and their womanhood."[1] Many Western readers, critiques, and politicians found in Nafisi's book, which appeared against the backdrop of the US invasion of Iraq, comforting proof of a universal humanism based on the Western neoliberal values of personal freedom and autonomy.[2]

Several years later, the granddaughter of former Soviet premier Nikita Khrushchev also wrote a book about reading Nabokov—but in the context of post-Soviet Russia. Nina Khrushcheva hoped to witness a transformation among post-Soviet Russian readers similar to the one Nafisi witnessed among her students in Tehran. Khrushcheva recounts how reading Nabokov helped her to dismantle her own Soviet-era mindset and to understand and appreciate core Western values, such as personal responsibility: "Instead of exalting in the spirit of compassion and sympathy, rebellion and submission, that Russian literary characters—certainly those in Gogol and Dostoevsky— are supposed to indulge themselves in, [Nabokov's characters] take responsibility for their own lives" (2007:1–2).

Unfortunately for Khrushcheva, her tale of reading does not have as happy an ending as Nafisi's. Khrushcheva notes sadly that Russian readers had by the early 2000s largely lost interest in Nabokov. And so, placed beside Nafisi's triumphant story, Krushcheva's tale offers a more sober assessment of the soft diplomacy of literature, reminding us of the utter unpredictability of the reception of "world literature" across languages and cultures. In fact, a close examination of the reception of literature in translation often tells us more about enduring cultural differences and the malleability of textual meaning than it does about a universal culture of humanism and global values.[3]

But, while post-Soviet Russian readers may have treated Nabokov with general indifference, another scion of world literature and cosmopolitan polyglot, Oscar Wilde, has met with surprising success there. Post-Soviet

---

[1] Available online at: http://www.smithsonianmag.com/people-places/Book_Review_-_ Veiled_Threat.html#ixzz19WsDer2M (accessed November 12, 2014).

[2] This reading, however, did not go uncontested. John Carlos Rowe in his review of Nafisi's book describes it as, "an excellent example of how neoliberal rhetoric is now being deployed by neoconservatives and the importance they have placed on cultural issues" (Rowe 2007:253).

[3] A spectacular example of the potential disparity between the domestic and international reception of a literary work is Milorad Pavić's *Dictionary of the Khazars*, discussed in Damrosch (2005). (See Chapter 7.)

Russia has witnessed a boom in new editions of Wilde's work in Russian translation, totaling more than sixty-five, as well as several collected volumes containing one or more works by Wilde. Approximately ten monographs dedicated to Wilde have been published in Russia, and several more that include Wilde in a study of multiple authors. Five biographies of the writer have been published in Russian translation (Parandowski, Brandreth, Ackroyd, Ellman, and Langlade), with Langlade's appearing in the prestigious series Zhizn' Zamechatel'nykh Liudei [Life of Noteworthy People], as well as in another edition. Ellman's biography has gone through at least three editions. Two editions of Wilde's letters have also appeared. So ubiquitous is Wilde in Russia today that Russian readers, conjectures the critic Aleksei Zverev, "might find it difficult to believe there were ever any lapses in the publication of his works in Russia" (2000c:373).

Lapses, however, there were, due in no small part to the author's homosexuality, making Wilde's popularity in today's Russia surprising given that homosexuals are "possibly the most stigmatized and oppressed minority group in contemporary Russia" (Chernetsky 2007:146), as evidenced most recently by the adoption in 2013 of a national law banning homosexual propaganda. The unprecedented boom in editions of Wilde's work in post-Soviet Russia, therefore, poses some interesting questions about what contemporary Russian readers are finding in the Irish-born homosexual Wilde that they could not find in the Russian-born and adamantly heterosexual Nabokov. Is Wilde, not Nabokov, the writer Khrushcheva was looking for, the real poster child for a new Russia, who could provide Russian readers with literary role models "of a kind dramatically different from those readers had come to expect in Russian literature: sufferers, revolutionaries, and madmen; men and women subservient to fate" (Khrushcheva 2007:1)? Could the story of Wilde in Russia provide another feel-good story, like Nafisi's, about the spread of Western values—up to and including tolerance of homosexuality—through literature?

Translating homosexuality

Before discussing the translation of works of Western gay literature in late-Soviet and post-Soviet Russia, I would like to discuss the particular challenges posed by translating homosexuality across languages and cultures. As Mona Baker points out in her translation textbook *In Other Words*, until only recently there was no neutral, that is, non-perjorative term to designate homosexuals in Arabic (1992:24). When new terms are introduced to fill the gap, they are often foreign borrowings.[4] Denis Altman cautioned that the use of terminology to describe (homo)sexuality in different cultures is not consistent, much of it is borrowed from the West and is often used "to describe a rather different reality" (1997:419). To the extent that "the language of queer politics is (American) English" (Fassin 2001:216), the adoption of such terms may at some level reflect and even symbolize US cultural hegemony. The problem of translating homosexuality is further exacerbated by the fact that what constitutes homosexuality is imagined differently across cultures and even within cultures (see Murray 2000). And so, it should only be expected that the translation of Western gay literature into languages and cultures outside the West will inevitably involve a complex negotiation of global aspirations and local concerns.

Keith Harvey's monograph *Intercultural Movements: American Gay in French Translation* (2003) analyzes the translation shifts that occured in the translation of "gay-themed" literature from English into French and French into English, providing a model for linking textual evidence to broader cultural beliefs and dispositions and underscoring the position of translated texts "as interfaces between competing ideological positions" (Harvey 2003:43). Harvey convincingly demonstrates a general tendency on the part of French translators and editors to tone down or neutralize the "camp talk" present in the source text, which served in the US context as a crucial marker of membership in the gay subculture. Harvey interprets this phenomenon as a reflection of a deeply ingrained concept within French culture of "universal"—that is, non-sectarian—French identity: "If the category of 'gay' is problematic in France, it follows that the notions of gay writing and gay literature are also disabled in the French cultural polysystem by a universalizing tendency in the Gallic conception of subjectivity" (2003:417).

---

[4] It is important to remember that Soviet Russia produced nothing akin to the Kinsey Report or the Masters and Johnson studies, which provided a more or less neutral language to facilitate public discussion of sexual matters, that is, a discourse that was neither moralizing nor obscene. The almost total silence of official Soviet culture on sexual matters delayed the emergence of such a "neutral" language, leaving largely intact the traditional discursive gap between the bawdy language of Russian folklore (burlesque), supplemented in the twentieth century by the prison slang of the Gulag, and the elevated, obfuscating language of high literature (silence), discussed in Lalo (2011). What few quasi-scientific terms there are in circulation are tainted by their Soviet origin, while the absence of a broad-based LGBTQ activist movement in Russia with access to mass media outlets has made the kind of repurposing of derogatory terms that occurred with *queer* in the West largely unthinkable.

Another important aspect of such transfers is the political and cultural power imbalances that inevitably influence and shape translations, especially translations from the Anglo-American world, making translation almost always an "unequal exchange" (Casanova 2010). Such power imbalances have generated strong resistance to US cultural hegemony in many parts of the world. As Eric Fassin comments, "opposition to gay and lesbian politics (even among moderate gays) [in France] is often formulated as a rejection of so-called US identity politics in the name of French political culture" (2001:216). Fassin contrasts the US model of citizenship—or national identity—based on group identities with the French universalist model, according to which differences in ethnicity and sexuality are consigned to the private sphere. A close reading of the shifting political rhetoric in the United States and France in the course of the 1990s, when debates about same-sex marriage and other issues of gay integration were raging on both sides of the Atlantic, ultimately reveals that "the politics of same-sex marriage *did not translate well*" (217; italics added).

The translation of the rhetoric of gay rights is especially fraught in today's Russia where the association of the United States with the minoritarian or communitarian model of homosexual identity is very strong, and the passage in 2013 of a federal law banning "homosexual propaganda" suggests a strong desire on the part of the Russian ruling elite to disable the public expression of a gay identity.[5] The motivations to do so are many and varied. The sudden reappearance of homosexuality in Russian media after decades of silence, for example, led many Russians to see homosexuality itself as a foreign borrowing, a pernicious effect of Western capitalism and democracy.[6] Homosexuality today continues to serve in Russia as a powerful symbol of the insidious spread of Western values (and, many Russians believe, of the "Western disease" of AIDS) and of Russia's diminished virility—reflected not only in its loss of superpower status but also in plummeting birthrates and declining longevity, especially for Russian men.[7] The first Russian anthology of gay fiction in fact featured short stories that all took place in some foreign land and involved romance with a foreigner. The anthology, aptly named

---

[5] The situation is similar with Western feminism. Beth Holmgren, for example, noted, "the problem with effectively translating the most basic Western terms like 'feminism', 'emancipation', and 'gender' for a slogan-wary Soviet audience" (1995:15).

[6] In fact, the slang term *der'mokrad*, a comic deformation of the word *demokrat*, or 'democrat', formed from the Russian words *der'mo*, meaning 'shit', and *krad*, meaning 'theft', was also used in the post-Soviet period to refer to homosexuals, who were perceived as radical Westernizers (see Saburoff 2008).

[7] The Russian association of homosexuality with a loss of virility is enabled by the still popular conception of homosexuality as gender inversion.

Drugoi, or *The Other*, suggested that Russian gays themselves had introjected the idea of homosexuality as somehow non-Russian.[8]

Such representations appear to confirm the historian Dan Healey's contention that since the late nineteenth century homosexuality has been discursively constructed in Russia within a "tripartite geography of perversity." Within this mapping, Russia was situated between a decadent (homosexual) West and a debauched (homosexual) East, producing Russia as "naturally and purely heterosexual" (2001:253). Within that discursive context, the notion of a gay identity appears as an attack on a universalist conception of Russianness. This helps to explain, at least in part, the opprobrium and even violence directed today toward an emerging gay subculture, perceived by many as an assault on Russia's traditional identity and on the collective nature of that identity—an attempt by one group to separate itself from the collective.

Russian animosity toward a Western-style model of community identity for homosexuals was expressed quite openly by the critic Mikhail Zolotonosov in his review of Kostia Rotikov's *The Other Petersburg* [*Drugoi Peterburg*, 1998]. Reacting to Rotikov's assertion that *The Other Petersburg* was a work of "gay folklore," Zolotonosov states unequivocally:

> There is no such thing as homosexual literature, neither fiction nor folklore, nor any other type, and there cannot be .... Homosexuality as a form of sexual life, as an ethos (based on play, in which men play roles of active and passive), as a psychology—that exists. But there are no means available for the construction of some particular literary form on the part of homosexual authors. There are particular thematic concerns, but no special literature or culture as a whole. (Zolotonosov 1999:197)

Similarly, the critic Evgenii Vitkovskii fulminated against Western scholarship on Oscar Wilde that studied the great man through the prism of individual identities, such as his Catholicism, his Irishness, and his homosexuality, producing in the end: "Lies, lies, nothing but lies" (2000:9).

To the extent that the general cultural context in Russia for the translation of Western gay literature could be described as hostile to the notion of a minoritizing gay identity, translations of works of Western gay literature and the paratextual material accompanying them could be expected to

---

[8]   Even in the relatively gay-friendly years preceding the Russian revolution, the hero of Russia's first gay novel, *Wings*, by Mikhail Kuzmin, ultimately finds sexual liberation not in his native city of St. Petersburg or in the Russian countryside, but in sunny Italy, and with a man of mysterious foreign origin.

display a particular set of strategies designed to neutralize the threat posed by that identity to a universalist Russian model of citizenship and to reflect in a variety of ways the specific nature of Russian homophobia.[9] Moreover, the dearth of positive homosexual characters in Russian literature and the absence of viable, non-pejorative terms for gays and lesbians that are generally accepted both within Russia's gay community and in Russian society at large cannot fail to shape the translation, marketing, and reception of Western gay literature in the context of post-Soviet Russia.[10]

Packaging Wilde

It may be tempting to some to see the post-Soviet interest in Wilde as an embrace of Western neoliberal values. According to this interpretation, Wilde, described by one contemporary Russian critic as "the world's greatest Individualist" (Obratsova 1997:5), is seen as offering Russian readers what Krushcheva had hoped they would find in Nabokov. At first glance, the story of Wilde in Russia does indeed appear to support the notion of (Western) literature as a humanizing, democratizing force insofar as the publication of Wilde's work in the Soviet era appears to be closely connected to liberalization trends.[11] For example, Wilde was "re-discovered" after a hiatus of over thirty years (with some minor exceptions) in the post-Stalinist Thaw period. One of the highpoints of that rediscovery was the publication in 1960 of a two-volume collected works of Wilde, accompanied by an essay on the author by Kornei Chukovsky, the renowned prerevolutionary translator of Wilde, who had,

---

[9] I am using "gay" here as an umbrella term to refer to the marketing of literary works and authors to an LGBTQ audience. Gay literature may be authored by individuals who are not openly gay, such as Walt Whitman, or who lived in a time before the emergence of a totalizing "gay" identity, such as Sappho or Michelangelo, but who are packaged for a contemporary gay-identified audience.

[10] I will be focusing below on the packaging of Western gay literature in Russian rather than on the translations themselves. There are, unfortunately, few works that analyze the actual translations of gay-themed literary works into Russian. One notable exception is Alexandra Berlina's 2012 study of Dmitrii Vedeniapin's translation of Michael Cunningham's novel *The Hours*. Through careful textual analysis and lexical research (including online polling), Berlina comes to the nuanced conclusion that, "though Vedeniapin did not want his translation to be anti-gay, he unwittingly transmits the hostility of a culture which has rendered him insensitive to gay discourse" (464).

[11] For statistics on the publication of Wilde's works in Russia, as well as any mention of Wilde in Soviet print media, see Roznatovskaia (2000). For excellent overviews of the reception of Wilde in pre-Soviet and Soviet Russia, see Pavlova (1986), Pavlova (1991), Bershtein (1998), Bershtein (2000), and Bullock (2013).

in the introduction to the 1912 edition, declared Wilde to be "our very own Russian writer" (1912:xxxiii).[12] The current boom in the publication of Wilde's work was also inaugurated by liberalization policies, adopted under perestroika. But, while the publication numbers are revealing and appear, at least superficially, to connect Wilde with political liberalization in Russia, a closer examination of not only the translations themselves but also of the paratextual and critical literature surrounding them—what I will refer to as the *packaging* of the author—suggests that Wilde and his homosexuality are being packaged for a contemporary Russian audience in ways very different from those used to package Wilde in the West.[13]

Publishing statistics provide a general outline of the Russian packaging of Wilde: as an author of children's literature and as a stylist. Indeed, almost half of the late-Soviet and post-Soviet editions feature his short stories for children, either alone or together with other works. The second most popular work of Wilde's, according to publication records, is the novel *The Picture of Dorian Gray*, which is not unrelated to the previous point for in Russia the novel is often published in a single edition with the tales, suggesting that it is being marketed to children or young readers. Moreover, several of the Russian editions of *Dorian Gray* were put out by the publishing house Detskaia Literatura (Children's Literature).

While children's literature was considered a "safe" haven from political censorship in Soviet Russia—one of the first of Wilde's works to be published in Russia after Stalin's death was a children's story in 1954—the designation of children's writer also had the effect of restricting the critical or interpretive approaches applied to Wilde's work, promoting the Soviet interpretation of Wilde as the author of didactic literature. As the influential Soviet critic Aleksandr Anikst asserted, "Wilde the theoretician declared the freedom of art from morality, but in his stories, Wilde the artist foists upon us a certain morality" (qtd. in Bullock 2013:248); in other words, the stories are edifying. The canonization of Wilde as a great English stylist, known for the clarity of his writing—he occupied a central place in English programs in post-Stalinist Russia, alongside writers such as John Galsworthy, Somerset Maugham, O. Henry, Jack London, and Theodore Dreiser (Bullock 2013: 243)—also served to restrict interpretations of his

---

[12] There were a few minor exceptions between 1922 and 1960.

[13] The concept of packaging literature is taken from Richard Watt's 2005 study of paratextual material accompanying works of francophone literature published in France, *Packaging Post/Coloniality: The Manufacture of Literary Identity in the Francophone World*. Like Watt, I take most of my material for analysis from the paratexts accompanying Russian publications of Wilde's works.

work. Whereas English interpretations of Wilde typically focus on the slipperiness of the author's language, highlighting his use of innuendo and double entendre, the Soviets' "deliberately superficial emphasis on style above all else" effected, as Phillip Ross Bullock contends, "the evisceration of all meaning from his language" (2013:243, 242)—at least in official readings of his work.

In Russia, for example, *Dorian Gray* is presented as a rather straightforward morality tale, albeit with a fantastic twist. In fact, in an introduction to a post-Soviet edition of the novel, critic Iurii Fridshtein describes it as a detective novel and compares it with the novels of Arthur Conan Doyle and Charles Dickens, noting that Conan Doyle wrote a favorable review of the novel (2010:301). (Conan Doyle was one of the most popular English-language authors in Soviet Russia.) In the West, however, the novel is generally seen as one of Wilde's most challenging works, deeply encoded with references to his homosexuality and also thoroughly decadent, in which every plotline leads to death. Moreover, Jeff Nunokawa argues, "the image of homosexual desire inscribed in and on *The Picture of Dorian Gray* [provides] an inaugural image of gay identity" (1991:313). Indeed, the prosecutor at Wilde's trial suggested that the novel, along with *Phrases and Philosophies*, was about homosexuality: "calculated to subvert morality and encourage unnatural vice" (qtd. in Dollimore 1987:58). Initial reaction of Western audiences to the novel as scandalous and shocking, as well as contemporary Western critics' attention to the work's decadent aspects and homosexual allusions—one critic uncovers evidence of "child abuse"—have surely made the work in the eyes of Western publishers unfit to market to young readers.

The post-Stalinist packaging of Wilde as a moralist and a stylist were meta-textual strategies that effectively functioned to foreclose the interpretation of Wilde's works as gay and/or decadent.[14] Surprisingly, perhaps, despite the lifting of censorship restrictions following the fall of the Soviet Union, this packaging of Wilde and of other gay writers remains widespread in

---

[14] The only more or less open treatment of Wilde's sexuality in the Soviet era occurred in a short study of Wilde by Chukovsky, which first appeared in the pre-revolutionary collection *Faces and Masks* [*Litsa maski*, 1914] and was then republished in a stand-alone biography of Wilde in the relatively censor-free year of 1922. In a chapter with the Latin title of "Modo vir, modo femina" [The Masculine Way, the Feminine Way], Chukovsky offers a gender-based discussion of Wilde's sexuality, which is, in Bullock's words, "thoroughly indebted to the kind of pseudo-psychological notions of sexuality as pathology that were so widespread around the turn of the century" (2013:259). Moreover, the use of Latin to shield delicate readers from direct contact with sexual content was a widely practiced strategy at this time. Consider Sir Richard Burton's use of Latin to refer to sexual practices in his translation of the *Arabian Nights*.

contemporary Russian publishing. Below I isolate and discuss the specific strategies employed by Russian translators, editors, publishers, and critics to domesticate the work of Wilde and other Western gay-identified authors for contemporary Russian readers. These strategies, largely inherited from the Silver Age and the Soviet period, have the effect of disabling readings of these works that would affirm the specificity of the gay experience and the centrality of sexuality, or the libido, to individual happiness. I consolidate these strategies into three basic groups, which I refer to as *erasure, aestheticization,* and *Russification.*[15]

Erasure

The erasure of references to homosexuality can take a variety of forms, ranging from overt and covert excision to obfuscation through the use of euphemism and innuendo. The excision of homosexual references was a common practice in Soviet Russia, at least from the 1930s on. Mikhail Gasparov documented the practice in reference to Russian translations of ancient Greek and Roman poetry, where any references to homosexuality were either omitted or changed to be heterosexual (Gasparov 1991). And, while recent archival work has lent some nuance to our understanding of the censorship of homosexual references in translated literature in the Soviet period (see Sherry 2015)—the practice was more uneven and porous than previously thought—Soviet society maintained almost total silence on the subject of homosexuality in the mass media, as well as in scholarly research. Igor Kon discusses the fact that it was impossible for Soviet historians and anthropologists to study—or even mention—homosexuality in ancient Greece and Rome (1997:354–355). When it was mentioned at all, it was done with great circumspection, which brings me to the second form of erasure: euphemism.

This form of erasure remains surprisingly popular in post-Soviet Russia, due, at least in part, to the practice of republishing pre-Soviet and even Soviet-era translations together with the original paratextual material (typically with all dates removed). Several post-Soviet editions of Sappho's verses, for example, are accompanied by introductions written by her early twentieth-century Russian translators, Vikentii Veresaev and Viacheslav Ivanov. Veresaev's essay from 1915 is included in both a 2000 and a 2001

---

[15] These strategies, of course, overlap. Euphemism, for example, can in some cases be considered a strategy of erasure and in others, of aestheticization. Similarly, much of the Russification of these works, specifically the playing down of the physical aspects of sexual desire, is achieved through aestheticization or erasure.

edition of Sappho's verse, while Ivanov's essay from 1914 appears in the same 2001 volume; a Russian translation of an essay on Sappho by the French scholar Théodore Reinach from the 1930s is included in the 2000 edition. Significantly, no dates are provided for these essays, and there is usually no contemporary essay that might help to historicize the positions of the prerevolutionary or Soviet-era commentators. The same is true of post-Soviet Russian editions of the poetry of Michelangelo. The 2001 Russian reedition, for example, contains an essay by Walter Pater from 1899, as the introduction, and an essay by the translator Abram Efros, first published in 1964, as the afterword.[16] Again, no dates are provided for either essay, and there is no contemporary commentary that could recontextualize Michelangelo's sexuality for a post-Soviet audience. Or consider the 1998 Russian translation of the US psychologist Alexander Lowen's *Love and Orgasm*. The text, originally published in 1965, contains discussions of homosexuality that today would be described as viciously homophobic and that have been thoroughly discredited by the American Psychiatric Association. Nevertheless, the Russian translation was published with those sections intact and with no commentary to situate Lowen's work within contemporary psychology. The absence of critical commentary in the form of an introduction or even footnotes lends an aura of unquestioned authority to these texts—indeed, Lowen's book was published in a Russian series titled Classics of Western Psychology.[17] This helps to explain why these texts are able to exert such a strong influence on the way homosexuality is understood and discussed in Russia today.

That influence is perhaps most evident in the extensive use of euphemism when referencing homosexuality. For example, when Veresaev in his introductory essay at last confronts the notion that Sappho may have been a lesbian, he resorts to the euphemistic discourse of his time: "All of these circumstances still do not give us the right to conclude that Sappho's relationship with her students possessed that *specific quality* [spetsificheskii kharakter] which in the present day is associated with the name of Sappho" (2000:13, italics mine).

In his afterword to the Russian translations of Michelangelo's poetry, Efros, too, eventually addresses—toward the end of page 34—the charge that Michelangelo experienced same-sex desire, but he does so in typical

---

[16] While Efros's afterword was first published in 1964, the essay must have been written at least a decade earlier as Efros died in 1954.

[17] This is not the case only with translations. The 1913 edition of Vasilii Rozanov's book-length study of homosexuality was republished in 1990, by the publisher Druzhba Narodov, again with no introductory material to historicize or contextualize his rather idiosyncratic views on the subject.

Soviet fashion, through the use of euphemism and innuendo. Efros quotes a contemporary of Michelangelo, Ascanio Condivi, who writes: "I heard afterward from those who had been present (at conversations with Michelangelo) that he spoke of that kind of love one reads about in Plato" (2001:223).

The use of Silver Age and Soviet-era euphemism to refer to homosexuality continues in the critical literature written today. While the gay-identified critics Aleksandr Shatalov and Yaroslav Mogutin make free use of the terms *homosexuality* and *homosexual* in reference to James Baldwin and his Russian translator Gennadii Shmakov, in the introduction to Baldwin's *Another Country*, Aleksei Zverev exhibits a rather anachronistic delicacy when discussing the topic, referring to homosexuals as "followers of a forbidden eros [priverzhentsy zapretnogo erosa]" (2000b:6).[18] Or consider the critic Sergei Shcherbakov's description of the offenses that led up to Wilde's imprisonment: "Of course, to take boys openly to restaurants when for a 'person of society' even a dalliance with one's own maid was considered indecent was a blatant challenge to that society" (2000:6). The court records, however, document in rather graphic detail Wilde's relations with these boys, which went well beyond taking them to restaurants.

Even in the introduction to the 2010 Russian edition of William Burrough's novel *Junkies*, the translator, Aleks Kervi, makes no mention of the theme of homosexuality, although Burroughs himself is unabashed in his portrayals of gay sex. There is, however, one reference to "sex" in the introduction (Kervi 2010:8), but it functions, one could argue, to obscure the specificity of gay sex.

Aestheticization

Another defining feature of the Russian treatment of homosexuality, one that is closely tied to erasure, is aestheticization, that is, the translation of physical desire into an aesthetic disposition, as evident in Efros's presentation of Michelangelo's homosexuality not as an expression of physical desire but as a kind of philosophical trope, a reflection of his Neoplatonic views:

> Michelangelo's Platonism was vital, not empirical; it was linked to the stages of his biography but not conditioned by them—it was more principled, broader, more profound; it was a manifestation of

---

[18] On the specific terminology-related problems posed by the translation of Western gay fiction into Russian, see Berlina (2012).

the artist's worldview, his experience of the world, not a veil, a curtain or a pseudonym for the facts of his everyday life, as the cruel slander of Pietro Aretino attempted to imply in regard to Michelangelo's friendship with Tommaso Cavalieri; the slander, however, only succeeded in embarrassing his contemporaries, not to mention his descendants. Aretino's calumny is an extreme case of *biografizm* [biographism]. (Efros 2001:226)

Elsewhere, Efros goes to great lengths to enforce a distinction between Michelangelo's relationship to Tommaso Cavaliera, which he describes as a "passionate attachment to a friend" (219), "a passionate friendship" (226), and a "friendship" (226), and his relationship with Vittoria Colonna, which he categorizes as "a great love" (226) and "an enormous love" (229).[19]

Efros, however, does not simply deny Michelangelo's homosexual desire. In a move typical of Russian scholarly discourse still today, he aestheticizes the artist's desire, de-emphasizing its physicality by contextualizing it in the philosophy of the time as "Neoplatonic eros" (225), according to which "earthly beauty is a reflection of heavenly beauty; mortal flesh is a temporary veil over the eternal soul; and sensual love is a distortion of divine eros" (229). The emphasis placed on Michelangelo's divine artistic yearnings over his earthly desires is suggested in the epigraph from the artist's contemporary Giorgio Vasari that opens Efros's Introduction: "He gladly read the Holy Scriptures, being an exemplary Christian, and respected the works of Girolamo Savonarola, having listened to his voice from the pulpit" (200). A Dominican friar, Savonarola was known for his burning of what he considered to be immoral art.

This specific strategy of erasing homosexuality by aestheticizing it is not only evident in reeditions of Soviet and pre-Soviet works. It is still alive and well among post-Soviet literary scholars and critics, as illustrated in the following remarks by Valerii Chukhno, a leading Russian specialist on Oscar Wilde, in his afterword to a 2003 Russian edition of Wilde's works:

The sources of Wilde's non-traditional sexual orientation should, obviously, be sought, as paradoxical as that may sound, in his *aestheticism*. Beauty meant so much for him that its association with one biological sex or another, including his own, did not mean very much

---

[19] In this, Efros follows Pater, who makes no mention at all of Cavalieri while dedicating several paragraphs to Colonna, whom he describes as an "ardent neo Catholic." This must have had great resonance in Pater's time with the Neo-Catholic movement led by the charismatic Cardinal John Newman in full flower.

to him. After meeting such a lovely creature as the young Lord Alfred Douglas, Wilde could not help but fall in love with him, seeing in him the *perfect incarnation of Beauty*. (2003: 435; italics mine)

Elsewhere, Chukhno describes Douglas's features as "ideal" (2003:439). This aestheticization—which, incidentally, was a strategy developed by Wilde himself "to disguise the erotic implications [of his relationship with Alfred Douglas]" (Foster 2001:88)—is a product of the general prudery of Russian academic writing and of the particular aversion felt toward overt (homo)sexual references, reflected in an avoidance of such terms as *gei, goluboi* or *gomoseksualist*, which would confer a minority identity on the individual. In A. G. Obratsova's lengthy introduction to the Russian edition of Wilde's letters, these words are never used, nor is the word lover (*liubovnik*), for that matter. The only reference in Vitkovskii's introduction is found in a passage in which the critic vituperates against the tendency of Western scholars to chop up the objects of biography into discrete "identities," quoted above. Chukhno goes only slightly further by referring to Douglas's "homosexual inclinations" and toward the end of his afterword cites Wilde's plea that his "homosexuality be considered a disease rather than a crime" (2003:457). In a 1993 review of the Russian translation of Peter Ackroyd's *The Trials of Oscar Wilde* by Aleksei Zverev, no direct mention is made of Wilde's homosexuality except for a single reference to "vice," although it was, obviously, at the center of the trials. An updated version of the article, published in 2000 as the introduction to a Russian reedition of Ackroyd's novel, reflected a slight change in norms: "vice" was changed to "Greek love" and the word *izvrashenets*, or "pervert," was added (Zverev 2000a:13). Still, the author obscures the actual facts of Wilde's sexuality by aestheticizing it as "the logical result of the cult of Beauty" (13).

Chukhno, too, pays little attention to the whole question of Wilde's sexuality, emphasizing instead the artistic, spiritual bond that united Wilde and Lord Alfred Douglas: "They conducted long, intimate [zadushevnye] conversations about art and literature, read their works to one another; they had common creative interests and shared a passion for the theater. After all, it was Alfred Douglas who translated Wilde's *Salomé* from French into English, and this play is still performed today in America, England and in other English-speaking countries in precisely this translation by Douglas" (2003:442).

Where the details of an author's sexual life are presented—as in the Russian translation of Jacques Langlade's biography of Wilde—Russian critics express indignance. In his introduction to Langlade's biography, Zverev models the kind of euphemistic treatment of the theme he would have wanted Langlade to employ: "Perhaps the only significant complaint that might arise among readers of this biography concerns the fact that too much attention is given to the intimate aspects of Wilde's life: so much so that the shocking details can lead us to forget about everything else" (Zverev 1999:7). Such comments suggest that the open discussion of sexual issues remains, at least in middle-class circles, profoundly *nekul'turno*, or vulgar.[20]

One sees a similar "aestheticizing" tendency in the introduction to a 1993 translation of Japanese writer Yukio Mishima's novel *The Golden Pavilion* by Grigorii Chkhartishvili, a translator and one-time editor of the prestigious journal *Inostrannaia Literatura* [Foreign Literature] who would later become famous as a writer of detective novels under the pseudonym Boris Akunin. Chkhartishvili ignores the homoerotic motifs in Mishima's works, which earned the Japanese writer a prominent place in the Western gay literary canon, focusing instead on the "aesthetic formula" driving Mishima's work (1993:8). Chkhartishvili describes the Japanese author as a "refined aesthete" (20) and *The Golden Temple*, as Mishima's "aesthetic manifesto" (13).

Russification

The most popular works of Wilde in Russia, following his children's stories, are undoubtedly his prison writings, *De Profundis* and *The Ballad of Reading Goal*. While not the most published works, they dominate the critical literature on Wilde in Russia, which presents the author for the most part as a "tragic hero" (Bullock 2013:242). This was an interpretation of Wilde that emerged in the prerevolutionary Silver Age. As Bullock points out, "Russian literary culture had been profoundly shaped by ideas of artistic suffering and self-sacrifice, the Christological overtones of which mapped closely onto the myth of Wilde himself (not for nothing did *The Ballad of Reading Goal* and *De Profundis* become his most widely translated and discussed works)" (238).

This is largely true of Wilde scholarship still today, where contemporary Russian scholars continue to lend the author's prison "confession," *De Profundis*, an especially authoritative place in the Wildean oeuvre, as revealing the "true" Wilde behind the masks donned in his previous works. Iurii Fridshtein calls *De Profundis* "perhaps [Wilde's] most brilliant literary work" (1993:105) and perhaps his most truthful. In a review of a new Russian edition of Wilde's letters that includes *De Profundis—De Profundis*

---

[20] For more on class-based representations of homosexuality in Soviet culture, see Kuntsman (2009).

was written in the form of a letter to Wilde's lover Lord Alfred Douglas—Fridshtein opens with the rather naïve Sentimentalist claim that "Nowhere does a person reveal himself as in letters. In letters, which are not intended to be studied by future generations, but rather are addressed to close friends, to people who form a part of the life of the one writing and sending these letters" (1993:104). In his afterword to a 2000 collection of Wilde's work, the translator, Valerii Chukhno, makes a similar claim: "We can see the *authentic* Wilde *only* in his famous *De Profundis*" (2003:432; italics added).[21] In his introduction to the 1999 Russian translation of Jacques Langlade's biography of Wilde, the translator, Zverev, asserts that *De Profundis* is the best possible biographical account of Wilde's life: "When there is such a significant autobiographical document, it is hard to accept other interpretations and versions. Wilde told about himself better than anyone else could. Every other interpretation will seem strained" (Zverev 1999:8). Zverev refers elsewhere to the "sincerity" of *De Produndis* (2000a:432–433). Shcherbakov similarly describes *De Profundis* and *Ballad of Reading Goal* as the "summits of [Wilde's] work, in which he presents not a mocking aesthete but a human being filled with humility [*smirenie*] and wisdom [*mudrost'*]" (2000:6).

The Russian reading of *De Profundis* as the sincere confession of a suffering artist makes it a perfect example of *zhiznetvorchesto*, or "life creation," the concept that a writer's life and work should form a seamless whole. This is a point Chukhno makes explicitly: "Oscar Wilde's life and Art, which he served with all the powers of his soul, were indissoluble, so inseparably intertwined that it is difficult to make out the boundary separating his life from his Art" (2003:433)—a view that leads most Russian critics not to queer Wilde's literary works but rather to aestheticize his homosexuality.

The popularity of *De Profundis* in Russia—and the interpretive centrality of the work—stands, however, in stark contrast to its reception in the West where, according to Foster, it "occupies a precarious place in Oscar Wilde's canon and for several reasons is often skirted by wary interpreters" (2001:85), who disregard it as anomalous and contradictory or read it as yet another Wildean "mask" or "pose."[22] Western lay readers,

---

[21] The critic Evgeniia Lavut (1997) also insists that Wilde's eclectic oeuvre can only be understood through his letters. See Philip Ross Bullock (2008:97–98) on the insincerity of the letters of Wilde's contemporary, the Russian composer Petr Chaikovsky. As Chaikovsky wrote in his diary, "I am never myself in my letters" (98).

[22] It should be pointed out here that Chukovsky, too, held the view that Wilde's persona in *De Profundis* was "a pose" (Bullock 2013:252). This view, however, is not the dominant one in contemporary post-Soviet scholarship.

too, tend to "disparage or dismiss *De Profundis*" (2001:85). The problem of *De Profundis* for Western scholars is that "Wilde seems to be writing against himself, constructing self-representations that appear to hide as much as they reveal" (2001:86). Russians, on the other hand, perceive the work as a sincere and largely unmediated outpouring of the author's soul—the "authentic Wilde," in Chukhno's words. Therefore, Russian scholars and critics tend to read the text in a more straightforward way, taking it at face value, so to speak. And so, while Western critics interpret Wilde's comparison of himself with Jesus Christ as "deeply implicated with irony" (Foster 2001:104), Russian critics do not.[23] As Vitkovskii notes, "The sad anniversary—one hundred years since the death of Oscar Wilde—fell in the same year as the two thousandth anniversary of the birth of Christ" (2000:24). And after declaring Wilde to be a great "Individualist," Obratsova then remarks, "Of course, the greatest, and first Individualist in history was Christ" (1997:5–6). Obratsova is here parroting Wilde's own words in *De Profundis* while stripping them of any hint of irony. Chukhno and Pal'tsev, too, draw an association between Wilde and Christ: Chukhno, by titling his preface to the 2009 Eksmo edition of Wilde's selected works "The Crown of Thorns of a Genius [Ternovy venets genii]" (2009:5), and Pal'tsev, by posing the rhetorical question, "Didn't he in 'The Soul of Man under Socialism' and in his 'Prison Confession' turn his mind, ever in search of truth, to the image of Christ and to the example He left of selfless service to Humankind?" (1993:10).

This Russian reading of *De Profundis* inscribes Wilde within traditional and still powerful Russian cultural scripts and frames based on the redemptive power of suffering. In *De Profundis*, the homosexual stands as a trope for the individual in modern society whose narcissism is redeemed through suffering (*stradanie*) and the humble acceptance of that suffering (*smirenie*), for which the sufferer is then rewarded with compassion (*sostradanie*) and granted Russian cultural citizenship.[24] As Kornei Chukovsky, the translator of the 1912 *Complete Collected Works of Oscar Wilde*, put it in the introduction: "when we heard from [Wilde] an anthem to the joy of suffering, we cried out: 'he is ours' [*on nash*], we opened our

---

[23] Indeed, Wilde's portrayal of himself "as a sorrowing aesthete spiritualized by suffering" (Foster 2001:102) invokes a motif that remains prominent in Russian portrayals of homosexuality even today (see Baer 2009). The agency accorded the homosexual in this scenario, it should be noted, is of a spiritual, not a political, in nature.

[24] For more on the narrative of redemptive suffering as it relates to homosexuality in post-Soviet Russia, see Baer (2009).

hearts to him" (1912:xxxiii). Zverev confirms the continuing popularity of this reading of Wilde when he writes, "Interest in Wilde is determined by sympathy for the underrated, the slandered, and the outcast" (1993:12). Elsewhere, he refers to Wilde as "a victim" (1993:374). Fridshtein argues that Wilde's incarceration exposed him to "a world of suffering the existence of which he had never suspected" (1993:105). But, rather than allowing himself to be crushed by the experience, the writer proved himself, "able not only to proudly bear his own humiliations and suffering but also to see that there were others suffering and in torment around him" (1993:105). Fridshtein highlights Wilde's "capacity for compassion" (2010:307), which leads readers, in return, to show compassion for Wilde. As Chukhno puts it, "*De Profundis* leaves no one indifferent, inspiring profound compassion [*sostradanie*] for a great writer who paid such a high price for his mistakes and errors" (2003: 458–459). (Chukhno's "mistakes" and "errors" are, of course, euphemisms for Wilde's sexual dalliances.)

The narrative arc implied by redemptive suffering is clearly drawn by Chukhno in his gloss of *De Profundis* as "the story of a brilliant soul [*dushi*], its ascent to unattainable heights and its fall into the depths of despair, and from those depths (de profundis), *he directs to us, and not just to Lord Alfred Douglas,* his words imbued with pain" (2003:433; italics mine). Although born in the Silver Age, this narrative of redemptive suffering remains dominant in post-Soviet Russian commentaries on Wilde, which tend to present "the traditional image of Wilde as a tortured artist who finds his way to God" (Lavut 1997:5). Obratsova actually describes Wilde with the religious term *muchenik-stradatel'*, or "Christian passion-sufferer" (1997:21), while Chukhno classifies *De Profundis* as a spiritual confession: "*De Profundis* can be considered the confession of a Great Sufferer, the repentance of a Great Sinner, and the autobiography of a Great Artist's soul" (2003:462). Obratsova opens her introduction to a 1997 edition of Wilde's letters with the following quotation from *De Profundis*: "You came to me to learn of the Pleasure of Life and the Pleasure of Art. Perhaps I am chosen to teach you something much more wonderful—the meaning of Suffering and its beauty" (1997:5). Without the slightest hint of irony, Obratsova notes, "Suffering [which she capitalizes throughout the essay] is the highest emotion available to a human being. It is at once an object and a sign of high Art, the highest degree of perfection. *Suffering is the only truth*" (1997:18; italics mine). Explaining the workings of the Orthodox concept of *smirenie*, or total acceptance of suffering, she writes: "Suffering and beauty can combine only in the event that a suffering individual takes on with greater sensitivity the suffering of others" (1997:18). As proof that

Wilde has experienced this brand of redemptive suffering, she points out that "'Wilde in the *Ballad of Reading Goal*' almost never uses the pronoun 'I', only 'we'" (1997:19).[25]

This process of Russification through suffering is also evident in the post-Soviet packaging—or rather repackaging—of the US writer James Baldwin,[26] who is presented in both the 1993 and 2000 Russian editions of his work as a suffering aesthete: one of the "saddest" writers in postwar Western literature (Zverev 2000b:8), who experienced "infinite loneliness" (2000b:5). Zverev goes on to describe Baldwin as "deeply lonely" and "sad" (2000b:5, 8). The love about which Baldwin writes in *Another Country*, notes the critic, "is tragic, often illegal, and if we are to judge by the accepted standards, abnormal, and was seen by the author and his heroes as truly another country against the backdrop of the surrounding pragmatism, emotional sterility and the doleful struggle for worldly success [zhiteskii uspekh]" (2000b:3). Here, the translator asserts the relevance of this work for a post-Soviet audience by drawing a link between 1950s America and a newly capitalist Russia.

Moreover, the social and literary constraints of 1950s America that shaped Baldwin's representation of homosexuality make this work especially congenial to a post-Soviet Russian audience. In *Giovanni's Room*, for example, the tortured nature of the same-sex relationships in the novel, the fact that the main character is bisexual, not exclusively homosexual, as well as the foreign element—the main character's lover is an Italian imigrant in France—aligns the work with the traditional Russian view of homosexuality as tragic, foreign, and not an exclusive identity. *Giovanni's Room* was one of the first works of Western gay literature to be published in post-Soviet Russia because, as Laurie Essig puts it, it is a story "that make[s] sense in Russia" (1999:94).

The strategy of Russification through suffering-inspired compassion is addressed directly in Aleksandr Shatalov and Yaroslav Mogutin's introduction to the 1993 edition of Baldwin's *Giovanni's Room*. Shatalov and Mogutin describe the translator, Gennadii Shmakov, in terms of the

---

[25] It is not surprising then that the most popular of Wilde's plays in Russia is far and away *Salomé*, connecting as it does to a rich tradition of suffering in Russian Decadence, as evident in the subtitle of Andrei Kurpatov's study of Roman Viktiuk's production of the play, entitled *Strakh, sladostratie, smert'* [Fear, Sensuality, Death]. The other plays, characterized by witty word play and frivolity, are given little scholarly attention in today's Russia and are not as widely available.

[26] Baldwin's play *Blues for Mister Charlie* was published in the Soviet journal *Inostrannaia Literatura* in 1966, which was possible because with this work Baldwin could be presented as a political activist, a critic of racism in the United States.

traditional Russian motif of the suffering, spiritually refined artist and intellectual. Shmakov, "a ballet, theater and literary critic, specialist in the work of Mikhail Kuzmin," and a friend of Nobel laureate Joseph Brodsky, who dedicated "one of his finest poems of recent years" to him, died from AIDS at the age of 48 (1993:13–14). His intellect, combined with his suffering, allowed Shmakov to produce a translation that "uniquely transformed James Baldwin's novel, introducing contemporary nuances, making the book closer to the Russian reader and, thanks to that, making Baldwin's image more humane and profound" (1993:14).

Wilde's Irishness is also deployed in the packaging of Wilde for a Russian audience. Post-Soviet Russian critics exploit Wilde's ethnic identity, a member of an oppressed ethnic minority in England, to encourage sympathetic identification on the part of Russian readers. In his introduction to a 2000 edition of Wilde's prose works, for example, Shcherbakov presents the soulful Irish-born artist as an outsider in the rigidly conformist society of nineteenth-century England, keying into traditional Russian discourse that contrasts the emotional, soulful Russian to the reserved, rational Westerner. Vitkovskii presents Wilde as a "passionate Celt" and then goes on to describe the tragedy of the Irish Wilde's imprisonment as a "distinctly English story," one that could have only taken place in a land where disputes are settled not by duels (as in Russia?) but in the courts (2000:13), a remark that calls to mind Nicolas Berdyaev's critique of the "Western cult of cold-blooded justice" (1962:87).

While the cult of suffering establishes a kind of metaphoric association between Wilde and Russian culture, other, more direct links are also made. Shcherbakov, for example, notes Wilde's interest in Russian culture, mentioning his play *Vera, or the Nihilists*, which, he conjectures, was not performed in Wilde's lifetime because "he describes Russian revolutionaries with too great a sympathy" (2000:5). (It should be noted, it was not performed in tsarist or Soviet Russia either.) He then adds that Wilde considered the Russian anarcho-communist Prince Petr Kropotkin "as a model human being" (2000:5). Indeed, Wilde refers to Kropotkin in *De Produndis* as "a man with a soul of that beautiful white Christ that seems coming out of Russia" (Wilde 1994:934).[27]

Others inscribe Wilde within the Russian literary canon, drawing direct links to Dostoevsky. Obratsova, for example, notes the influential role

---

[27] But, this tendency to group Kropotkin, Dostoevsky, and Wilde under the Russian banner of redemptive suffering is only possible if one ignores Kropotkin's damming criticism of Dostoevsky's great novels. As Irina Sirotkina explains, "The prince-anarchist P. A. Kropotkin (1942–1921) called Dostoevsky's later novels 'unwholesome,' with every character 'suffering from some psychical disease or from moral perversion'" (2002:48).

played by the Russian writer during Wilde's formative years at Oxford. His favorite Russian novel, she points out, was Dostoevsky's *The Insulted and Injured*, and his favorite heroine was Natasha from that same novel. She connects Wilde again with Dostoevsky a little later in her introduction: "Did he [Wilde] believe, like his favorite Russian writer, that 'beauty saves the world.' To a great extent—yes." (1997:10).[28] Nikolai Pal'tsev, too, in his lengthy introduction to volume two of a two-volume collection of Wilde's works, draws a connection between Wilde and Dostoevsky, first comparing *Dorian Gray* to *Crime and Punishment*, and then Lord Henry to Ivan Karamazov (1993:10).

Dostoevsky, in fact, serves as an important frame of reference for domesticating other gay authors, as well. Chkhartishvili, for example, attempts to Russify the Japanese author Yukio Mishima by connecting him to Dostoevsky. In the eight sections of the introduction, Chkhartishvili uses five citations from Dostoevsky's fiction as epigraphs—three from *The Possessed*, one from *Brothers Karamazov*, and another from *The Idiot*—as well as one from Nicolas Berdyaev's essay on Stavrogin, the anti-hero of Dostoevsky's *Possessed*. Chkhartishvili makes the connection with Dostoevsky explicit in the body of the introduction where he writes, "The tempter of Mizogutin [the hero of Mishima's novel *The Golden Temple*] is not Mephistopheles or Woland, but an offshoot of an impoverished line of that ancient species; it is rather Sologub's 'petty demon,' Ivan Karamazov's devil, or the demon recalled by Stavrogin" (1993:16).[29] Similarly, in the short translator's afterword to the 2001 Russian translation of Jean Genet's *Funeral Rites*, G. Zinger describes the main character as not entirely a surprise for the Russian reader: "Many of his features can be observed in Sologub's *Petty Demon* and in Bulgakov's *Heart of a Dog*" (2001:380).

Depoliticizing homosexuality

The overall effect of *erasure*, aestheticization, and Russification is to depoliticize homosexuality, as reflected in the canonization of *De Profundis* as the master text in Wilde's oeuvre. Russian interpretations of Wilde's

---

[28] This association of Wilde and Dostoevsky, while frequently referenced in the post-Soviet critical literature on Wilde, has its roots in the prerevolutionary period with N. Ia. Abramov's monograph *Religiia krasoty i stradaniia: O. Uail'd i Dostoevskii* [The Religion of Beauty and Suffering: O. Wilde and Dostoevskii], published in St. Petersburg in 1909.

[29] A Russian biography of Mishima, by Nikolai Nadezhdin, which appeared in the series Informal Biographies, includes a chapter on Mishima and Dostoevsky (2009:74–75).

homosexuality through the lens of *De Profundis* diminish Wilde's agency to the extent that in *De Profundis* "Wilde often phrases his actions as passive submission," exhibiting "polarities of victimization and self-destruction" (Foster 2001:98, 107). But, while many Western critics, like Foster, see this passivity as yet another pose, Russian critics take it as a sign of Wilde's spiritual transformation. The rhetoric of passivity adopted by Wilde in *De Profundis* aligns very closely with the traditional Russian conception of individual agency, or rather "non-agentivity, as indexed by the term *sud'ba*, or 'fate,'" described by the cultural anthropologist Anna Wierzbicka as "the feeling that human beings are not in control of their lives and that their control over events is limited; a tendency to fatalism, resignation, submissiveness; a lack of emphasis on the individual as an autonomous agent, 'achiever', and controller of events" (1992:395).

It is perhaps no coincidence then that Obratsova entitles her introduction to Wilde's letters: "Oscar Wilde: Man and Fate" [Oskar Ual'd: Chelovek i sud'ba]. Shcherbakov suggests a similar notion of fate when he points out that Wilde's prison works could never have been written had Wilde "not ended up in prison" (2000:6); in other words, this suffering was necessary in order for Wilde to produce his greatest work. Fate is also a recurring theme in Chukhno's writing on Wilde. Noting the similarity of Alfred Douglas to Dorian Gray—the eponymous hero of a novel Wilde had written before ever meeting Douglas—Chukhno notes, "It is as if the writer had foreseen his tragic fate with the young lord" (2003:438). Chukhno insists that if Wilde had never met Douglas, he would have found someone else with whom he could play out "suicidal tendencies slumbering in his soul" (2003:444). And later, Chukhno writes, "Wilde decided to meet his fate with his head held high" (2003:451). Fridshtein not only agrees that Wilde's fate was inevitable but also notes that Wilde by his own actions "hastened fate" and "sped up his tragic dénouement" (2010:299). Fridshtein compares Wilde's situation during the months leading up to his arrest with that of Pushkin during the months leading up to his fatal duel with D'Anthès, when jealous onlookers watched these great men "fly toward the abyss" (2010:299). We see a similar invocation of fate in the paratextual material accompanying the Russian translation of Baldwin's *Another Country*, where Baldwin is described as "driven by fate" (Zverev 2000b:8). Zverev later writes, "Fate dogs Baldwin's characters like the madman with a razor in the poetry of Arsenii Tarkovsky" (2000b:8)—a famous Soviet-era poet and dissident.

One can discern in Russian discourse on homosexuality in general and on Wilde in particular some acknowledgment of a homosexual identity while vigorously denying it any political or sexual agency, making it into an essentially tragic destiny. In the post-Soviet Russian imagination, the homosexual, such as Wilde in *De Profundis*, enters the public sphere in a way very much like the one sketched out by Dostoevsky for the murderer Raskolnikov in *Crime and Punishment*—through public repentance. In such a scenario, homosexuality becomes visible, public, at the moment it is renounced. According to the logic of *smirenie*, the only agency available is acceptance of one's fate.

Moreover, while Russian scholars see Wilde's most important work as *De Profundis*, in which Wilde appears to renounce his homosexual lifestyle, scholars in the West often draw a direct and productive association between Wilde's mature aesthetics and his embrace of his homosexuality. Dollimore, for example, notes that "Wilde's major writing, including that which constitutes his transgressive aesthetic, dates from 1886, when, according to Robert Ross, he first practiced homosexuality" (1991:623). Foster, in fact, reinterprets *De Profundis* not as an act of submission but rather as a complex assertion of political and social agency. In *De Profundis*, Foster writes, "Wilde was trying to demonstrate not so much that he was above the world, but that he had been—and still could be—an agent in a world that required duplicity and disguise for survival" (2001:86–87).

The lopsided critical attention paid to *De Profundis* in Russia and the interpretation of that text as a straightforward expression of *smirenie* minimize any sense of *political* agency, presenting his incarceration as redemptive. Indeed, the almost total neglect of Wilde's political writings in post-Soviet Russia is perhaps no less significant than the inordinate critical attention paid to *De Profundis*. Conspicuously absent in post-Soviet editions of Wilde is his essay "The Soul of Man under Socialism." While it may be tempting to read this absence as a simple reflection of post-Soviet ambivalence over Russia's socialist past, it may also reflect the fact that the view of suffering—and of personal agency—presented there is diametrically opposed to the one ostensibly organizing *De Profundis*. As Dollimore notes in his essay on Wilde and Gide, "Wilde begins *The Soul of Man under Socialism* (1987) by asserting that a socialism based on sympathy alone is useless" (1987:50). And later: "Wilde also dismisses the related pieties, that humankind learns wisdom through suffering, and that suffering humanizes" (1987:51). To quote Wilde himself: "Pain is not the ultimate mode of perfection. It is merely provisional and a protest. It has reference to wrong, unhealthy, unjust surroundings" (Wilde 1994:1103). Interestingly, "The Soul of Man under Socialism" was far more popular in Russia at the time of its first publication than it was in England, where it was read as "a joke in bad taste" (Dollimore 1987:60). In Russia, it underwent several editions during the twenty years following its original publication but then disappeared in the 1920s.[30]

The popularity of "The Soul of Man under Socialism" in tsarist Russia suggests that the Russian interpretation of Wilde then was more complex and more "political" than it is today. And, if the depoliticization of Wilde distinguishes the post-Soviet interpretation of the author from prerevolutionary Russian interpretations, it also distinguishes it from Soviet interpretations, which presented Wilde—when he was at last allowed to be published—as an anti-bourgeois radical, "an author formed by the crisis of bourgeois, capitalist society" (Bullock 2013:247). And so, we can say that the depoliticization of Wilde represents something uniquely post-Soviet: the struggle for privacy, which has undoubtedly impeded the emergence of an LGBT activist movement there.

The promotion of privacy over political engagement in fact characterizes the packaging of many Western gay authors in post-Soviet Russia. We see it clearly in Chkhartishvili's (1993) introduction to Mishima's novel *The Golden Temple*. The epigraph—taken from the entry on Mishima in the third edition of the *Great Soviet Encyclopedia*—must have seemed ironic to early post-Soviet readers. Chkhartishvili uses the entry to invoke the politicized Soviet-era interpretation of the writer, which was common after his spectacular suicide by *seppuku* following a raid on an army base. Mishima is described in the entry as someone "fascinated with blood, horror, cruelty, and perverted sex" who "prosthelytized fascist ideas" (qtd. in Chkhartishvili 1993:5), fascism, of course, being the ultimate mark of foreignness in official Soviet culture. This political interpretation of Mishima's life and work was especially strong in the Soviet Union, where, "Soviet ideologists were even more delighted over the sensation surrounding Mishima's death. Interpreted in a specific way this story perfectly completed the [Soviet] picture of the outside world, so wildly dangerous to the Countries of Victorious Communism" (6). The Soviet press saw Mishima's political protest and "so-called suicide" as yet another sign of the political reaction gaining ground throughout the world, as evidenced by various nationalist, neo-fascist, and racist movements: "Is it any wonder, then, that this author's works began to be translated into Russia only after a delay of many years, and that his name was for many long years the talk of the town Soviet internationalist propaganda" (7). Chkhartishvili rejects the Soviet political interpretation of Mishima's life and work in favor of an aesthetic, thoroughly apolitical one. Ultimately, Chkhartishvili asserts, "Mishima was

---

[30] For more on the reception of Wilde's essay in Soviet Russia, see Bullock 2013: 241–242.

always weak in terms of ideology; something else is crucial: the harmony of his phrasing, the clarity of his images, an entire aesthetic panoply" (24).

The connection between homosexuality and privacy is even more clearly drawn in the introduction to the translations of James Baldwin's novels *Giovanni's Room* and *Another Country*. Baldwin was not unknown to Russian readers when these translations appeared, but his reputation in Soviet Russia had been based on his more political works, understood in the narrow sense of the term, such as *Blues for Mister Charlie*, a play based on the murder of Emmet Till, the fourteen-year-old African American boy who was brutally murdered in Mississippi for having allegedly flirted with a white woman. The play was published in Russian translation in the prestigious journal *Inostrannaia Literatura* [Foreign Literature] in 1966. The lifting of censorship restrictions in the early 1990s, however, allowed another Baldwin—a tragic, apolitical, homosexual one—to be introduced to post-Soviet Russian readers. The publication in 1993 of Shmakov's translation of *Giovanni's Room*, which had circulated in *samizdat* since the late 1960s, was eventually followed by V. Bernadskaia's translation of *Another Country* in 2000.

If the Soviet Baldwin was politically engaged, the post-Soviet Baldwin is decidedly not. Zverev writes in the introduction to *Another Country* that when the novel was first published, its themes were perceived to be primarily of "sociological or political interest" (2000b:3). "Only a few years later," Zverev asserts, "when racial antagonisms had begun to calm down, one saw that Baldwin's novel was written about something completely different: about love" (3). Above all, he claims, the novel was "lyrical." "Not wanting his characters to illustrate specific phenomena or tendencies," as in the social novel, Zverev claims, "[Baldwin] simply creates several human destinies that turn out in all different ways but always with an unhappy ending. *And these destinies don't personify anything except the world as the American author sees it*" (7–8; italics added). In Zverev's opinion, Baldwin was able to achieve this because he wrote in another time, "when you didn't need to prove that literature was something different from a philosophical treatise or a statistical table" (10). Baldwin's fiction, then, appears as a model for a post-Soviet literature intent on depoliticizing the literary field. In Zverev's words, *Another Country* is a "deeply private/personal story" (7).

The struggle for individual or personal freedom is also an important theme in Chkhartishvili's introduction to *The Golden Temple*. In discussing Mishima's fascination with the Marquis de Sade, Chkhartishvili presents Sade as a figure who is utterly free, quoting Appolonnaire's description of Sade as "the freest spirit of all those who ever lived" (1993:25). For Mishima,

Chkhartishvili contends, Sade was an individual "without a mask" (30).[31] The twin themes of freedom and honesty, or sincerity, are also underscored for Chkhartishvili by Mishima's focus on individuals in all their uniqueness, not as social or national types, a view, incidentally, echoed by Zverev in regard to Baldwin. Chkhartishvili describes Mishima's early novella *Death in the Middle of Summer* as an utterly apolitical "laboratory study of the emotional suffering of a single (utterly ordinary) representative of the species Homo sapiens" (18–19).

Chkhartishvili's description of Mishima's hero bears a striking resemblance to Aleksandr Shatalov's description of the East German transvestite Charlotte von Mahlsdorf in his introduction to the Russian translation of her memoir *Ich bin meine eigene Frau* [I Am My Own Wife]. Whereas the first English translation of the memoir, *I Am My Own Woman: The Outlaw Life of Berlin's Most Distinguished Transvestite Charlotte von* Mahlsdorf (1994), presented von Mahlsdorf as a defiant activist, the Russian text presents her as someone intent on protecting her private life. As Shatalov writes, unlike many transvestites, von Mahlsdorf "was directed less toward outward effect […] than toward a search for inner harmony" (Shatalov 2000:6). Elsewhere, he asserts that the book and the film about her life "made this modest German worker […] *against her will* into the most famous European transvestite" (5; italics added). This theme of the private is underscored in the Russian subtitle: *The Secret Life of Berlin's Most Famous Transvestite*. To the extent that the Russian subtitle was modeled after the English one, not the original German, which was simply "ein Leben" [A Life], then the substitution of *secret* for *outlaw* supports not only the argument that von Mahlsdorf, the public activist, was repackaged in the Russian edition as a private individual but also that this defense of privacy necessarily limited the available forms of political engagement in post-Soviet Russia.[32]

This return to privacy, however, should not be understood exclusively in negative terms as a rejection of political engagement but can also be understood in positive terms as a quest for authenticity, sincerity, and for a protected private sphere. This is suggested by Shatalov in his introduction to Edmund White's *A Boy's Own Story*, which appeared in Russian translation in 2000. Shatalov, like Chkhartishvili, never invokes the gay canon, instead

---

[31] To fit Chkhartishvili's comments within the broader post-Soviet rehabilitation of de Sade, see Morozova (2000) and Khramov (2006).

[32] For an interesting discussion of the similarities between Western discourse regarding sexual secrecy (homosexuality) and Soviet-era discourse regarding political secrecy (dissidence), see Moss (1995). Post-Soviet culture was characterized, one could say, by the replacement of political secrecy with sexual secrecy.

inscribing White's autobiographical novel within a broader literary tradition, mentioning, in particular, J.D. Salinger's *Catcher in the Rye*. The comparison with Salinger's novel is telling for since its publication in Russian in 1960, *Catcher in the Rye* has occupied a prominent position within the Russian alternative canon of foreign literature. According to Nikolai Kratsev, "The Russian translation by Rita Rait-Kovaleva became a fixture in the library of virtually every Soviet intellectual" (2010:online). Soviet readers, explains the philosopher Boris Paramonov, "took close to their hearts [Caufield's] rebellion against the conventionalism of the society, against the alienation of people and the artificial social values which one had to follow in their social lives" (qtd. in Kratsev 2010:online). Shatalov situates the plight of White's homosexual within a Russian narrative of the individual's quest for authenticity, for genuine experiences in a corrupt and corrupting world.

The theme of moral honesty is in fact a consistent one in the paratextual literature accompanying Russian translations of Western gay literature, suggesting a parallel between the Soviet *intelligent* who refused to live "by lies" and the homosexual yearning to live honestly, without masks or subterfuge. Zverev, for example, describes the amorous relationship described in Baldwin's *Another Country* as "nepoddel'naia liubov'," or "not fake," and Baldwin, Zverev declares, was "an intellectual in the full sense of the word" (Zverev 2000b:10). In other words, the post-Soviet Baldwin, like the post-Soviet Wilde, is a moral not a political figure, or to put it somewhat differently, politics is here figured, not unlike the way it was among members of the Soviet intelligentsia, in terms of personal morality and individual integrity. As such, it reflects broader literary and cultural trends or positions that can be described as a rejection of Soviet-era engaged literature in favor of an "escape into privacy."[33] But, as Zverev's reference to "the doleful struggle for worldly success" (2000b:3) in his introduction to *Another Country* makes clear, this escape into privacy is also a critique of post-Soviet capitalism.

For many Russian gays and lesbians, too, the right to privacy was seen as one of the great promises of the post-Soviet era, after the brutal intrusions by the Soviet regime on the private lives of its citizens. And so, Lev Klein,

---

[33] As Kirill Medvedev describes it in an article entitled "Beyond the Poetics of Privatization," which appeared in the *New Left Review* in 2013: "Amid the mass depoliticization of the post-Soviet period, the dominant stance among writers was to assume an intrinsic incompatibility between poetry and politics, referring back to the Soviet era as a negative example. In the 1990s, the notion that politics and art should be kept separate was based on the idea that the country was moving irreversibly towards liberal democracy, leaving poets free to concentrate on their art" (2013:online).

author of an enormous book-length study of homosexuality *The Other Love* [*Drugaia liubov'*], uses the introduction as an opportunity not to "come out" but rather to make the case for homosexuality's place in the private realm: "The question of my sexual orientation—whether I am homosexual or not—can be of interest only to that person who has a personal interest [personal'nye vidy] in me—only that person needs to know whether his orientation is suitable or not" (2000:16).

The post-Soviet attempt to break with the Soviet past and its literature of social engagement is also evident in Andrei Kuprin's introduction to the 2000 Russian edition of E. M. Forster's *Maurice*, where he notes that "Forster was never a 'public' figure" (2000:18). He then goes on to say, "A statement was attributed to Forster, which was never understood or accepted by his contemporaries: 'If I had to choose whether to betray my country or a friend, I hope that I would betray my country'" (18). "I have no doubt," the translator concludes, "that when the reader turns the last page of this book, he will understand and accept what Forster had to say" (18)—marking a total reevaluation of the Soviet relationship between the private and the public, the personal and the political.

Conclusion

What becomes evident in the examination of post-Soviet translations of Western gay fiction is the tension between Russian readers' and publishers' attraction to foreign literature and their skepticism regarding Western political and social models. And, while the translation of Western gay fiction in contemporary Russia represents, at some level, a celebration of post-Soviet freedom from censorship, the relentless domestication of these texts suggests an ambivalence toward gay-themed literature—which the Russian public is ready to accept only on its own, largely apolitical, terms.

Moreover, those terms apply not only to the packaging of Western translated literature but also to the reception of Russia's own emergent gay literature, as reflected in a review of the collection *Russian Gay Prose of 2007* [Russkaia gei-proza 2007] published in the popular Russian weekly *Moskovskii Komsomolets*:

> Awaiting you in this book is not agitation [agitka], sniveling, or debauchery ... But an encounter with foreign [chuzhie] experiences. To put it more eloquently, gay prose is composed of the sparks and dust produced by the clatter arising from the homosexual's difficult life. What makes this book interesting? Its poeticity, its "atmosphere." (online)

In a few short sentences, the author of this review sketches the outlines of the Russian strategy of domestication in regard to gay literature: it must be apolitical (no agitation), full of suffering (the difficult life of the homosexual), with an attention to form (poeticity). Applied to Western gay literature, these domestication strategies work to align many of the foundation texts of a Western gay subculture with post-Soviet Russian attitudes toward sexuality, literature, and politics, reminding us that in the end the spread of world literature reveals at least as much about local beliefs and reading practices as it does about the existence of universal values.

I should mention here that I do not wish to suggest that Western interpretations of Wilde are somehow "right" and the Russian interpretations, "wrong." Rather, a focus on the ways Russians have packaged Western gay literature should encourage Western readers to acknowledge the ways in which that literature has been packaged in the West. There is no literature that is not packaged. Moreover, the packaging of literature as "gay" is complicated and contested in the West, as well. And so, this analysis is not meant to suggest that Russians are misreading Wilde, but rather that by studying the ways in which literary works are packaged, inscribed within certain cultural scripts and frames, we can see how those scripts and frames enable and disable certain interpretations at a level so covert as to make those interpretations seem natural and self-evident. Moreover, the association of homosexuality with a protected private sphere, promoted in the Russian packaging of many of these works of Western gay literature, may solidify the foundations of a political positioning not only against rising authoritarianism but also against the dehumanizing forces of neoliberal economics, making these representations of homosexuality, for all their dependence on pre-Soviet and Soviet discursive traditions, something uniquely post-Soviet.

7

Unpacking *Daniel Stein*:
Where Post-Soviet Meets Postmodern

If we depart from the national point of view, inverting the normal vision
and placing the practice of translation in the universe of international
literary exchanges, that is, in the world literary field, we can formulate the
hypothesis that translation as normally defined is a preconstructed object,
a sort of screen-notion which prevents appreciation of the real stakes of the
international circulation of literary texts.

Pascale Casanova (2010:287)

A number of translation scholars have drawn a rather direct connection between the recent spate of fictional portrayals of translators and translation and the postmodern condition. As Karen Littau puts it, "Translation with its Babel myth and its confusion of languages emerges as a privileged trope for the postmodern, precisely because it, too, is a site where the difficult acknowledgement of the divisions between texts, languages, traditions, cultures, and peoples occur" (2010:437). Dirk Delabastita and Rainier Grutman make a similar point in the introduction to the 2005 special issue of *Linguistica Antverpiensia*, entitled *Fictionalizing Translation and Multilingualism*: "Like (and often along with) 'travel', 'translation' has [...] become a master metaphor epitomizing our present *condition humaine*, evoking our search for a sense of self and belonging in a perplexing context of change and difference" (2005:23). That human condition, they note, is intimately tied to "the postmodern critique of Western rationality and empirical research" (2005:29). Quite simply, when translators appear as characters in fictional texts, they challenge, if only implicitly, their traditional invisibility in cultural exchanges, becoming a part of the story. As such, they may serve as an effective vehicle for a postmodern critique of traditional textual hierarchies that privilege the original and the author of the original over translations and translators. The translator as literary character, with his or her own personal problems and professional aspirations—and very often in an emotionally fraught relationship with the source text author—serves as the very embodiment of the postmodern notion that "all acts of reading, or acts of translation are collaborative acts of writing, are versionings" (Littau 2010:446).

To the extent that fictional translators represent the embodiment of postmodern themes, it would appear that Russia, too, is fully participating in this postmodern moment: fictional translators can be found in many works of contemporary Russian literature and film (see Baer 2005). Boris Akunin's dashing detective Erast Fandorin knows several Western European languages, as well as Japanese, and often serves as an *ad hoc* translator when the need arises. Alexandra Marinina's detective hero, Nastia Kamenskaia, translates detective fiction from English, French, and German in her spare time. Viktor Pelevin's obsession with the globalization of markets and, specifically, the phenomena of public relations and advertising, is reflected in comic (mis)translations and disgressions on the topic of the translatability of Russian culture. And Liudmila Ulitskaya's novel *Daniel Stein, Interpreter* features a multilingual Jewish Catholic priest and Holocaust survivor who saves 300 Jews from the Nazis by exploiting his position as an interpreter and later sets out to translate the Catholic liturgy—with some notable omissions—into Hebrew for his congregation in Israel. Stein's daring assertions of his agency as a translator, among other traits, have led many critics and scholars to label the novel a "postmodern classic," effectively mystifying the relationship between Post-Soviet and postmodern.[1]

Defining postmodernism

Postmodernity emerged in the West as a "widespread current in art and literature, and also an entire world-view" in the late 1960s (Seldon 1989:71). For many writers, critics, and philosophers, postmodernity was seen as a function of the massive dislocations and technical advances that accompanied late capitalism, postcolonialism, and globalization, producing a profound sense of ontological uncertainty and fluidity, which were reflected both in hybrid literary and artistic forms and in new "cosmopolitan" identities. With its tendency toward self-reflection and self-parody, postmodernism challenges meta-narratives, as well as traditional categories of identity-formation, perhaps chief among them, nationality.

---

[1] For more on the stakes involved with conflating the various "post" phenomena, see Anthony Appiah's "Is the Post- in Postmodernism the Post- in Postcolonial?"(1991) and David Chiani Moore's (2001) "Is the Post- in Postcolonial the Same as the Post- in Post-Soviet? Toward a Global Postcolonial Critique."

Raman Seldon describes the effects of postmodernism in the following way: "Human shock in the face of the unimaginable (pollution, holocaust, the death of the 'subject') results in a loss of fixed points of reference. Neither the world nor the self possesses unity, coherence, meaning. They are radically 'de-centered'" (1989:72).

It is perhaps no coincidence then that writers and critics seized on the term postmodernism in Russia in the late 1980s and early 1990s when all the verities and master narratives of Soviet history and culture were turned on their head. And while novels by Vladimir Sorokin and Vladimir Pelevin, for example, did indeed reflect the general ontological uncertainty that marked Western examples of postmodernity, it was not long before scholars and critics began to caution against the blanket use of postmodernism in reference to late Soviet and early post-Soviet cultural products. As early as 1993, the US scholar Marjorie Perloff questioned whether Russian postmodernism might be considered an oxymoron, and in 1994, Nancy Condee and Vladimir Padunov argued that Russian postmodernism had a different teleology from its Western counterpart. In 1999, Mark Lipovetsky published his book-length study *Russian Postmodernist Fiction: Dialogue with Chaos*, in which he outlines a Russian postmodern tradition. Paraphrasing Lipovetsky's argument, Eliot Borenstein, the translator and editor of the volume, notes in the introduction:

> [For Lipovetsky] Russian postmodernism is both an integral part of a worldwide phenomenon and a product of the Russian cultural reality. Lipovetsky firmly links postmodernism to the modernist tradition, tracing such key postmodern features as self-referentiality to their roots in Russian metafiction of the 1920s, which addresses two issues at once, one "global," the other "local." [...] His demonstration of postmodernism's Russian modernist roots disarms national critics who claim that postmodern is merely an ill-suited Western import. (Borenstein 1999:xvi)

In 2000, the Japanese Slavist Tetsuo Mochizuki asserted that, "Russian postmodernism is by no means a mere import of the European trend, but has its roots in Russia's cultural history" (2000:online). And, as Tine Peeters remarks, "Postmodernism in Russia is evidently not an exact copy of Western postmodernism. It is rather a site of appropriation and transformation of globalized cultural forms, just as Russian Byronism was not simply a translation of an English literary trend, but a genuinely Russian phenomenon." And, therefore, Peeters concludes, "One could say that even the most Westernized postmodern writers are still profoundly Russian"

(Peeters 2004:online). This is reflected in Rosalind Marsh's assessment that "the major difference between Russian and Western postmodernism is not primarily a response to modern capitalism, as in the West, but rather represents a total rejection of Soviet ideology and the aesthetics of Socialist realism" (2007:87). Russian writers and critics, too, questioned the applicability of Western postmodernism to the post-Soviet situation (see Tsukanov and Viazmitinova 1999).

Through analysis of Liudmila Ulitskaya's 2007 novel *Daniel' Shtain, Perevodchik* [Daniel Shtain, Translator], its English translation, and the reception of that translation, I will trace below the fundamental incompatability of these two postmodernisms in order to reveal what Casanova calls, "the real stakes of the international circulation of literary texts" (2010:287).

A postmodern classic?

Ulitskaya's novel achieved a great deal of attention in the media in both Russia and the West. First published in Russian in 2006, it was awarded the prestigious national literary award Bol'shaia Kniga in 2007; it appeared in 2011 in an English translation by the seasoned translator Arch Tait, under the title *Daniel Stein, Interpreter*, for which Tait won the PEN Literature in Translation Award. Following the publication of the English translation, Western scholars and critics raced to declare the novel a postmodern tour de force. Michael Autrey's review in *Booklist* describes it thusly:

> a postmodern epistolary novel [that] tells the 'true' story of the improbable, heroic life of a Polish Jew who translates for the Gestapo, saves part of a ghetto, escapes execution, hides in a convent, converts to Catholicism, joins the partisans, emigrates to Israel, and re-founds the Church of St. James, a community for which he performs mass in Hebrew. He offends church officials and violates orthodoxies, but Daniel is a sort of saint, doing the work of Christ. Two popes and a terrorist make cameo appearances. (Autrey 2011:21)

The reviewer for the *Daily Beast* called it "a refreshing affirmation of the beauty of hybridity" (Rosenthal 2011:online), while the reviewer for the *Washington Post* described the novel as "a feat of love and tolerance" (Bukiet 2011:online). The Russian literary scholar Benjamin Sutcliffe, focusing on the hybridity of Ulitskaya's characters, also saw the novel as "an elaborated argument for tolerance" (2009:496), and Bread Leigh's review on his Russia blog *Bears & Vodka* offered similar praise. "Ultimately," Leigh writes:

> the book is about pluralism. It's about religious tolerance and anti-dogmatism. It's about a man who speaks several languages, preaches in all of them, and relates to people free of catechism but full of faith. It's about how there is no single right answer, no single truth. The format and the cast of characters reinforce all these themes. [...] But I think there's another reason for the enthusiastic critical response. Daniel Stein stands apart in post-Soviet Russian literature because it isn't trying to deal with the fallout of an empire, or of an ideology. It's not trying to show the corruption of early-stage capitalism. It's not trying to shock with language, sex, or violence. In short, *it's not about post-Soviet Russia*. (Leigh 2010; italics mine)

Although I will argue that the novel is indeed very much about post-Soviet Russia, I must begin by admitting that the temptation to canonize Ulitskaya's novel as a postmodern classic is entirely understandable. The author herself appears to engage directly with postmodern preoccupations on the level of both form and content. The fact that it is a "fictional" biography of the Jewish priest and Holocaust survivor Oswald Rufeisen, conveyed in fragments of letters, newspaper articles, conversations, lectures, and sermons authored by a host of international characters, challenges traditional notions of novelistic narrative structure and point of view. The fact that Ulitskaya herself appears occasionally to comment in letters to friends or to her publisher on the progress of the novel highlights the constructed nature of the work and exposes her own personal and professional motivations, while denying her any absolute authority—she is just another character. The novel, one could say, contains no authoritative authorial voice. As Ulitskaya, the character, writes to her agent: "I'm not a real writer, and this book isn't a novel. It's a collage. I cut out pieces of my own life and the lives of others and I paste them 'without paste'—caesura!" (2006:469).[2] And, while one could argue that Stein is the most authoritative voice in the novel, the moniker *perevodchik*, or 'translator', associates him from the start with the notion of mediation. In this way, as Margarita Levantovskaya argues, "Ulitskaya's broad application and investment in the allegorical value of translation makes a powerful contribution to early and

---

[2]   All translations from *Daniel' Shtain, perevodchik* are mine unless otherwise indicated.

current views of translation as a useful paradigm for thinking about not only textual but also social and political issues surrounding such concepts as authenticity and interpretation" (2012:93).

Many of the characters display what David Damrosch referred to in reference to Milorad Pavić's novel *Dictionary of the Khazars* as "flamboyant multilingualism" and are difficult to categorize. Born into now fallen empires that were characterized by a mix of ethnicities, languages, dialects, and confessions, these characters fit uncomfortably within more rigid postwar nationalist categories. Consider, for example, Eva Makanian, who is a central figure in the novel and whose reflections open the book. After having been asked at a party whether she was Polish—because of her accent—Eva muses: "This question always took me somewhat aback. It was hard for me to answer. Instead of a short reply, do I launch into a lengthy story about how my mother was born in Warsaw and I was born in Belorussia, Father unknown. About how I spent my childhood in Russia and landed in Poland for the first time in 1954, then returned to Russia to study at the university. About how I moved from there to West Germany and then, finally to America..." The reply she finally gives eschews national categories altogether: "I was born in Emsk. In Chernaia Pushcha." (Ulitskaya 2006:9).[3]

Moreover, the fact that Daniel Stein, like Rufeisen, is initially denied citizenship in the State of Israel because of his conversion to Catholicism, despite being ethnically Jewish and a Holocaust survivor, also problematizes the whole idea of national identity, revealing it to be constructed, not essential or given; and Stein's increasingly antagonistic relationship with the Catholic hierarchy over articles of faith does indeed suggest, as Leigh argues, that the beloved priest is deeply antidogmatic. This is a point of view that is supported by Rufeisen's own comments recorded in the 1990 biography by Nechama Tec, *In the Lion's Den*: "My idea is to fight for a return to pluralism in the Church, with the hope that in Judeo-Christianity there will also be a return to pluralism. Somehow the two tendencies of pluralism will allow for the creation of a church that will have a Jewish character. The Church as it is now is not capable of accepting pluralism" (1990:241). Indeed, the intertextual reference in the biography's title to the Old Testament story of Daniel serves to underscore the shared culture of the two religious traditions.

Such a postmodern reading of *Daniel Stein* is actively encouraged from the start by the English translation of the novel's title. In Russian, the

---

[3]   Emsk is Ulitskaya's fictional name for the actual town of Mir. Ulitskaya may have avoided using the real name of the town given the fact that *mir* in Russian, and other Slavic languages, mean "peace" and "world." Ironically, using the real name might have seemed like a heavy-handed fictionalization to reflect the broad themes of the novel.

word *perevodchik* is a rather mundane description of an occupation. As the great Soviet translator Samuil Marshak put it, "We sense in the word *perevodit'* [to translate] something technical, not creative. This is perhaps fully justified in those cases when we are referring to the translation of a document, a letter or a conversation from one language into another" (Marshak 1959:245). Without an adjective specifying "written" or "spoken," *perevodchik* can refer to either a translator or an interpreter, whereas in English there is an unavoidable lexical distinction that must be made between the two. Therefore, the decision to translate *perevodchik* as "interpreter," one might say, broadens the horizon of expectations for the English reader by making possible a figurative reading that is discouraged in the Russian.[4] The notion of the translator as "interpreter" in the figurative sense is empowering and stands very much at the heart of postmodern reassessments of the translator's agency. This point was articulated by George Steiner in his seminal work *After Babel*:

> 'Interpretation' as that which gives language life beyond the moment and place of immediate utterance or transcription, is what I am concerned with. The French word *interprète* concentrates all the relevant values. An actor is *interprète* of Racine; a pianist gives *une interprétation* of a Beethoven sonata. Through engagement of his own identity, a critic becomes *un interprète*—a life-giving performer—of Montaigne or Mallarmé. As it does not include the world of the actor, and includes that of the musician only, the English term interpreter is less strong. But it is congruent with French when reaching out in another crucial direction. Interprète/interpreter are commonly used to mean translator. This, I believe, is the vital starting point. (1992:28)

That metaphoric interpretation of interpreter is also supported by the rather enigmatic cover design of the English translation: the silhouette of a male figure shown walking alongside a high stone wall. By invoking the idea of physical borders and border crossing, the image sooner evokes an interpreter, who is often positioned physically beside or between the speakers, than it does a translator. The Russian cover, incidentally, has no image.

While the choice of "interpreter" for the title of the English translation can be said to broaden the interpretive resonance of the title, in another

---

[4] There exists another translation of this novel by a Russian émigré, Irina Erman. She chose to translate the title as *Daniel Stein, Translator*. Bread Leigh, on his blog Bears & Vodka, gives the same translation, rendering *perevodchik* as "translator" rather than "interpreter."

sense, it narrows English reader's horizon of expectations by referencing Stein's work as an interpreter for the Nazis during the Second World War, thereby assigning his radical translation of the Catholic liturgy into Hebrew a secondary status. The cover photos of Tec's biography of Rufeisen also reference his role as an interpreter for the Nazis, suggesting the preferred Western interpretation of Rufeisen's life as a member of the resistance. Finally, the addition of "A Novel" to the English title appears to settle the question, provocatively left open by Ulitskaya, of whether this is a work of fact or fiction.

Postmodern or post-Soviet?

While this postmodern reading of the novel may seem obvious to the English reader and appears to be confirmed by the title and the cover design, it is in fact a reading that is predicated on ignoring a number of themes in the novel that point to an alternative, distinctly Russian interpretation of Ultiskaya's fictional project. I will discuss three major themes that are to a greater or lesser extent lost in translation but that serve to define Ulitskaya's source text as post-Soviet—as opposed to postmodern. In other words, I argue that Ulitskaya's source text does not relegate Stein to an ambiguous "space between," but rather thoroughly inscribes him within traditional Russian cultural scripts and frames.

Let me begin by contextualizing translation itself within a Russian cultural context. The Western scholars quoted at the beginning of this article interpret the current interest in fictional translators as a symptom of our postmodern condition marked by, among other things, the death of the author and the end of metanarratives. Russian writers, however, have been deeply concerned with issues of translation since at least the early eighteenth century, following Peter I's policy of forced Westernization. Translation became a matter of national survival. In 1703, Peter issued an edict with instructions to translators on how to practice their craft, and in 1768, Catherine II founded The Society for the Translation of Foreign Works (Sobranie dlia perevoda inostrannykh knig) to support the translation of foreign works into Russian. Translation has since that time been seen by many Russians as service to the nation. As Vilen Komissarov puts it: "Literary translations [in the late eighteenth century] were expected [...] to meet important social and cultural needs. Translators regarded their work as a service to their country, and they expressed this belief in forewords and prefaces to their translations. They believed that their mission was to enlighten and instruct their compatriots, to set moral standards and to create a new Russian literature. From that time on literary translation always enjoyed a high status in Russian culture" (Komissarov 1998:543).

And while for some Romantic writers, translation was seen as an embarrassing reminder of Russia's belated modernity—as the poet Kiukhel'beker lamented in his 1824 essay "On the Direction of Our Poetry, Especially Lyrical Poetry, over the Last Decade," "who but our run-of-the-mill translators will translate translators?" (Kiukhel'beker 2013:21)—for others, it represented a means to overcome that belatedness—consider Dostoevsky's portrayal of Pushkin as a universal man, capable of taking in foreign influences and rendering them thoroughly Russian, allowing Russian culture to speak the "last word" to the world. Russian translators, like Vasilii Zhukovsky, took enormous liberties with the content of the source texts they translated, seeing translation primarily as a vehicle for enriching Russia's "young" culture. It is customary for Russians still today to claim that Russian translations of Western classic authors such as Shakespeare surpass the originals. As Andrew Wachtel puts it, "Members of the Russian cultural elite proposed a model that emphasized their nation's peculiar, spongelike ability to absorb the best that other peoples had to offer as the basis for a universal, inclusive national culture" (1999:52). Translation through Russian, then, was seen as the path to a universal culture that, in Dostoevsky's formulation in his 1880 speech at the unveiling of the Pushkin monument in Moscow, would allow Russia "to utter the ultimate word of great, universal harmony" (1985a:980). The imperialist assertion of Russian cultural superiority here suggests a crucial distinction between Russian universalism (absorption into Russian culture) and cosmopolitan postmodernism (as disintegration and fragmentation).

And so, one could argue that Russia's preoccupation with translation has more to do with Russia's sense of belated modernity, stretching back to the time of Peter I, than it does with contemporary postmodern concerns. As Svetlana Boym notes, "The notions of the 'nomadic self' and 'transcendental homelessness' might sound familiar to the reader of Western modernist and postmodern theory; in the Russian context, however, they date back to the nineteenth century and signify an opposition to the modern ideology of individualism and to modernization in general" (1995:134). In that light, Daniel Stein's work as a translator and interpreter appears as less radical, or at least, less postmodern.

My second point concerns Ulitskaya's fictional interventions in the life of Oswald Rufeisen. In fact, she herself admits, "For me, it was more important to follow the truthfulness of the literary narration rather than the historical truth" (qtd. in Braungardt 2009). Those interventions, I would argue, rather than constructing him as a postmodernist avant la lettre, as Western critics would have it, serve to *Russify* the Jewish Catholic priest, specifically by associating him with the great nineteenth-century writer and intellectual Lev Tolstoy. For example, Ulitskaya draws this connection on a meta-literary plane where it is easy to see parallels between the eclectic form of Ulitskaya's novel and that of Tolstoy's magnum opus *War and Peace*, which was famously described by the American writer Henry James as a "baggy monster" (1934:84). Moreover, the birthplace of Eva Makanian, one of the main characters in the novel, and in some ways the symbolic center of *Daniel Stein*, is the town of Chernaia Pushcha (Dark Forest), which is the almost perfect semantic inverse of Tolstoy's famous residence Iasnaia Poliana (Clear Meadow).

More direct references to Tolstoy, however, concern Stein's rather idiosyncratic translation of the Roman Catholic liturgy into Hebrew and his subsequent excommunication from the Roman Catholic Church. Both of these plotlines were largely invented by Ulitskaya; while it is true that Oswald Rufeisen refused to recite the creed at high mass and avoided references to the Holy Trinity, he did not undertake a translation of the liturgy into Hebrew and died in the good graces of the Church. Ulitskaya's additions serve to "Russify" Stein, situating him within the tradition of the Russian, then Soviet, intelligentsia.

Stein's translation of the liturgy is a radical one for at least two reasons. First, he removes those articles of faith in which he no longer believes, specifically the Credo or Creed. Second, he undertakes this translation into Hebrew, which for most of his congregation is not their native language. In a sense, he creates this Hebrew version of the liturgy for a congregation he hopes may one day emerge in Israel—Hebrew-speaking Christians. This project makes him a suspicious character in the eyes of the Jewish authorities and of the Catholic Church. For this, Ulitskaya's Stein is excommunicated.

Most educated Russian readers would easily recognize this reference to Tolstoy who undertook his own idiosyncratic translation of the gospels and was eventually excommunicated. Moreover, Stein's refusal to translate the Credo, Latin for "I believe," references Tolstoy's first published explanation of his new religious views entitled "What I Believe." Like Stein's, Tolstoy's translation is an abridgment; the author sought to remove accretions to Christ's original teachings, combining the four gospels into one. As he explained in the preface to his translation, entitled *The Life of Jesus. The Gospel in Brief*: "Studying Christianity, I found next to this source of the pure water of life an illegitimate intermixture of dirt and muck that had obscured its purity for me; mingled with the high Christian teaching I found foreign and ugly teaching from church and Hebrew tradition" (2011:xxii). Tolstoy's translation then is not an example of postmodern play; rather, it is, like Stein's translation of the liturgy, an attempt to return Christianity to its source or origin, to remove the obfuscating interventions of churches. While Tolstoy acknowledges that we have only versionings of the gospels (the first version of the canonical Bible, after all, was itself a translation, written in Greek, not in the actual language of Jesus, Aramaic), he is convinced that through careful reading and study he can convey the ultimate "meaning" of Christ's teaching. (In an ironic twist of fate, Tolstoy's translation of the gospels was first published in an abridged French translation, which Tolstoy considered a "perversion of his writing" (Condren 2011:xi).) In any case, this association of Stein with Tolstoy presents the Jewish priest less as a postmodernist than as an honorary member of the Russian intelligentsia, which has for centuries now been the standard bearer of the dream of a Russian universal culture, imagined in stark opposition to a Western-style pluralism.

The fact that Stein has no concrete associations with Russia does not invalidate this reading or obscure the references to Tolstoy, for this connection is based on an idealistic vision of the Russian intelligentsia defined not in terms of ethnicity or class but as an imagined community of readers. As Boym explains, "It is culture and education that constitute a Russian community. However, what distinguishes Russians is not so much *what* they read but *how* they read—by passionately transgressing the boundaries between life and fiction, by wishing to live out literature and, with its help, change the world" (1995:139). Like Ulitsksaya's novel, Stein's translations—both for the Nazis and for his congregation in Israel—exhibit a passionate transgression of the boundaries between life and fiction, between truth and lies. In other words, the Jewish Catholic Daniel Stein reads—and translates—like a Russian *intelligent*. In this way, he embodies a uniquely Russian universalism, capable of synthesizing all the greatest works produced in the world, which Dostoevsky saw as epitomized in the life and works of Russia's greatest poet, Pushkin.

The third and final point that allows me to draw a clear distinction between a post-Socialist and a postmodern reading of *Daniel Stein* concerns the character Eva Makanian. Eva is one of only two characters in the novel living in the United States, which turns out to be a rather significant fact. For most of the novel, Eva is estranged from her mother who was a zealous member of the resistance during the Second World War, when she gave birth to Eva in a forest, and an even more zealous communist after the War. Eva is vaguely discontented with her life. Divorced from her first husband, she comes to suspect her second husband, Grisha, of having an affair with her adolescent son, Grisha's stepson. The suspicion grows apace with her increasing disenchantment with the United States and its cultural values.

The family moves from Boston to Los Angeles, deeper into the belly of the beast, where Eva comes to an imperfect peace with her son's homosexuality, eventually allowing her son and his boyfriend to move into her house. While on the surface, everything appears copacetic, Eva is troubled by her son's lifestyle and by her own tacit acceptance of it. She eventually approaches Daniel Stein for advice.

Eva later recounts his advice to her friend Esther: "Daniel said that he, too, like me, experiences a profound horror [*tikhii uzhas*] before this vice and had never encountered homosexuals. And he said that it would be better if Aleks lived on his own so as not to involve me in his relationships. Because I need to save myself from destruction [*razrusheniia*]" (Ulitskaya 2011:437). Father Stein's use of "horror" and "destruction" is striking insofar as it equates the events of the Second World War with a homosexual lifestyle. After that, Eva appears only once more in the novel; in a letter to Esther that is included right after the transcript of their conversation, she recounts that her estranged husband was seriously injured in a car accident and that she was now "living like an automaton" (439). After that, she disappears from the novel. The absence of any reply from Eva regarding Brother Daniel's advice suggests that she is unable to follow through with it but is also unable to fully reconcile herself to her son's lifestyle. She is condemned then to live out her life in a state of moral uncertainty and anxiety. This plotline is distinguished from the many others in the novel by the fact that in every other instance the characters follow Brother Daniel's advice, and it invariably brings joy and peace to their troubled lives. Homosexuality, it turns out, represents the limit of Brother Daniel's tolerance and of his antidogmatism, a point that has been largely ignored by Western critics who prefer to see the novel as a postmodern celebration of pluralism and hybridity. Sutcliffe admits—in a footnote—that his decision not to treat the problematic theme was intentional, although he offers no explanation: "This discussion does not address gays, another marginalized and often victimized group in Russian society" (2009:501).[5] We can only assume it would have complicated his presentation of Ulitskaya as a US-style liberal.[6]

---

[5] None of the scholarly articles dedicated to Ulitskaya's novel and published in the West (Sutcliffe 2009, Vojvodić 2011, and Letkovskaya 2012) has treated the motif of homosexuality in the novel and how it relates to the themes of religious and ethnic identity and tolerance. Sutcliffe acknowledges the motif but chooses to ignore it.

[6] Sutcliffe describes *Daniel Stein* on his facebook page as "Ulitskaya's masterpiece on the Holocaust and tolerance" (accessed November 13, 2014).

The limits of tolerance

A key to understanding this rather depressing subplot is suggested in Ulitskaya's short story "Golubchik" ["Darling"], first published in 1995. This story also recounts the seduction of a young boy by his stepfather and so provides a rather direct intertextual reference. The title is a play on words. The Russian root *golubchik*, meaning "darling" or "dear," has as its root *goluboi*, or "light blue," which in Russian slang means "gay." Moreover, as a form of address, *golubchik* is most often used by adults with children but has also been appropriated by Russian gays as a campy sign of intimacy among themselves. In the story, the stepfather, a respected musicologist, not only initiates his stepson into adult sexual relations but also schools him in the intricacies of classical music, presenting a classical Greek model of age-stratified homosexual relations. After his stepfather's death, Slava is adrift. He has an intense, spiritual relationship with a female music student, Zhenya, but the now adult Slava has physical desires that cannot be satisfied by music alone. He begins cruising Moscow parks and eventually picks up a stranger, dressed, not coincidentally, in a cowboy shirt. Of approximately the same age, Slava and his partner represent what is referred to as an "egalitarian" relationship, which is often associated with global (Western) gay culture. Moreover, when they make love, it is violent and, Ulitskaya implies, soulless insofar as, during their lovemaking, Slava no longer hears music in his head—a child prodigy with an innate feel for music, Slava before this moment has always heard music in his head. The story ends tragically with Slava being brutally murdered while cruising in a park.

The work is a damming portrayal not of homosexuality per se but of a homosexual lifestyle that is indexed in the story as American (remember his lover's cowboy shirt) and soulless (it stops the music). This interpretation reflects the general sentiment among post-Soviet Russian writers and intellectuals who, while attributing an innate artistic sensitivity and refinement to homosexuals, condemn US-style gay identity not as a sin or as a crime but as profoundly "nekul'turno" [uncultured]— one of Vasily Aksyonov's characters in the short story "Around Dupont Circle" refers to the US gay subculture as *vul'garno* [vulgar]. This negative assessment stems from the view that an exclusive gay identity is egotistical, narcissistic, a reflection of the inflated individualism of Western and, in particular, US culture. As Boym notes, "Individualized sexuality is a part of the Romano-Germanic individualized worldview, while communal rhythmical pathos is part of the realm of Eurasia" (1995:153). More simply put, global gay culture is seen not only as un-Russian, but as a symptom of US cultural imperialism.

I imagine few readers would interpret "Golubchik" as an expression of a postmodern consciousness. In fact, Ulitskaya makes it clear that the subject of her story is the crisis of Russian national identity in a post-Soviet world. For example, she names the stepfather Nikolai Romanovich, a rather obvious reference to the last tsar Nikolai Romanov, inscribing the tale within modern Russian history and suggesting historical parallels between the chaos following the fall of the Romanov dynasty and the chaos that accompanied the fall of the Soviet Union, when the achievements of Russian high art were cheapened, debased, pushed aside in the post-Soviet marketplace, now filled with cheap cultural products from the West. (Slava, incidentally, is not only a nickname for Vladislav but is also the Russian word for "glory," a term widely used in Soviet-era slogans.) Moreover, Ulitskaya's specific enplotment of the theme—a stepfather seducing a stepson—confirms popular Russian notions that (1) homosexuals are pedophiles (the 2013 law banning homosexual propaganda was presented as a defense of Russia's children), and that (2) women—in this case, the wife—are often the other unwitting victim of male homosexual desire.[7]

The theme of homosexuality in *Daniel Stein*, then, is neither an example of postmodern diversity nor is it an "innocent" detail meant to add "local color"—a taste of life in twenty-first century Los Angeles. Rather, it belongs to a broad post-Soviet discourse on homosexuality that plays an important role in post-Soviet national and territorial bordering. Ulitskaya's insistent connection of homosexuality with the United States, for example, reflects and reinforces a post-Soviet symbolic geography that defines Russia against the United States so as to (re)inscribe Russia within a European cultural zone. But, it is also an assertion of the uniqueness of Russian culture within Europe, its spirituality and soulfulness, which can be traced back to the nineteenth century. In *How Russians Read the French*, Priscilla Meyer demonstrates how the rewriting of contemporary French novels by Russia's greatest nineteenth-century writers, Lermontov, Dostoevsky, and Tolstoy, functioned to distinguish Russian culture from its French counterpart, in particular, from what the Russians saw as a cynical and sensational take on human sexuality. As Meyer puts it, "Russia's distanced evaluation of French Romanticism, which rejected the world and diction of the solitary solipsist and of French realism, with its tendency to sensational sociological exposé, helped Russian writers define both their sense of national identity and their conception of the purpose of literary art" (2010:218). She goes on to

---

[7]   For more on the presentation of women and children as the innocent victims of male homosexuality, see, in particular, the work of Russian psychologist Dilia Enikeeva (2003).

note, "the very necessity of turning to the French for models in creating a national Russian literature made the desire [on the part of Russian writers] to highlight their own distinctiveness even more acute than the difference between worldviews alone would have done" (2010:210).

Within that context, the contemporary disdain for homosexuality as an exclusive identity, a lifestyle with its own subculture, can be interpreted as an expression of a distinctly Russian notion of universalism, with its roots in nineteenth-century Russian thought on Russia's unique historical destiny. This universalism, based on a common high literary culture, infused with spiritual values as opposed to religious dogma, should not be confused with Western notions of pluralism. In Russia today, among gays and straights, liberals and conservatives, global gay culture, based on the US model of exclusive and totalizing sexual identities, functions as a powerful, negatively charged metonym for a soulless and egotistical West, and so, "Russian gay rights activists have to fight for the very recognition of LGBT people as a social group" (Sharova 2010:74).

To read the subplot of Eva and her son à la russe, then, is to see in Brother Daniel's advice as a pointed rejection of a hegemonic US culture celebrating diversity and pluralism in favor of a traditional Russian notion of (heterosexual) universalism. This assertion of Russia's difference—its untranslatability, if you will—in the midst of a work that appears to celebrate the endless proliferation of versionings would seem to suggest a limit to pluralism. Moreover, beneath the postmodern veneer of multilingualism, global migration, and the critique of authoritarian institutions in Ulitskaya's novel, Daniel Stein himself changes little. His fundamental character is fixed; there is nothing "fluid" about him. "The hero," in the words of the Slavist Jasmina Vojvodić, "remains essentially identical to himself" (2011:141). In this way, one could argue, Daniel Stein serves as an embodiment of the concept of Russian culture as synthesizing and universal, transcending ethnic identities while nonetheless reflecting a deep suspicion of Western-style pluralism and postmodern hybridity.

Misreading Russia

Despite the warnings of scholars regarding the application of postmodernity to post-Soviet Russia, writers, readers, and critics find it hard to resist the temptation. Consider, for example, the Ukrainian interpreter in Jonathan Foer Safron's best-selling novel *Everything is Illuminated*. When asked how well he speaks English, he replies: "I'm fluid," instead of fluent. Fluid is, of course, a buzzword in writing on postmodernity, used to describe a subjectivity liberated from restrictive and exclusive identity categories, be they ethnic, national, colonial, economic, gender-based, or even sexual— Homi Bhabha's "hybrid" (1994) and Julia Kristeva's "happy cosmopolitan." (1991:3) And so, Sasha's substitution of fluid for fluent functions as a kind of metaliterary Freudian slip, revealing the author's intention to present post-Soviet Ukraine as his postmodern playground.

And Foer is not alone. Surprising as it may seem against a backdrop of sexism, homophobia, and resurgent nationalism, a number of Western scholars and journalists who traveled in Russia in the early 1990s "discovered" a liberating postmodern fluidity in the subjectivity of post-Soviet subjects. The US anthropologist Laurie Essig, for example, declared: "sexuality in Russia is too fluid to be 'trapped.'" It is, she implies, queer avant la lettre, postmodern. The Russianist Luc Beaudoin came to a similar conclusion, claiming that the "gendered construction of Russian gay men is somewhat more fluid [than the construction of American gay male identity]" (2–6:229). The Canadian filmmaker Steven Kokker traveled to post-Soviet Russia in search of what he called a "sexually fluid generation," as did the British novelist Duncan Fallowell who, after spending one hot summer in St. Petersburg, declared, "People's sense of identity is liquid. Russia itself is a liquid" (1994:302). The US journalist David Tuller shared Fallowell's assessment: "For through my travels and interviews," Tuller explains, "and, especially, my weekends at the dacha—where we partied, chugged vodka, and chatted all night—I experienced, in startling and unexpected ways, a different kind of sexual freedom than I had found in the golden gay enclaves of New York and San Francisco" (1996:42). Frank Browning declared Tuller's Russia to be a "liberating alternative" to the gay ghettoes of the West (qtd. on the cover of Tuller 1996).[8]

Sarah Rubin Suleiman, who spent her childhood in Budapest, was perhaps the first to admit to misreading postcommunist Eastern Europe as postmodern. In an article written in 1993 entitled "The Politics of Postmodernism after the Wall (Or What Do We Do When the Ethnic Cleansing Starts)," Suleiman takes to task Western scholars, herself included, who projected their postmodern political aspirations onto other peoples

---

[8] This projection of sexual freedom onto the East, and onto Russia, in particular, has in fact a long history. Alexander Etkind, for example, traces the influence on Freud's thinking of "the Russian stereotype," "a conception held by Westerners that Russia is an exotic place where even the most incredible excesses are possible, be they political or sexual" (1997:88). And Freud, whose most famous patients were Russian, is purported to have commented: "These Russians are like water; they fill any containers, but do not retain the form of any" (qtd. in Etkind 1997:225).

and societies, in particular, those emerging from under the communist yoke: "The idea of a postmodern paradise where one can try on identities like costumes in a shopping mall, appears to me now as not only naïve, but intolerably thoughtless in a world where whole populations are murdered for the sake of ethnic identity" (1993:51). The fall of communism did not usher in a new postmodern hybrid subjectivity so much as it gave new life to traditional ethnic, ethno-nationalist, and ethno-religious identities. Indeed, subsequent research in the field of Sexuality Studies has revealed that the sexuality of post-Soviet subjects is constrained if not by a notion of exclusive sexual orientations, then by the no less restrictive categories of active/passive and masculine/feminine (see Baer 2009:36–41).

The misreading of postcommunist as postmodern was also the subject of David Damrosch's article "Death in Translation," which compares the international reception of Milorad Pavić's critically acclaimed *Dictionary of the Khazars* to its reception back home in Serbia. The theme of translation runs throughout the work—indeed it is presented as a translation of three different encyclopedias in three different languages using three different scripts—and this is certainly one of the factors contributing to its "status as a work of international postmodernism." Damrosch points out, however, that, "the book's international success involved the neglect or outright misreading of its political content" (2005:381). Specifically, the celebration of the novel's playful postmodernity is predicated on a certain blindness— an inability or unwillingness on the part of international critics to see the theme of Serbian nationalism, and specifically Serbian ressentiment over its perceived oppressed status as the majority ethnic group in multiethnic Yugoslavia. Damrosch notes that Catalan readers are likely to pick up on this theme, and I would imagine Russian readers, as well. In any case, Pavić's novel, Damrosch maintains, "contains a political polemic that had been hidden in plain sight from international audiences who had welcomed the novel as 'an Arabian Nights romance,' 'a wickedly teasing intellectual game,' and an opportunity 'to lose themselves in a novel of love and death,' as the flyleaf of the American edition describes the book" (2005:381).

Conclusion

The tendency on the part of the English readers and critics to read Ulitskaya's novel as a plea for postmodern pluralism may reflect a general tendency in the West to see World Literature as a utopian space where national limits, as Goethe suggested, are transcended. (1994) The degree to which works of literature in translation ever truly transcend national limits is a matter of debate, but it seems clear that the postmodern discourse surrounding the reception of Ultiskaya's novel in English has obscured a Russian interpretation that recognizes a distinct limit to Western pluralism in the form of tolerance for homosexuality. Not coincidentally, Ulitskaya's short story "Golubchik" has yet to be translated into English, and I suspect it never will be, reminding us that any study of cross-cultural exchange must pay attention not only to what gets translated—and to how those translations are packaged—but also to what does not get translated.

Bibliography

Abramovich, Nikolai. 1909. *Religiia krasoty i stradaniia. O. Uaľd i Dostoevskii* [The Religion of Beauty and Suffering. Oscar Wilde and Dostoevsky]. St. Petersburg: Losev.

Adorno, Theodor. 1991. "Words from abroad." In *Notes to Literature*, Vol. 2, Rolf Tiedermann (ed.) and Shierry Weber Nicholson (trans.), 185–199. New York: Columbia University Press.

Akhmatova, Anna. 2013. "On Lozinskii" (1955). In *Russian Writers on Translation*, Brian James Baer and Natalia Olshanskaya (eds), 98–99. Manchester: St. Jerome.

Aksenov, Vasilii. 1996. "B raione ploshchadi Diupon" [Around Dupont Square]. In *Negativ polozhiteľnogo geroia. Rasskazy*, 253–69. Moscow: Vagrius.

Altman, Dennis. 1997. "Global Gaze/Global Gays." *GLQ* 3: 417–436.

Alvarez, R. and C. Vidal (eds). 1996. *Translation, Power, Subversion*. Clevedon, Philadelphia, Adelaide: Multilingual Matters.

Anderson, Benedict. 1991. *Imagined Communities. Reflections on the Origin and Spread of Nationalism*. London: Verso.

Antokoľskii, Paveľ. 1963. "Cherny kleb masterstva" [The Black Bread of Craftsmanship]. *Masterstvo Perevoda* 3, 5–10. Moscow: Sovetskii pisateľ.

Antokoľskii, Paveľ, Mutar Auezov, and Maksm Ryľskii. 1955. "Khudozhestvennye perevody literatur narodov SSSR." In *Voprosy Khudozhestvennogo perevoda. Sbornik statei* [Questions of Literary Translation. A Collection of Articles], Vladimir Rosseľs (ed.), 5–44. Moscow: Sovetskii pisateľ.

Appiah, Anthony. 1991. "Is the Post- in Postmodernism the Post- in Postcolonial?" *Critical Inquiry* 17:336–357.

Apter, Emily. 2013. *Against World Literature. On the Politics of Untranslatability*. London and New York: Verso.

Arnault, Antoine-Vincent. 1825. "Fable XVI. La Feuille." In *Oeuvres de A.V. Arnault*, Vol. 4, *Fables et poésies diverses*, 168. Paris: Bossange Père.

Arnault, Antoine-Vincent. 1823. *Les loisirs d'un banni*, Auguste Imbert (ed.). Paris: Les Marchands de Nouveautés.

Arnault, Antoine-Vincente. 1794. *Marius à minturnes, tragédie en trois actes*. Paris: Maradan.

Arnault, Antoine-Vincente. 1792. *Lucrèce, tragédie, en cinq actes, en vers*. Paris: Cailleau.

Asimakoulos, Dmitri and Margaret Rogers (eds). 2011. *Translation and Opposition*. Bristol/Buffalo/Toronto: Multilingual Matters.

Autrey, Michael. 2011. "Review of *Daniel Stein, Interpreter* by Liudmila Ulitskaya. Booklist (15 March 2011): 21.

Baer, Brian James. 2011. "Translation Theory and Cold War Politics: Roman Jakobson and Vladimir Nabokov in 1950s America." In *Contexts, Subtexts and Pretexts: Literary Translation in Eastern Europe and Russia*, Brian James Baer (ed.), 171–186. Amsterdam and Philadelphia: John Benjamins.

Baer, Brian James. 2006. "Literary Translation and the Construction of a Soviet Intelligentsia." *The Massachusetts Review* 47(3): 537–560.

Baer, Brian James. 2005. "Translating the Transition: The Translator-detective in Post-Soviet Fiction." *Linguistica Antverpiensia* 4: 243–254.

Baiburova, R. M. 2000. "Moskovskie masony epokhi prosveshcheniia—Russkaia intelligentsiia XVIII v." [Moscow Masons in the Age of the Enlightenment—The Russian Intelligentsia of the 18th Century]. In *Russkaia Intelligentsia. Istoriia i sud'ba* [Russian Intelligentsia. History and Fate]. T. B. Kniazevskaia (ed.), 243–250. Moscow: Nauka.

Baker, Mona. 2010. Editor's Introduction to Karen Littau's "Translation in the Age of Postmodern Production: From Text to Hypertext." In *Critical Readings in Translation Studies*, Mona Baker (ed.), 435–437. London and New York: Routledge.

Baker, Mona. 1992. *In Other Words. A Coursebook on Translation*. London and New York: Routledge.

Bakhtin, Mikhail M. 1981. "Discourse in the Novel." In *The Dialogic Imagination. Four Essays*, Michael Holquist (ed.) and Caryl Emerson and Michael Holquist (trans.), 259–422. Austin: University of Texas Press.

Barta, Peter I. (ed.). 2001. *Gender and Sexuality in Russian Civilization*. London: Routledge.

Barthes, Roland. 1992. "The Death of the Author (1968)." In *Modern Literary Theory. A Reader*, Philip Rice and Patricia Waugh (eds), 114–121. London and New York: E. Arnold.

Barthes, Roland. 1986. "The Reality Effect." In *The Rustle of Language*, Richard Howard (trans.), 141–148. New York: Hill and Wang.

Bassnett, Susan and Harish Trivedi (eds). 1999. *Post-Colonial Translation*. London and New York: Routledge.

Beaudoin, Luc. 2006. "Raising a Pink Flag: The Reconstruction of Russian Gay Identity in the Shadow of Russian Nationalism." In *Gender and National Identity in Twentieth-Century Russian Culture*, Helena Goscilo and Andrea Lanoux (eds), 225–240. DeKalb: Northern Illinois University Press.

Beck, Karin. 2007. *Beyond the Napoleonic Principle: Two Modes of Language Use as Bilingualism in Leo Tolstoy's* War and Peace. Unpublished Ph.D. dissertation, Columbia University.

Belinsky, Vissarion. 2013. "Vissarion Belinskii (1811–1848)." In *Russian Writers on Translation*, Brian James Baer and Natalia Olshanskaya (eds), 31–39. Manchester: St. Jerome.

Berdyaev, Nicolas. 1962. *The Russian Idea*, introduction by Alexander Vucinich. Boston: Beacon Press.

Berlina, Alexandra. 2012. "Homosexuality in the Russian Translation of *The Hours*." *Sexuality and Culture: An Interdisciplinary Quarterly* 16(4):449–466.

Bermann, Sandra. 2005. Introduction. In *Nation, Language, and the Ethics of Translation*, Sandra Bermann and Michael Wood (eds), 1–10. Princeton and Oxford: Princeton University Press.

Bershtein, Evgenii. 2000. "'Next to Christ': Oscar Wilde in Russian Modernism." In *The European Reception of Oscar Wilde*, Stefano Evangelista (ed.), 285–300. London: Continuum.

Bershtein, Evgenii. 1998. "The Russian Myth of Oscar Wilde." In *Self and Story in Russian History*, Laura Engelstein and Stephanie Sandler (eds), 168–188. Ithaca and London: Cornell University Press.

Bhabha, Homi. 1994. *The Location of Culture*. London and New York: Routledge.

Billiani, Francesca. 2007. Introduction. In *Modes of Censorship and Translation: National Contexts and Diverse Media*, F. Billiani (ed.), 1–26. Manchester: St. Jerome.

Binyon, T. J. 1992. Introduction. In *A Hero of Our Time*, V. Nabokov in collaboration with D. Nabokov (trans.), xi–xxii. New York: Alfred A. Knopf.

Blackledge, Adrian and Angela Creese. 2010. *Multilingualism. A Critical Perspective*. London and New York: Continuum.

Blommaert, Jan and Chris Bulcaen. 2001. "Encounters." In *The Making of Authority. Languages and Publics*, Susan Gal and Kathryn Woolard (eds), unnumbered pages. Manchester: St. Jerome.

Bobrick, Benson. 2001. *Wide as the Waters: The Story of the English Bible and the Revolution It Inspired*. New York: Simon and Schuster.

Bogdanov, K., R. Nikolozi, and Iu. Murashov (eds). 2013. *Dzhambul Dzhabaev. Prikliucheniia kazakhskogo akyna v Sovetskoi strane. Stat'i i materialy* [Dzhambul Dzhabaev. Adventures of a Kazakh Akyn in the Land of the Soviets. Articles and Material]. Moscow: Novoe Literaturnoe Obozrenie.

Borenstein. Eliot. 1999. "Editor's Introduction: Postmodernism, Duty-free." In Mark Lipovetsky, *Russian Postmodernist Fiction. Dialogue with Chaos*, Eliot Borenstein (ed. and trans.), xv–xviii. New York: M. E. Sharpe.

Boym, Svetlana. 1995. "From the Russian Soul to Post-Soviet Nostalgia." *Representations* 49 (Winter): 133–166.

Braudel, Fernand. 1988. *The Identity of France*. Volume I. *History and Environment*, Siân Reynolds (trans.). New York: Harper & Row.

Braungardt, G. M. 2009. "Review of *Daniel Stein* by Liudmila Ulitskaia. *NDR Kultur* (May 29)." Available online at: http://www.ndr.de/kultur/literatur/buchtipps/nbdanielstein100.html (accessed 2 Jan 2003).

Briggs, Anthony. 2002. "Translating Tolstoy." *Tolstoy Studies Journal*, 14: 100–118.

Brodski, Bella. 2007. *Can these Bones Live? Translation, Survival, and Cultural Memory*. Stanford, CA: Stanford University Press.

Bromfield, Andrew and Jennifer Coates. 2007. "A Note on the Translation." In *War and Peace. Original Version*, Leo Tolstoy (ed.) xi–xviii. New York: Harper Collins.

Brooks, Jeffrey. 2000. *Thank You, Comrade Stalin! Soviet Public Culture from Revolution to Cold War*. Princeton: Princeton University Press.

Buden, Boris. 2013. "Nothing to Complete: Something to Start." In *Post-Post-Soviet? Art, Politics & Society in Russia at the Turn of the Decade*, Marta

Dziewanska, Ekaterina Degot, and Ilya Budraitskis (eds), 183–193. Warsaw: Museum of Modern Art in Warsaw.

Bukiet, Melvin Jules. 2011. "*Daniel Stein, Interpeter* Reviewed." *Book World.* *Washington Post* (10 May). Available online at: http://www.washingtonpost .com/entertainment/books/book-world-daniel-stein-interpreter-reviewed/2011/03/17/AFVSZtgG_story.html (accessed 30 April 2012).

Bullock, Philip Ross. 2013. "Not One of Us?: The Paradoxes of Translating Oscar Wilde in the Soviet Union." In *The Art of Accommodation. Literary Translation in Russia*, Leon Burnett and Emily Lygo (eds), 235–264. Bern: Peter Lang.

Bullock, Philip Ross. 2008. "Ambiguous Speech and Eloquent Silence: The Queerness of Tchaikovsky's Songs." *19th-Century Music* 32 (Summer) 1: 94–128.

Burnett, Leon. 1985. "The Survival of Myth: Mandel'shtam's 'Word' and Translation." In *The Manipulation of Literature: Studies in Literary Translation*, Theo Hermans (ed.), 164–197. New York: St. Martin's Press.

Burnett, Leon and Emily Lygo. 2013. "The Art of Accommodation: Introduction." In *The Art of Accommodation: Literary Translation in Russia*, Leon Burnett and Emily Lygo (eds), 1–30. Oxford and Bern: Peter Lang.

Burson, Jeffrey D. 2005. "Mandate of the Fatherland: Denis Fonvizin's Translation of Neo-Confucianism into the Politics of Enlightened Absolutism under Catherine the Great." *Vestnik. Journal of Russian and Asian Studies.* Available online at: http://www.sras.org/denis_fonvizin_s_translation_of_neo-confucianism (accessed 2 July 2012).

Burt, Richard. 1998. "(Un)Censoring in Detail: The Fetish of Censorship in the Early Modern Past and the Postmodern Present." In *Censorship and Silencing: Practices of Cultural Regulation*, Robert C. Post (ed.), 17–41. Los Angeles, CA: Getty Research Institute.

Casanova, Pascale. 2010. "Consecration and Accumulation of Literary Capital: Translation as Unequal Exchange." In *Critical Readings in Translation Studies*, Mona Baker (ed.), 285–303. London and New York: Routledge.

Chamberlain, Lori. 2000. "Gender and the Metaphorics of Translation." In *The Translation Studies Reader*, Lawrence Venuti (ed.), 314–329. London and New York: Routledge.

Chénier, André. 1862. "Près des bords où Venise est reine de la mer." In *Poésies de André Chénier*, Edition Critique, L. Becq de Fouquières (ed.), 412. Paris: Charpentier.

Chernetsky, Vitaly. 2007. *Mapping Postcommunist Cultures: Russia and Ukraine in the Context of Globalization.* Montreal and Kingston: McGill-Queen's University Press.

Chernyshchevskii, Nikolai. 2013. "Schiller as Translated by Russian Poets" (1856). In *Russian Writers on Translation. An Anthology*, Brian James Baer and Natalia Olshanskaya (eds), 57–58. Manchester: St. Jerome.

Chester, Pamela and Sibelan Forrester (eds). 1996. *Engendering Slavic Literatures.* Bloomington: Indiana University Press.

Cheyfitz, Eric. 1991. *The Poetics of Imperialism: Translation and Colonization from the Tempest to Tarzan*. Oxford: Oxford University Press.

Chkhartishvili, Grigorii. 1993. "Zhizn' i smert' Iukio Misimy, ili kak unichtozhit' khram" [The Life and Death of Yukio Mishima, or How to Destroy the Temple]. In *Zolotoi Khram*, Iukio Misima (ed.), [Golden Temple], G. Chkhartishvili (trans.), 5–34. St. Petersburg: Azbuka.

Choldin, Marianna Tax. 1985. *A Fence around the Empire. Russian Censorship of Western Ideas under the Tsars*. Durham: Duke University Press.

Chuilleanáin, Eiléan Ní, Cormac Ó Cuilleanáin and David Parris (eds). 2009. *Translation and Censorship*. Dublin: Four Courts Press.

Chukhno, Valerii. 2009. "Ternovy venets genii" [The Crown of Thorns of a Genius]. In *Oskar Uail'd. Stiki. P'esy. Povesti. Aforizmy i paradoksyi* [Oscar Wilde. Verses. Plays. Stories. Aphorisms and Paradoxes], 5–8. Moscow: Eksmo.

Chukhno, Valerii. 2003. "Ispoved' dushi. Posleslovie" [The Confession of a Soul. An Afterword]. In *Oskar Uail'd. De Profundis*, 431–462. Moscow: Eksmo-Press.

Chukovskaya, Lydia. 2002. *The Akhmatova Journals. Volume I. 1938–1941*, Milena Michalski and Sylva Rubashova (trans.). Evanston, IL: Northwestern University Press.

Chukovskii, Kornei. 1922. *Poet i palach* [The Poet and the Executioner]. Petersburg: Epokha.

Chukovskii, Kornei. 1912. "Oskar Uail'd. Etiud" [Oscar Wilde. A Study]. In *Polnoe sobranie sochinenii Oskara Uail'da* [Complete Collected Works of Oscar Wilde], Vol. 1, K. I. Chukovskii (ed.), i–xxxiii. St. Petersburg: A.F. Marks.

Chukovskii, Kornei and Andrei Fedorov. 1930. *Iskusstvo perevoda* [The Art of Translation]. Leningrad: Academia.

Clark, Katerina. 2011. *Moscow, the Fourth Rome: Stalinism, Cosmopolitanism, and the Evolution of Soviet Culture, 1931–1941*. Cambridge, MA: Harvard University Press.

Clark, Katerina. 2001. "Germanaphone Intellectuals in Stalin's Russia: Diaspora and Cultural Identity in the 1930s." *Kritika* 2(3): 529–551.

Clark, Katerina. 1984. *The Soviet Novel*. Chicago, IL: University of Chicago Press.

Clark, Katerina and Evgeny Dobrenko, with Andrei Artizov and Oleg Naumov. 2007. *Soviet Culture and Power: A History in Documents, 1917–1953*. New Haven, CT: Yale University Press.

Clowes, Edith W. 2011. *Russia on the Edge. Imagined Geographies and Post-Soviet Identity*. Ithaca and London: Cornell University Press.

Coetzee, J. M. 1996. *Giving Offense. Essays on Censorship*. Chicago and London: University of Chicago Press.

Condee, Nancy. 2009. *The Imperial Trace. Recent Russian Cinema*. Oxford: Oxford University Press.

Condee, Nancy and Vladimir Padunov. 1994. "Pair-a-dice Lost: The Socialist Gamble, Market Determinism, and Compulsory Postmodernism." *New Formations* 22: 72–94.

Condren, Dustin. 2011. Foreword. In *The Gospel in Brief. The Life of Jesus*, Leo Tolstoy (ed.), Dustin Condren (trans.), vii–xiv. New York: Harper Perennial.

Conroy, Pat. 2007. Introduction. In *War and Peace*, Leo Tolstoy (ed.),7–17. New York: Signet Classics.

Cornwall, Neil. 1998. *Reference Guide to Russian Literature*. Chicago, IL: Fitzroy Dearborn.

Costlow, Jane T., Stephenie Sandler, and Judith Vowles (eds). 1992. *Sex and the Body in Russian Culture*. Stanford, CA: Stanford University Press.

Crane, Mary Thomas. 1993. *Framing Authority: Sayings, Self, and Society in Sixteenth-century England*. Princeton, NJ: Princeton University Press.

Cronin, Michael. 2006. *Translation and Identity*. London and New York: Routledge.

Cronin, Michael. 2003. *Translation and Globalization*. New York: Routledge.

Cummings, William. 2005. "Rethinking the Translation in Translation Studies: Questions from Makassar, Indonesia." In *Asian Translation Traditions*, Eva Hung and Judy Wakabayashi (eds), 195–210. Manchester: St. Jerome.

Damrosch, David. 2009. "Introduction: All the Time in the World." In *Teaching World Literature*, David Damrosch (ed.), 1–11. New York: MLA.

Damrosch, David. 2005. "Death in Translation." In *Nation, Language, and the Ethics of Translation*, Sandra Bermann and Michael Wood (eds), 380–398. Princeton and Oxford: Princeton University Press.

Danilin, Iu. 1973. *Beranzhe i ego pesni* [Béranger and His Songs]. Moscow: Khudozhestvennaia literature.

Dashkova, Polina. 2002. *Nikto ne zaplachit. Roman* [No One Will Cry. A Novel]. Moscow: Astrel'/ACT.

Debreczeny, Paul. 1997. *Social Functions of Literature. Alexander Pushkin and Russian Culture*. Stanford, CA: Stanford University Press.

Delabastita, Dirk and Rainier Grutman. 2005. "Introduction. Fictional Representations of Multilingualism and Translation." *Linguistica Antverpiensia* 4: 11–34.

Delvecchio, Anna. 2011. *Translation as a Catalyst for the Russification of Ukrainian under Imperial and Soviet Rule*. Unpublished Doctoral Dissertation, University of Ottawa.

Derzhavin, Konstantin. 1961. "Tvorenie Dante" [Dante's Oeuvre]. In *Dante Alig'eri. Bozhestvennaia komediia* [Dante Aligheri. The Divine Comedy], 5–13. Moscow: Khudozhestvennaia Literatura.

Dingwaney, Anurdha and Carol Maier (eds). 1995. *Between Languages and Cultures: Translation and Cross-Cultural Texts*. Pittsburgh, PA: University of Pittsburgh Press.

Dobrenko, Evgeny. 2011. "Naideno v perevode: rozhdenie sovetskoi mnogonatsional'noi litartury iz smerti avtora" [Found in Translation: The Birth of Soviet Multinational Literature from the Death of the Author]. *Neprikosnovennyi zapas* 78(4): 235–262.

Dobrenko, Evgeny. 1997. *The Making of the State Reader. Social and Aesthetic Contexts of the Reception of Soviet Literature*. Trans. Jesse M. Savage. Stanford, CA: Stanford University Press.

Dolack, Thomas. 2011. "'A Dream of Light in the Eternal Darkness': Karolina Pavlova's Translations from the German." In *Translating Women: Gender and Translation in the 21st Century*, Louise von Flotow, 37–56. Ottawa, ON: University of Ottawa Press.

Dollimore, Jonathan. 1991. *Sexual Dissidence. Augustine to Wilde, Freud to Foucault.* Oxford: Oxford University Press.

Dollimore, Jonathan. 1987. "Different Desires: Subjectivity and Transgression in Wilde and Gide." Textual Practice 1(1): 48–67.

Dontsova, Dar'ia. 2003. *Krutye Nasledniki* [Hard-boiled Heir]. Moscow: Eksmo.

Dostoevskii, Fedor M. 1981. "Muzhik Marei" [The Peasant Marei]. In F. M. Dostoevskii (ed.). *Polnoe sobranie sochinenii v tridstati tomakh* [F. M. Dostoevsky. Complete Collection of Works in Thirty Volumes], Vol. 23, V. G. Bazanov (ed.), 47–50. Leningrad: Nauka.

Dostoevskii, F. M. 1973. *Prestuplenie i nakazanie. Rukopisnye redaktsii* [Crime and Punishment. Manuscript Redactions],Vol. 7. In F. M. Dostoevskii. (ed.) *Polnoe sobranie sochinenii v tridstati tomakh* [F. M. Dostoevsky. Complete Collection of Works in Thirty Volumes]. V. G. Bazanov (ed.). Leningrad: Nauka.

Dostoevsky, Fyodor. 1999. *Crime and Punishment*, Sydney Monas (trans.). New York: Signet Classic.

Dostoevsky, F. M. 1985a. *The Diary of a Writer*, Boris Brasol (trans.) Salt Lake City, UT: Peregrine Smith Books.

Dostoevsky, Fyodor. 1985b. *The House of the Dead*, David McDuff (trans.). London and New York: Penguin.

Dowler, Wayne. 1982. *Dostoevsky, Grigor'ev, and Native Soil Conservatism.* Toronto and Buffalo: University of Toronto Press.

Efros, A. M. 2001. *"Poeziia Mikelandzhelo"* [The Poetry of Micheangelo]. In *Mikelandzhelo. Tvorets. Risunki i stikhotvoreniia* [Michelangelo. Creator. Drawings and Poems], 201–234. Moscow: Eksmo-Press.

Egolin, A. M. 1969. *Nekrasov i poety-demokraty 60-80ykh godov XIX veka* [Nekrasov and the Poet-Democrats of the 60–80s of the XIX Century]. Moscow: Khudozhestvennaia Literatura.

Enikeeva, Dilia. 2003. *Gei i lesbiianki* [Gays and Lesbians]. Moscow: Astrel'.

Erlich, Iza S. 1981. "'The Peasant Marey.' A Screen Memory." In *The Psychoanalytic Study of the Child*, Vol. 36. Albert J. Solnit et al. (eds), 381–389. New Haven, CT: Yale University Press.

Essig, Laurie. 1999. *Queer in Russia: A Story of Sex, Self, and the Other.* Durham: Duke University Press.

Etkind, Alexander. 2011. *Internal Colonization. Russia's Imperial Experience.* Cambridge: Polity.

Etkind, Alexander. 1997. *Eros of the Impossible: The History of Psychoanalysis in Russia.* Boulder, CO: Westview Press.

Etkind, Efim. 2012. *La traductrice* [The Translator], Sophie Benech (trans.). Paris: Éditions Interférences.

Etkind, Efim. 1997. "Introduction." In *Mastera poeticheskogo perevoda*, E. Etkind (ed.), 5–57. Moscow: Akademicheskii Proekt.

Etkind, Efim. 1978. *Notes of a Non-Conspirator*, Peter France (trans.). Oxford: Oxford University Press.

Etkind, Efim. 1968. Introduction. In *Mastera russkogo stikhotvornogo perevoda* [Maters of Russian Verse Translation], E. Etkind (ed.), 5–72. Leningrad: Sovetskii pisatel'.

Even-Zohar, Itamir. 2010. "The Position of Translated Literature within the Literary Polysystem. Theory." In *The Translation Studies Reader*, Lawrence Venuti (ed.), 192–197. London and New York: Routledge.

Fadeev, Aleksandr. 2013a. "For the Cause of World Peace (1949)." In *Russian Writers on Translation*, Brian James Baer and Natalia Olshanskaya (eds), 84. Manchester: St. Jerome.

Fadeev, Aleksandr. 2013b. "Answers to Questions from English Writers" (March 6, 1947). In *Russian Writers on Translation. An Anthology*, Brian James Baer and Natalia Olshanskaya (eds), 57–58. Manchester: St. Jerome.

Fadeev, Aleksandr. 1960. "Torzhestvo razuma i spravedlivosti" [The Triumph of Reason and Justice] (September 23, 1947). In *Sobranie sochinenii v 5-i tomakh. Tom chetvertyi. Stati' i rechi* [Collected Works in Five Volumes, Vol. 4. Articles and Speeches], E. F. Knipovich, V. M. Ozerov, and K. A. Fedin (eds), 442–447. Moscow: Khudozhestvennaia Literatura.

Fallowell, Duncan. 1994. *One Hot Summer in St. Petersburg*. London: Jonathan Cape.

Fassin, Eric. 2001. "Same Sex, Different Politics." *Public Culture* 13(2): 215–232.

Fateev, P. S. 1969. *Mikhail Mikhailov – Revolutsioner, pisatel', publitsist* [Mikhail Mikhailov—Revolutionary, Writer, Publicist]. Moscow: Mysl'.

Fawcett, Peter. 1998. "Ideology and Translation." In *Routledge Encyclopedia of Translation Studies*, Mona Baker (ed.), 106–111. London and New York: Routledge.

Felch, Susan M. 2011. " 'Halff a Scrypture Woman': Heteroglossia and Female Authorial Agency in Prayers by Lady Elizabeth Tyrwhit, Anne Lock, and Anne Wheathill." In *English Women, Religion, and Textual Production, 1500–1625*, Micheline White (ed.), 147–166. Farnham, Surrey, and Burlington, Vermont: Ashgate.

Figes, Orlando. 2007. "Tolstoy's Real Hero." *New York Review of Books* 54(18). Available online at: http://www.nybooks.com/articles/20810 (accessed 1 October 2009).

Fish, Stanley. 1980. "Interpreting the Variorum." In *Is There a Text in This Class?*, 147–174. Cambridge, MA: Harvard University Press.

Fitzpatrick, Sheila. 1974. "Cultural Revolution in Russia, 1928–1932." *Journal of Contemporary History* 9(1): 33–52.

Florovsky, Georges. 1979. *Ways of Russian Theology*, trans. by Robert L. Nichols. Available online at: http://www.myriobiblios.gr/texts/english/florovsky_ways.html (accessed 2 July 2010).

Foster, David. 2001. Oscar Wilde, *De Profundis*, and the Rhetoric of Agency. *Papers on Language and Literature* 37(1): 85–110.

Frank, Joseph. 2010. *Dostoevsky. A Writer in His Time*. Princeton, IL: Princeton University Press.

Freud, Sigmund. 1966. "*Psychopathology of Everyday Life.*" In *The Basic Writings of Sigmund Freud*, A. Brill (ed. and trans.), 35–178. New York: The Modern Library.

Fridshtein, Iurii. 2010. "Oskar Uail'd: Teatr dlia odnogo aktera" [Oscar Wilde: Theater for a Single Actor]. In *Oskar Uail'd. Portret Doriana Greia* [Oscar Wilde. The Picture of Dorian Gray], A. Abkina (trans.), 298–311. St. Petersburg: Azbuka-klassika.

Fridshtein, Iurii. 1993. Review of *Oskar Ual'd. Pis'ma raznykh let* [Oscar Wilde. Letters from Various Years]. *Inostrannaia Literatura* 11: 104–105.

Friedberg, Maurice. 1997. *Literary Translation in Russia. A Cultural History*. University Park, PA: Penn State Press.

Gabrielyan, Nina. 2013. Interview with Nina Gabrielyan. *Noev kovcheg* 19.225 (Oct 16–31). Available online at: http://noev-kovcheg.ru/mag/2013-19/4148 .html#ixzz2pXGNDXWN (accessed 5 Jan 2014).

Gabrielyan, Nina. 2004. *Master of the Grass*. In *Glas New Russian Writing*, Vol. 33, Kathleen Cook (trans.), 1–76. Bedford: Glas.

Gabrielyan, Nina. 2001. *Khoziain travy*. Moscow: Eksmo.

Gal, Susan and Kathryn Woolard. 2001. "Constructing Languages and Publics. Authority and Representation." In *Languages and Publics. The Making of Authority*, Susan Gal and Kathryn Woolard (eds), 2–12. Manchester: St. Jerome.

Gallagher, Aoife. 2009. "Pasternak's Hamlet: Translation, Censorship and Indirect Communication." In *Translation and Censorship: Patterns of Communication and Interference*, Eilean Ni Chuilleanain, Cormac O Cuilleanain, and David Parris (eds), 119–131. Portland, OR: Four Corners Press.

Gasparov, Mikhail. 1997. "Pervochtenie i perechtenie" [First Reading and Re-reading]. In *Izbrannye Trudy*, M. L. Gasparov (ed.), Vol. 2. Moscow: Izyki russkoi kul'tury.

Gasparov, Mikhail. 1991. "Klassicheskaia filologiia i tsenzura nravov" [Classical Philology and the Censorship of Mores]. *Literaturnoe obozrenie* 11: 4–7.

Gavchuk, Iurii. 1963. "Tri napravleniia russkogo poeticheskogo perevoda" [Three Trends in Russian Poetry Translation]. *Masterstvo Perevoda* 3, 353–358. Moscow: Sovetskii pisatel'.

Gheith, Jehanne M. 2004. *Finding the Middle Ground. Krestovskii, Tur, and the Power of Ambivalence in Nineteenth-Century Russian Women's Writing*. Evanston, IL: Northwestern University Press.

Ginzburg, Evgenia. 1995. *Journey into the Whirlwind*, Paul Stevenson and Max Hayward (trans.). New York and London: Harcourt.

Glasse, Antonia. 1985. "Kiukhel'beker." In *Handbook of Russian Literature*, Victor Terras (ed.), 241–242. New Haven: Yale University Press.

Glazov-Corrigan, Elena. 1994. "A Reappraisal of Shakespeare's Hamlet: In Defence of Pasternak's *Doctor Zhivago.*" *Forum for Modern Language Studies* 30(3): 219–238.

Goethe, Johan Wolfgang von. 1994. *Conversations of Goethe with Johan Peter Eckermann*, J. K. Moorhead (ed.), John Oxenford (trans.). Cambridge, MA: Da Capo Press.

Gogol, Nikolai. 2013. "What Is the Ultimate Essence of Russian Poetry?" (1946). In *Russian Writers on Translation. An Anthology*, Brian James Baer and Natalia Olshanskaya (eds), 28–29. Manchester: St. Jerome.

Goldberg, Jonathan. 1997. *Desiring Women Writing. English Renaissance Examples.* Stanford, IL: Stanford University Press.

Goodrich, Jaime. 2014. *Faithful Translators. Authorship, Gender, and Religion in Early Modern England.* Evanston, IL: Northwestern University Press.

Goriachkina, M. S. 1963. "N. D. Khvoshchinskaia (V. Krestovskii – psevdonim)." In *V. Krestovskii. Povesti i rasskazy* [V. Krestovskii. Novellas and Stories]. M. A. Goriachkina (ed.), 3–32. Moscow: Khudozhestvennaia literatura.

Goscilo, Helena and Andrea Lanoux (eds). 2006. *Gender and National Identity in Twentieth-Century Russian Culture.* DeKalb: Northern Illinois University Press.

Gosse, Étienne. 1818. "Fable XX, et la dernière. L'Arbre exotique." In *Fables.* Paris: Chaumerot.

Grafton, Anthony (with April Shelford and Nancy Siraisi). 1992. *New Worlds, Ancient Texts. The Power of Tradition and the Shock of Discovery.* Cambridge, Massachusetts, and London: Belknap Press of Harvard University Press.

Greene, Thomas M. 1982. *The Light in Troy: Imitation and Discovery in Renaissance Poetry.* New Haven, CT: Yale University Press.

Greenfeld, Liah. 1992. *Nationalism. Five Roads to Modernity.* Cambridge, MA: Harvard University Press.

Greenleaf, Monica. 1998. "Found in Translation: The Subject of Batiushkov's Poetry." In *Russian Subjects. Empire, Nation, and the Culture of the Golden Age*, M. Greenleaf and S. Moeller-Sally (eds), 51–80. Evanston, IL: Northwestern University Press.

Greenleaf, Monica. 1994. *Pushkin and Romantic Fashion. Fragment, Elegy, Orient, Irony.* Stanford, CA: Stanford University Press.

Gromova, T. V. (ed.). 1995. *Tsenzura v tsarskoi Rossii i Sovetskom Soiuze. Materialy konferentsii, 24–27 maia 1993 g. Moskva* [Censorship in Tsarist Russia and the Soviet Union. Conference Materials, May 24–27, 1993. Moscow]. Moscow: Rudomino.

Grutman, Rainier. 2006. "Refraction and Recognition. Literary Multilingualism in Translation." *Target* 18(1): 17–47.

Grutman, Rainier. 2002. "Les motivations de l'hétérolinguisme: Réalisme, compositions, esthétique" [The Motivations of Heteroglossia. Realism. Compositions. Aesthetics]. In *Eteroglossia e plurilinguismo letterario* [Heteroglossia and Literary Multilingualism]. Vol. 2. *Plurilinguismo e letteratura*, Furio Brugnolo and Vincenzo Orioles (eds), 329–349. Rome: Il Calamo.

Gumperz, John J. 1982. *Discourse Strategies*. Cambridge: Cambridge University Press.

Gutbrodt, Fritz. 2003. *Joint Ventures: Authorship, Translation, Plagiarism*. Bern and New York: Peter Lang.

Haber, Erika. 2003. *The Myth of the Non-Russian: Iskander and Aitmatov's Magical Universe*. Lanham, MD: Lexington Books.

Harussi, Yael. 1989. "Women's Social Roles as Depicted by Women Writers in Early Nineteenth-Century Russian Fiction," *Issues in Russian Literature before 1917. Selected Papers of the Third World Congress for Soviet and East European Studies*, J. Douglas Clayton (ed.), 35–48. Columbus, OH: Slavica.

Harvey, Keith. 2003. *Intercultural Movements. "American Gay" in French Translation*. Manchester: St. Jerome.

Hayes, Julie Candler. 2009. *Translation, Subjectivity, and Culture in France and England, 1600–1800*. Stanford, CA: Stanford University Press.

Healey, Dan. 2001. *Homosexual Desire in Revolutionary Russia. The Regulation of Sexual and Gender Dissent*. Chicago, IL: University of Chicago Press, 2001.

Heilbron, Johan. 2010. "Towards a Sociology of Translation: Book Translation as a Cultural World System." In *Critical Readings in Translation Studies*, Mona Baker (ed.), 304–316. London and New York: Routledge.

Henry, James. 1934. "Preface to *The Tragic Muse*." In *The Art of the Novel. Critical Prefaces*, 79–97. New York: Charles Scribner's Sons.

Hermans, Theo. 2010. "The Translator's Voice in Translated Narrative." In *Critical Readings in Translation Studies*, Mona Baker (ed.), 193–212. London and New York: Routledge.

Hermans, Theo. 1985. "Images of Translation: Metaphor and Imagery in the Renaissance Discourse on Translation." In *The Manipulation of Literature: Studies in Literary Translation*, Theo Hermans (ed.), 103–135. New York: St. Martin's Press.

Hirsch, Francine. 2005. *Empire of Nations. Ethnographic Knowledge and the Making of the Soviet Union*. Ithaca: Cornell University Press.

Hobsbawn, Erik and Terence O. Ranger (eds). 1992. *The Invention of Tradition*. Cambridge: Cambridge University Press.

Hofstede, Geert, et al. 1998. *Masculinity and Femininity. The Taboo Dimension of National Cultures*. London and New Delhi: Sage.

Hokenson, Jan Walsh and Marcella Munson. 2007. *The Bilingual Text: History and Theory of Literary Self-translation*. Manchester: St. Jerome.

Holmgren, Beth. 1995. "Bug Inspectors and Beauty Queens: The Problems of Translating Feminism into Russian." In *Post-communism and the Body Politic*, Ellen E. Berry (ed.), 15–31. New York: New York University Press.

Holquist, Michael. 1994. "Corrupt Originals. The Paradox of Censorship." *PMLA* 109(1): 14–25.

Holub, Miroslav. 1994. "The Poet and Human Solidarity." In *Comparative Criticism. An Annual Journal*. Special Issue: Revolutions and Censorship, E. S. Shaffer (ed.), 3–6. Cambridge: Cambridge University Press.

Hosington, Brenda M. 2011. "Lady Margaret Beaufort's Translations as Mirrors of Practical Piety." In *English Women, Religion, and Textual Production, 1500–1625*, Micheline White (ed.), 185–204. Farnham, Surrey, and Burlington, Vermont: Ashgate.

Hosking, Geoffrey. 1997. *Russia. People and Empire*. Cambridge: Harvard University Press.

Idel'baev, M. Kh. 2004a. "Perevody proizvedenii Salavata Iulaeva" [Translations of the Works of Salavat Iulaev]. In *Salavat Iulaev. Entsyklopediia* [Salavat Iulaev. Encyclopedia], 248–249. Ufa: Bashkirskaia Entsyklopediia.

Idel'baev, M. Kh. 2004b. "Stikhoslozhenie Salavata Iulaeva" [Verse Composition of Salavat Iulaev]. In *Salavat Iulaev. Entsyklopediia*, 344–345. Ufa: Bashkirskaia Entsyklopediia.

Iskander' Fazil. 1993. *Pshada. Znamia* 8: 3–36.

Iulaev, Salavat. 2004. "Moi Ural" [My Urals]. In *Salavat Iulaev. Stikhotvoreniia* [Salavat Iulaev. Verses]. (ed.), Ufa: Kitap.

Jaffe, Alexandra. 2010. "Locating Power: Corsican Translators and Their Critics." In *Critical Readings in Translation Studies*, Mona Baker (ed.), 263–282. London and New York: Routledge.

Jedamski, Doris. 2005. "Translation in the Malay World: Different Communities, Different Agendas." In *Asian Translation Traditions*, Eva Hung and Judy Wakabayashi (eds), 211–246. Manchester: St. Jerome.

Jusdanis, Gregory. 1991. *Belated Modernity and Aesthetic Culture. Inventing National Literature*. Minneapolis, MN: University of Minnesota Press.

Kahf, Mohja. 2010. "Packaging 'Huda': Sha'rawi's memoirs in the United States reception environment." In *Critical Readings in Translation Studies*, Mona Baker (ed.), 28–46. London and New York: Routledge.

Kalashnikova, Elena. 2008. *Po-russki c liubov'iu. Besedy s perevodchikami* [In Russian with Love. Conversations with Translators]. Moscow: Novoe Literaturnoe Obozrenie.

Kálmán, G. C. 1986. "Some Borderline Cases of Translation." *New Comparison* 1: 117–22.

Kanzer, Mark. 1947. "Dostoevsky's 'Peasant Marey'" *American Imago* 4: 78–87.

Karamzin, Nikolai M. 1993. *Istoriia gosudarstva rossiiskogo*. I–IV. Moscow: Zolotaia alleia.

Karataev, M. 1938. "O tvorchestve Dzhambula" [On Dzhambul's Oeuvre]. In *Dzhambul. Pesni i peomy* [Dzhambul. Songs and Poems], 7–14. Moscow: Khudozhestvannaia Literatura.

Karlin, Daniel. 2005. *Proust's English*. Oxford: Oxford University Press.

Karlinsky, Simon. 1986. *Marina Tsvetaeva. The Woman, Her World, and Her Poetry*. Cambridge Studies in Russian Literature. Cambridge: Cambridge University Press.

Kashkin, Ivan. 1955. "V bor'be za realisticheskii perevod" [In the Struggle for Realist Translation]. In *Voprosy Khudozhestvennogo perevoda. Sbornik statei* [Questions of Literary Translation. A Collection of Articles], V. Rossel's (ed.), 120–164. Moscow: Sovetskii pisatel'.

Katz, Michael R. 2008. "War and Peace in our Time." *The New England Review* 29(4). Available online at: http://cat.middlebury.edu/~nereview/29-4/29-4Katz.htm (accessed 1 Oct 2009).

Kelly, Catriona. 2009. "Sapho, Corinna, and Niobe: Genres and Personae in Russian Women's Writing, 1760–1820." In *A History of Women's Writing in Russia*, Adele Marie Barker and Jehanne M. Gheith (eds), 37–61. Cambridge: Cambridge University Press.

Kelly, Catriona. 2001. *Russian Literature: A Very Short Introduction*.Oxford: Oxford University Press.

Kervi, Aleks. 2010. "Predislovie perevodchika" [Translator's Preface]. In *Uil'iam Berrouz. Dzhanki* [William Burroughs. Junkies], 5–9. Moscow: ACT.

Kholmskaia, Ol'ga. 1959. "Pushkin i perevodcheskie diskussii pushkinskoi pory" [Pushkin and Translation-related Discussions in the Age of Pushkin]. *Masterstvo Perevoda* 1, 305–367. Moscow: Sovetskii pisatel'.

Khotimsky, Maria. 2011. *A Remedy for Solitude: Russian Poet-Translators in the Soviet and Post-Soviet Eras*. Unpublished Doctoral Dissertation, Harvard University.

Khramov, Evgenii. 2006. "Pochemu Sad?" [Why Sade?]. In *Markiz de Sad. 120 dnei Sodoma* [Marquis de Sade. 120 Days of Sodom], E. Khramov (trans.), 5–10. Moscow: Geleo.

Khrushcheva, Nina. 2007. *Imagining Nabokov: Russian between Art and Politics*. New Haven and London: Yale University Press.

Khvoshchinskaya, Nadezhda. 2000. *The Boarding School Girl*, Karen Rosneck (trans.). Evanston, IL: Northwestern University Press.

Kiukhel'beker, Vil'gel'm. 2013. "On the Direction of Our Poetry, Especially Lyrical Poetry, over the Last Decade (1824)." In *Russian Writers on Translation. An Anthology*, Brian James Baer and Natalia Olshanakaya (eds), 21–23. Manchester: St. Jerome.

Klein, Lev. 2000. *Drugaia liubov'* [Another Love]. Saint Petersburg: Folio Press.

Kokker, Steve. 1999. "Andrei: A Family Tradition and Denis: Raised on Mother's Milk." In *Military Trade*, Steven Zeeland (ed.), 77–106. Binghamton: Haworth Press.

Komissarov, Vilen. 1998. "Russian Tradition." In Routledge *Encyclopedia of Translation Studies*, Mona Baker (ed.), 541–549. London and New York: Routledge.

Kon, Igor'. 1997. *Seksual'naia kul'tura v Rossii. Klubnichka na berezke* [Sexual Culture in Russia. A Strawberry on a Birch Tree]. Moscow: OGI.

Kopper, John M. 1994. "Dante in Russian Symbolist Discourse." *Comparative Literature Studies* 31(1): 25–51.

Kratsev, Nikolai. 2010. "Salinger's Catcher in the Rye Resonated behind Iron Curtain as well." *Radio Free Europe/Radio Liberty* (29 January). Online. Available at: www.rferl.org/content/Salingers_Catcher_In_The_Rye_Resonated_Behind_Iron_Curtain_As_Well/1943025.html (accessed 2 May 2011).

Kristeva, Julia. 1991. *Strangers to Ourselves*, Leon Roudiez (trans.). New York: Columbia University Press.

Kronitiris, Tina. 1997. *Oppositional Voices: Women as Writers and Translators in the English Renaissance*. New York and London: Routledge.

Kuntsman, Adi. 2009. " 'With a Shade of Disgust': Affective Politics of Sexuality and Class in Memoirs of the Stalinist Gulag." *Slavic Review* 68(2):308–328.

Kuprin, Andrei. 2000. "Predislovie. Kniga zhizni Eduarda Forstera" [Foreword. The Book of Life of Edward Forster]. In *E. M. Forster. Moris. Roman. Rasskazy* [E. M. Forster. Maurice. A Novel. Stories], A. Kuprin (trans.), 5–18. Moscow: Glagol.

Kurpatov, Andrei. 2003. *Salomeia i Oskar Uail'd Romana Viktiuka: Strakh, sladostratie, smert'* [Roman Viktiuk's Salomé and Oscar Wilde: Fear, Sensuality, Death]. St. Petersburg: Triada.

Laird, Sally. 1999. *Voices of Russian Literature: Interviews with Ten Contemporary Writers*. Oxford: Oxford University Press.

Lakoff, George. 1987. *Women, Fire and Dangerous Things: What Categories Reveal about the Mind*. Chicago and London: University of Chicago Press.

Lalo, Alexei. 2011. *Libertinage in Russian Culture and Literature: A Bio-History of Sexualities at the Threshold of Modernity*. Leiden: Brill.

Lavut, Evgeniia. 1997. "Neizvestnyi Oskar Vaild" [The Unknown Oscar Wilde]. *Knizhnoe obozrenie "Ex Libris NG"* 15 (17 September): 5.

Layton, Susan. 1994. *Russian Literature and Empire: Conquest of the Caucasus from Pushkin to Tolstoy*. Cambridge: Cambridge University Press.

Lefevere, Andre. 1992. *Translation, Rewriting, and the Manipulation of Literary Fame*. London: Routledge.

Leigh, Bread. 2010. "Reviewed: *Daniel Stein, Translator*." *Bears & Vodka*. Available at: http://bearsandvodka.com/?p=1401 (accessed 30 April 2012).

Leighton, Lauren. 1994. *The Esoteric Tradition in Russian Romantic Literature*. University Park, PA: The Pennsylvania State University Press.

Leighton, Lauren. 1991. *Two Worlds, One Art*. DeKalb, IL: Northern Illinois University Press.

Leites, Aleksandr M. 1995. "Khudozhestvennyi perevod kak iavlenie rodnoi kul'tury" [Literary Translation as a Phenomenon of the Target Culture]. *Voprosy Khudozhestvennogo perevoda. Sbornik statei* [Questions of Literary Translation. A Collection of Articles], V. Rossel's (ed.), 97–119. Leningrad: Sovetskii pisatel'.

Lermontov, Mikhail. 2004. *A Hero of Our Time*, Marian Schwartz (trans.). New York: The Modern Library.

Lermontov, Mikhail. 1992. *A Hero of Our Time*, V. Nabokov in collaboration with D. Nabokov (trans.) New York: Alfred A. Knopf.

Lermontov, Mikhail. 1959. *Geroi nashego vremeni* [A Hero of Our Time]. In *M. Iu. Lermontov. Izbrannye sochineniia v dvukh tomakh. Tom vtoroi. Dramy i proza* [M. Iu. Lermontov. Selected Works in Two Volumes. Vol. 2. Dramas and Prose], 365–498. Moscow: Khudozhestvennaia Literatura.

Levantovskaya, Margarita. 2012. "The Russian-speaking Jewish Diaspora in Translation: Liudmila Ulitskaya's *Daniel Stein, Translator*." *Slavic Review* 71(1): 91–107.

Levin, Iurii. 1988. *Shekspir i russkaia literatura XIX veka* [Shakespeare and Russian Nineteenth-century Literature]. Leningrad: Pushkinskii Dom.

Lewis, Phillip. 2004. "The Effects of Translation." In *The Translation Studies Reader*, Lawrence Venuti (ed.), 256–75. Second edition. London and New York: Routledge.

Lieven, Dominic. 2000. *Empire: The Russian Empire and Its Rivals*. London: John Murray.

Lipovetsky, Mark. 1999. *Russian Postmodernist Fiction. Dialogue with Chaos*, Eliot Borenstein (ed. and trans.) New York: M. E. Sharpe.

Littau, Karen. 2010. "Translation in the Age of Postmodern Production: From Text to Intertext to Hypertext." In *Critical Readings in Translation Studies*, Mona Baker (ed.), 435–449. London and New York: Routledge.

Liubimov, Nikolai. 1963. "Perevod – Iskusstvo" [Translation—an Art]. *Masterstvo Perevoda* 3, 233–234. Moscow: Sovetskii pisatel'.

Loseff, Lev. 1984. *On the Beneficence of Censorship: Aesopian Language in Russian Literature*. Munich: Verlag Otto Sanger in Kommission.

Lotman, Iurii. 2010. *Nepredskazuemye mekhanizmy kul'tury* [The Unpredictable Workings of Culture]. Tallinn: TLU Press.

Lotman, Iurii. 1992. "Russkaia literatura na frantsuzskom iazyke" [Russian Literature in French]. In *Izbrannye stat'i*, Iu. M. Lotman (ed.), Vol. 3, 350–368. Tallinn: Aleksandra.

Lotman, Juri. 1984. "The Decembrist in Everyday Life." In Ju. Lotman and B. Uspenskij, *The Semiotics of Russian Culture*, Ann Shukman (ed.), C. R. Pike (trans.), 71–124. Ann Arbor, MI: Michigan Slavic Contributions.

Lowen, Alexander. [1965]1998. *Liubov' i orgazm* [Love and Orgasm], E. Pole (trans.). Classics of Western Psychology. Moscow: ACT.

Mahlsdorf, Charlotte von. 1997. *Ia sam sebe zhena. Tainaia zhizn' Sharlotty fon Mal'sdorf, samogo izvestnogo berlinskogo transvestita* [I Am My Own Wife. The Secret Life of Charlotte von Mahlsdorf, Berlin's Most Famous Transvestite], Aleksandr Shatalov (trans.). Moscow: Glagol.

Mahlsdorf, Charlotte von. 1994. *I Am My Own Woman. The Outlaw Life of Charlotte von Mahlsdorf, Berlin's Most Distinguished Transvestite*, Jean Hollander (trans.). Pittsburgh, PA: Cleis Press.

Malmstad, John E. and Nikolay Bogomolov. 1999. *Mikhail Kuzmin. A Life in Art*. Cambridge, MA: Harvard University Press.

Marinina, Aleksandra. 2002. *Stilist* [The Stylist]. Moscow: Eksmo.

Marrese, Michelle Lamarche. 2010. " 'The Poetics of Everyday Behavior' Revisited: Lotman, Gender, and the Evolution of Russian Noble Identity." *Kritika* 11(4): 701–739.

Marsh, Rosalind. 2011. "The Hunt for the Hairy Mammoth?' Woman-Centered and Feminist Prose in Post-Soviet Russia. In *New Women's Writing in Russia*,

Central and Eastern Europe: Gender, Generation, and Identities, R. Marsh (ed.), 407–457. Newcastle: Cambridge Scholars Publishing.

Marsh, Rosalind. 2007. *Literature, History and Identity in Post-Soviet Russia, 1991–2006*. Bern: Peter Lang.

Marshak, Samuil. 1962/1990. "Poeziia perevoda" [The Poetry of Translation]. In *Sobranie sochinenii v chetyrekh tomakh* [Collected Works in Four Volumes], Vol. 4, *Vospitanie slovom. Stat'i, zametki, vospominaniia* [Educated by the Word. Essays, Notes, Reminiscences], S. V. Mikhalkov (ed.), 212–216. Moscow: Pravda.

Marshak, Samuil. 1959. "Iskusstvo poeticheskogo portreta" ["The Art of the Poetic Portrait"]. *Masterstvo perevoda* 1, 245–250. Moscow: Sovetskii pisatel'.

Martin, Terry. 2001. *The Affirmative Action Empire. Nations and Nationalism in the Soviet Union, 1923–1939*. Ithaca: Cornell University Press.

Medvedev, Kirill. 2013. "Beyond the Poetics of Privatization." *New Left Review* (August–September). Available online at: http://newleftreview.org/II/82/kirill-medvedev-beyond-the-poetics-of-privatization (accessed 16 Nov 2014).

Mehrez, Samia. 1992. "Translation and the Postcolonial Experience: The Francophone North African Text." In *Rethinking Translation*, Lawrence Venuti (ed.), 120–138. New York: Routledge.

Merkle, Denise (ed.). 2002. *Censure et traduction dans le monde occidental/ Censorship and Translation in the Modern World. TTR* 15.2.

Meyer, Priscilla. 2010. *How Russians Read the French. Lermontov, Dostoevsky, Tolstoy*. Madison, WI: University of Wisconsin Press.

Meylaerts, Reine. 2010. "Multilingualism and Translation." In *Handbook of Translation Studies*. Volume I, Yves Gambier and Luc van Doorslaer (eds). Amsterdam/Philadelphia: John Benjamins.

Miller, Robin Feuer. 1984. "Imitations of Rousseau in *The Possessed.*" *Dostoevsky Studies* 5: 77–89.

Miner, Stephen Merritt. 2001. "Where the West Begins. Two New Books Look at Russia and Its Place in History." *New York Times on the Web* (1 July).

Mochizuki, Tetsuo. 2000. "Synthetic Research on Russian Postmodernism in the Nineties." Available online at: http://kaken.nii.ac.jp/en/p/10410107/2000/6/en (accessed 28 April 2012).

Mogutin, Yaroslav and Alexander Shatalov. 1993. "Nechto vrode liubvi. Predislovie" [Something Like Love. A Foreword]. In *Dzhaims Bolduin. Komnata Dzhovanni. Roman* [James Baldwin. Giovanni's Room. A Novel], G. Shmakov (trans.), 5–14. Moscow: Glagol.

Monas, Sydney. 1961. *The Third Section. Police and Society under Nicholas I*. Cambridge, MA: Harvard University Press.

Monticelli, Daniele. 2013. "From Authorship to Anonymous Translation. Patterns of De-authorization in Post-Soviet Estonia." Paper delivered at the conference *Beyond Transfiction: Translations and Their Authors*, University of Tel Aviv, May 7–8, 2013.

Moore, David Chioni. 2001. "Is the Post- in Postcolonial the Same as the Post- in Post-Soviet? Toward a Global Postcolonial Critique." *PMLA* 116(1):111–128.

Morozova, Elena. 2000. "Markiz de Sad i ego knigi" [The Marquis de Sade and His Books]. In *Markiz de Sad. Prestupleniia liubvi, ili bezumstva strastei* [Marquis de Sade. Crimes of Love, or the Madness of Passion], E. Morozova (trans.), 5–20. St. Petersburg: Azbuka.

Morris, Meaghan. 1997. Introduction. In *Translation and Subjectivity: On Japan and Cultural Nationalism*, Naoki Sakai (ed.), ix–xxii. Minneapolis, MN: University of Minnesota Press.

Moss, Kevin. 1995. "The Underground Closet: Political and Sexual Dissidence in East European Culture." In *Post-communism and the Body Politic*, Ellen E. Berry (ed.), 229–251. New York: New York University Press.

Murav, Harriet. 2005. "The Jew as Translator in Soviet Russia." *Cardozo Law Review* 26:2401–2414.

Murav, Harriet. 1994. *Holy Foolishness. Dostoevsky's Novels and the Poetics of Cultural Critique*. Palo Alto, CA: Stanford University Press.

Murray, Stephen O. 2000. *Homosexualities*. Chicago, IL: University of Chicago Press.

Nabokov, Vladimir. 1981a. "Russian Writers, Censors, and Readers." In *Lectures on Russian Literature*, F. Bowers (ed.), 1–13. San Diego, New York, and London: Harcourt Brace and Company.

Nabokov, Vladimir. 1981b. "Russian Writers, Censors, and Readers." In *Lectures on Russian Literature*, F. Bowers (ed.), 1–12. San Diego, New York, and London: Harcourt Brace and Company.

Nabokov, Vladimir. 1975. The Translator's Introduction. In *Eugene Onegin. A Novel in Verse*. Volume I, 1–88. Princeton, NJ: Princeton University Press.

Nabokov, Vladimir. 1973. "A Russian Beauty." In *A Russian Beauty and Other Stories*, S. Karlinsky and D. Nabokov (trans.), 1–8. New York: McGraw-Hill.

Nadezhdin, Nikolai. 2009. *Iukio Misima. "Nichego vyshe chesti"* [Yukio Mishima. "Nothing Higher than Honor"]. Moscow: Osipenko A. I.

Nafisi, Azar. 2003. *Reading Lolita in Tehran: A Memoir in Books*. New York: Random House.

Nandy, Ashis. 1994. *The Illegitimacy of Nationalism*. Delhi: Oxford University Press.

Nikitenko, Aleksandr. 1975. *Diary of a Russian Censor*, Helen Jacobson (ed. and trans.). Amherst, MA: University of Massachusetts Press.

Niranjana, Tejaswini. 1992. *Siting Translation: History, Post-Structuralism, and the Colonial Context*. Berkeley, CA: University of California Press.

Nunokawa, Jeff. 1991. "'All the Sad Young Men': AIDS and the Work of Mourning." In *Inside/out: Lesbian Theories, Gay Theories*, Diana Fuss (ed.), 311–323. New York and London: Routledge.

Obratsova, A. G. 1997. "Oskar Uail'd: Lichnost' i sud'ba" [Oscar Wilde: Identity and Fate]. In *Oskar Uail'd. Pis'ma* [Oscar Wilde. Letters], A. Obratsova and Iu. Fridshtein (eds), 5–22. Moscow: Agraf.

Offord, Derek. 1999. *Nineteenth-century Russia. Opposition to Autocracy*. Essex: Longman.

Oushakin, Serguei. 2001. "The Terrifying Mimicry of Samizdat." *Public Culture* 13(2): 191–214.

Ozerov, Lev. 1963. "Pesn'—dusha naroda" [Song—The Soul of the Folk]. *Masterstvo perevoda* 3, 202–212. Moscow: Sovetskii pisatel'.

Ozkirimli, U. 2000. *Theories of Nationalism. A Critical Introduction*. Basingstoke: Palgrave.

Palat, Madhavan K. 1989. "The Russian Conquest of Inner Asia," *Societat Catalana d'Economia (Filial de l'Institut d'Estudios Catalans), Annuari* 7: 120–127.

Pal'tsev, Nikolai. 1993. "Khudozhnik kak kritik, kritika kak zhudozhestvo" [The Artist as Critic, Criticism as Art]. In *Oskar Uail'd. Izbrannye proizvedeniia* [Oscar Wilde. Selected Works], N. N. Baryshnikova (ed.), 3–20. Moscow: Respublika.

Patterson, Annabel. 1984. *Censorship and Interpretation. The Conditions of Writing and Reading in Early Modern England*. Madison, WI: University of Wisconsin Press.

Pavlova, T. V. 1991. "Oskar Uail'd v russkoi literature (konets XIX - nachalo XX v.)" [Oscar Wilde in Russia (Beginning of the 19th–End of the 20th Centuries)]. In *Na rubezhe XIX i XX vekov: iz istorii mezhdunarodnykh sviazei russkoi literatury. Sbornik nauchnykh trudov* [On the Border of the 19th and 20th Centuries: From the History of International Relations of Russian Literature. A Collection of Scholarly Works]. Leningrad: Nauka.

Pavlova, T. V. 1986. *Oskar Uail'd v Rossii (konets XIX - nachalo XX veka)* [Oscar Wilde in Russia (Beginning of the 19th–End of the 20th Centuries)]. Unpublished Doctoral Dissertation, University of Leningrad.

Paz, Octavio. 1992. "Translation: Literature and Letters." In *Theories of Translation: An Anthology of Essays from Dryden to Derrida*, Rainer Schulter and John Biguenet (eds), 152–162. Chicago: University of Chicago Press.

Peaver, Richard. 2007. Introduction. In *War and Peace*, Leo Tolstoy (ed.), vii–xxvi. New York: Vintage Classics.

Peeters, Tine. 2004. "The Postmodern Situation in Russia." *Slavica Gandensia* 31. Available online at: http://russianpostmodernism.blogspot.com/ (accessed 29 May 2012).

Perloff, Marjorie. 1993. "Russian Postmodernism: An Oxymoron?" *Postmodern Culture* 3(2):online.

Perry, Catherine. 2003. *Persephone Unbound. Dionysian Aesthetics in the Poetry of Anna de Noailles*. Cranbury, NJ: Rosemont Publishing.

Peterson, Annabel. 1984. *Censorship and Interpretation. The Conditions of Writing and Reading in Early Modern England*. Madison, WI: University of Wisconsin Press.

Polonsky, Rachel. 1997. "Translating Whitman, Mistranslating Bal'mont." *Slavic and East European Journal* 75(3): 401–421.

Pushkin, Alexander. 1986. *Pushkin on Literature*, Tatiana Wolff (ed., trans.). Rev. edition. London: Athlone Press.

Rafael, Vincente L. 2007. "Translation in Wartime." *Public Culture* 19(2): 239–246.
Rafael, Vincente L. 2005. *The Promise of the Foreign. Nationalism and the Technics of Translation in the Spanish Philippines*. Durham: Duke University Press.
Remnick, David. 2005. "Translation Wars." *The New Yorker*, 18(35): 98–109.
Renan, Ernst. 1990. "What is a Nation?" In *Nation and Narration*, Homi K. Bhabha (ed.), 8–22. New York and London: Routledge.
Rice, James L. 1989. "Psychoanalysis of 'Peasant Marei.': Some Residual Problems." *Russian Literature and Psychoanalysis*, Daniel Rancour-Laferriere (ed.), 245–261. Amsterdam and Philadelphia: John Benjamins.
Richter, Eva and Bailin Song. 2005. Translating the Concept of 'Identity.'" In *Translation and Cultural Change: Studies in History, Norms, and Image-Projection*, Eva Hung (ed.), 91–110. Amsterdam and Philadelphia: John Benjamins.
Rosenholm, Arja. 1996. "The 'Woman Question' of the 1860s, and the Ambiguity of the 'Learned Woman.'" In *Gender and Russian Literature. New Perspectives*, Rosalind Marsh (ed.), 112–128. Cambridge: Cambridge University Press.
Rosenthal, Randy. 2011. "A Faith without Boundaries." Available online at: http://www.thedailybeast.com/articles/2011/04/23/daniel-stein-fire-season-and-other-books-reviewed.html (accessed 30 April 2012).
Rossel's, Vladimir M. 1964. "Radi shumiashchikh zelenykh vetvei" [For the Sake of Rustling Green Branches]. *Masterstvo perevoda* 4, 12–33. Moscow: Sovetskii pisatel'.
Rosslyn, Wendy. 2000. *Feats of Agreeable Usefulness: Translations by Russian Women, 1763–1825*. Fichtenwalde: Verlag F. K. Göpfert.
Rotikov, K. K. 1998. *Drugoi Peterburg*. St. Petersburg: Liga-Plius.
Rousseau, Jean-Jacques. 1997. *The Social Contract and Other Late Political Writings*, Victor Gourevitch (ed. and trans.). Cambridge: Cambridge University Press.
Rowe, John Carlos. 2007 "Reading Reading Lolita in Tehran in Idaho." *American Quarterly* 59.2: 253–275.
Rozencveig, Victor. 1993. "Three Masters of Russian Translation." *Meta* 38(4): 643–657.
Roziner, Felix. 1991. *A Certain Finkelmeyer*, Michael Henry Heim (trans.) New York: W.W. Norton.
Roznatovskaia, Iu. A. 2000. *Oskar Uail'd v Rossiii. Bibliograficheskii ukazatel', 1892–2000* [Oscar Wilde in Russia. A Bibliographic Index, 1892–2000]. Moscow: Rudomino.
Rudd, Charles A. 1982. *Fighting Words. Imperial Censorship and the Russian Press, 1804–1906*. Toronto, ON: University of Toronto Press.
Saburoff, Ivan. 2008. "Toward a Russian Gay Lexicon." Special Issue. *How Do We Read Queer Russia?*, Dan Healey (ed.). *kultura* 2: 10–11. Available online at: http://www.kultura-rus.uni-bremen.de/kultura_dokumente/ausgaben/englisch/kultura_2_2008_EN.pdf (accessed 23 June 2015).
Safron, Jonathan Foer. 2003. *Everything is Illuminated. A Novel*. New York: Harper Perennial.

Said, Edward. 1977. *Orientalism*. London: Penguin.

Sandler, Stephanie. 1983. "The Poetics of Authority in Pushkin's 'André Chénier.'" *Slavic Review* 42(2): 187–203.

Sandomirskaia, V. B. 1978. "Perevody i perelozheniia Pushkina iz A. Shen'e" [Pushin's Translations and Adaptations from Chénier]. In *Pushkin. Issledovaniia i materialy* [Pushkin. Research and Materials]. Vol. 8, 90–106. Leningrad: Nauka.

Santaemilia, José and Luise Von Flotow (eds). 2011. *Women and Translation. Geographies, Voices, and Identities*. Special Issue. *Monti* 3.

Schwartz, Marian. 2004. Translator's Preface. In *Mikhail Lermontov. A Hero of Our Time*, xvii–xxi. New York: Modern Library Classics.

Scotto, Peter. 1992. "Prisoners of the Caucasus: Ideologies of Imperialism in Lermontov's 'Bela.'" PMLA 107: 246–260.

Seidman, Naomi. 2006. *Faithful Renderings. Jewish-Christian Difference and the Politics of Translation*. Chicago, IL: Chicago University Press.

Seldon, Raman. 1989. *A Reader's Guide to Contemporary Literary Theory*. Second edition. Lexington: University Press of Kentucky.

Selim, Samah. 2010. "Pharoah's Revenge: Translation, Literary History and Colonial Ambivalence." In *Critical Readings in Translation Studies*, Mona Baker (ed.), 319–336. London and New York: Routledge.

Semevskii, V. I. 1922. *M. V. Butashevich-Petrashevskii i Petrashevtsy* [Butashevich-Petrashevskii and the Petrashevtsy]. Part I. Moscow: Zadruga.

Senderovich, Savely. 1982. *Aleteiia. Elegiia Pushkina "Vospominanie" i problem ego poetiki* [Aletheia. Pushkin's Elegy "Vospominanie" and the Problems of its Poetics]. Wiener Slawistischer Almanach Sonderband 8. Vienna: A. Hansen-Löve.

Seruya, Theresa, ed. 2008. *Translation and Censorship in Different Times and Landscapes*, T. Seruya and M. Lin Moniz (eds), xi–xix. Newcastle: Cambridge Scholars Publishing.

Shalamov, Varlam. 1994. *Kolyma Tales*. Trans, John Glad. New York and London: Penguin.

Shalamov, Varlam. (1963)2013. "The National Borders of Poetry and Free Verse." In *Russian Writers on Translation. An Anthology*, Brian James Baer and Natalia Olshanskaya (eds), 118. Manchester: St. Jerome.

Sharova. Veronika. 2010. "Byt' ili ne byt' gei praidu. Opyt dvukh stolits Rossii" [Is Gay Pride to Be or Not to Be? The Experience of Russia's Two Capitals]. *Gendernye Issledovaniia* 2–21: 72–89.

Shatalov, Aleksandr. 2000. Predislovie [Foreword]. In *Edmund Uait. Istoriia odnogo mal'chika* [Edmund White, A Boy's Own Story], V. Kogan (trans.), 5–8. Moscow: Glagol.

Shatalov, Aleksandr. 1997. "Introduction." In *Ia sam sebe zhena. Tainaia zhizn' Sharlotty fon Mal'sdorf, samogo izvestnogo berlinskogo transvestita* [I Am My Own Wife. The Secret Life of Charlotte von Mahlsdorf, Berlin's Most Famous Transvestite], Aleksandr Shatalov (trans.). Moscow: Glagol.

Shatalov, Aleksandr and Iaroslav Mogutin. 1993. " 'Something like Love.' A Foreword." In *Dzheims Balduin. Komnata Dzhovanni* [James Baldwin. Giovanni's Room], G. Shmakov (trans.), 5–14. Moscow: Glagol.

Shcherbakov, Sergei. 2000. "Oskar Uail'd." In *Oskar Uail'd*, 3–6. Moscow: Zvonnitsa-MG.

Sherry, Samantha. 2015. *Discourses of Regulation and Resistance: Censoring Translation in the Stalin and Khrushchev Era Soviet Union*. Edinburgh: University of Edinburgh Press.

Shlapentokh, Vladimir. 1990. *Soviet Intellectuals and Political Power. The Post-Stalin Era*. Princeton, NJ: Princeton University Press.

Shneidman, N. N. 1995. *Russian Literature, 1988–1994: The End of an Era*. Toronto, ON: University of Toronto Press.

Shread, Carolyn. 2011. "Transformations of Violence: Metaphorics Gains and Plastic Regeneration in Marie Vieux-Chauvet's Les Rapaces." In *Re-gendering Translation. Transcultural Practice, Gender/Sexuality and the Politics of Alterity*, Christopher Larkosh (ed.), 50–71. Manchester: St. Jerome.

Simon, Sherry. 2000. Introduction. In *Changing the Terms. Translating in the Postcolonial Era*, Sherry Simon and Paul St-Pierre (eds), 9–29. Ottawa, ON: University of Ottawa Press.

Simon, Sherry. 1996. *Gender in Translation. Cultural Identity and the Politics of Transmission*. London and New York: Routledge.

Simon, Sherry. 1994. *Le Trafic des langues: Traduction et culture dans la littérature québecoise* [The Traffic in Languages: Translation and Culture in Quebecois Literature]. Montreal, QC: Boreal.

Sinyavsky, Andrei. 1988. *Soviet Civilization. A Cultural History*, Joanne Turnbull (trans.). New York: Arcade Publishing.

Sirotkina, Irina. 2002. *Diagnosing Literary Genius. A Cultural History of Psychiatry in Russia, 1880–1930*. Baltimore and London: The John Hopkins University Press.

Sobol, Valeria. 2011. "The Uncanny Frontier of Russian Identity: Travel, Ethnography, and Empire in Lermontov's 'Taman.' " *Russian Review* 70 (January): 246–260.

Solomon, Karla Thomas. 1999. "Nadezhda Khvoshchinskaia (1824–1889)." In *Russian Women Writers*, Christine D. Tomei (ed.), 261–283. New York: Garland.

Solov'ev, Vladimir. 1900. "Rodina russkoi poezii. Po povodu elegii 'Sel'skoe kladbishche' (Posviashchaetsia P. V. Zhukovskomu)" [The Birthplace of Russian Poetry. On the Elegy "A Country Churchyard" (Dedicated to P. V. Zhukovsky)]. In *Stikhotvoreniia Vladimira Solov'eva* [The Poetry of Vladimir Solov'ev]. 3rd edition, 151–152, St. Petersburg: M. M. Stasiulevich.

Spechler, Dina. 1982. *Permitted Dissent in the USSR: Novy Mir and the Soviet Regime*. New York: Praeger.

Staritsyna, Zoia. 1969. *Beranzhe v Rossii XIX vek* [Béranger in Russia. 19th century]. Moscow: Vysshaia Shkola.

Stavans, Ildar. 2005. "On Censorship: A Conversation with Ildar Stavans." Interview by Albin, Verónica. *Translation Journal* 9.3 (July). Online. Available at: http://accurapid.com/journal/33censorship1.htm (accessed 23 Jan 2010).

Steiner, George. 1992. *After Babel. Aspects of Language and Translation.* Oxford and New York: Oxford University Press.

Stewart, Susan. 1994. *Crimes of Writing. Problems in the Containment of Representation.* Durham: Duke University Press.

Strauss, Leo. 1952. *Persecution and the Art of Writing.* Glencoe, IL: The Free Press.

Sturge, Kate. 2004. *'The Alien Within': Translation into German during the Nazi Regime.* Munich: Iudicium.

Suleiman, Sarah Rubin. 1997. "The Politics of Postmodernism after the Wall (Or What Do We Do When the Ethnic Cleansing Starts)." In *International Postmodernism. Theory and Literary Practice*, J. W. Bertens, H. Bertens, and D. Foukeme (eds), 51–64. Amsterdam and Philadelphia: John Benjamins.

Suleiman, Sarah Rubin. 1992. *Subversive Intent: Gender, Politics, and the Avant-garde.* Cambridge and Oxford: Harvard University Press.

Sutcliffe, Ben. 2009. "Liudmila Ulitskaia's Literature of Tolerance." *Russian Review* 68: 495–509

Tarkovskii, Arsenii. 2013. "The Opportunities of Translation (1973)." In *Russian Writers on Translation*, Brian James Baer and Natalia Olshanskaya (eds), 119–121. Manchester: St. Jerome.

Tarkovskii, Arsenii. 1982. "Perevodchik" [The Translator]. In *Izbrannoe: Stikhotvoreniia, poemy, perevody* (1929-1979) [Selections: Lyric Verse, Narrative Poems, Translations], 69. Moscow: Khudozhestvennaia Literatura.

Taylor, Juliette. 2005. "'A Distortive Glass of Our Distorted Glebe': Mistranslation in Nabokov's Ada." *Linguistica Antverpiensia* 4: 265–78.

Tec, Nechama 1990. *In the Lion's Den. The Life of Oswald Rufeison.* Oxford: Oxford University Press.

Theim, Jon. 1995. "The Translator as Hero in Postmodern Fiction." *Translation and Literature* 4(2): 207–218.

Thompson, Eva. 2000. *Imperial Knowledge. Russian Literature and Colonialism.* Westport, CT: Greenwood Press.

Todd, Willam Mills III. 1978. *Literature* and Society in *Imperial Russia, 1800–1914.* Stanford, CA: Stanford University Press.

Tolstoi, Lev. 1961. *Voina i mir* [War and Peace]. In *Sobranie sochinenii v dvadtsati tomakh* [Collected Works in Twenty Volumes]. Vol. 4–7. Moscow: Khudozhestvennaia Literatury.

Tolstoy, Leo. 2011. *The Gospel in Brief. The Life of Jesus*, Dustin Condren (trans.). New York and London: Harper Perennial.

Tolstoy, Leo. 2007. *War and Peace.* Original Version, Andrew Bromfield (trans.). New York: Harper Collins.

Tolstoy, Leo. 1964. *War and Peace*, Rosemary Edmonds (trans.). London: Penguin Books.

Tomashevsky, Boris. 1925. *Teoriia literatury* [Theory of Literature]. Moscow and Leningrad: Gosizdat.

Tomaszkiewicz, Teresa. 2002. "La traduction des textes déjà censurés." *TTR* 15(2): 171–189.

Toury, Gideon. 1995. "Pseudotranslations and Their Significance." In *Descriptive Translation Studies and Beyond*, 40–52. Amsterdam and Philadelphia: John Benjamins.

Trivedi, Harish. 2006. "In Our Own Time, on Our Own Terms: 'Translation' in India." In *Translating Others*, Volume 1, Theo Hermans (ed.), 102–119. Manchester: St. Jerome.

Trofimova, Elena and Ellen I. Goff. 1994. "Gabrielyan, Nina Mikhailovna." In *Dictionary of Russian Women Writers*, Maria Ledkovsky, Charlotte Rosenthal, and Mary Zirin (eds), 189–190. Westport, CT: Greenwood Press.

Tsukanov, Andrei and Liudmila Viazmitinova. 1999. "Postmodernistskii fragment. Postmodernizm – Ideia dlia Rossii?" [A Postmodern Fragment. Postmodernism–an Idea for Russia?]. Interview with Il'ia Il'in. *Novoe Literaturnoe Obozrenie* 39: 241–253.

Tuller, David. 1996. *Cracks in the Iron Closet: Travels in Gay and Lesbian Russia*. Chicago, IL: University of Chicago Press.

Tumanik, E. N. 2008. "Perevod Biblii Dekabristom A. N. Murav'evym" [The Translation of the Bible by A. N. Murav'ev]. *Gumanitarnye nauki v Sibiri* 2, 11–14.

Twarog, Leon. 1971. "Literary Censorship in Russia and the Soviet Union." In *Essays on Russian Intellectual History*, L. B. Blair (ed.), 98–123. Austin and London: University of Texas Press.

Tymoczko, Maria. 2010a. Foreword. In *Translation, Resistance, Activism*, Maria Tymoczko (ed.), vii–ix. Amherst and Boston: University of Massachusetts Press.

Tymoczko, Maria. 2010b. "Ideology and the Position of the Translator: In What Sense Is a Translator 'In Between'?" In *Critical Readings in Translation Studies*, Mona Baker (ed.), 213–228. London and New York: Routledge.

Tymoczko, Maria and Edwin Gentzler (eds). 2002. *Translation and Power*. Amherst: University of Massachusetts Press.

Tynianov, Iurii. 1938. Introduction. In *Vil'gel'm Kiukhel'beker, Prokofii Liapunov. Tragediia V. Kiukhelbekera* [Vil'gel'm Kiukhel'beker, Prokofii Liapunov. A Tragedy by Vil'gel'm Kiukhel'beker], 5–23. Leningrad: Sovetskiii pisatel'.

Tyulenev, Sergey. 2011. "Women-Translators in Russia." *MonTI* 3: 75–105.

Ulitskaia, Liudmila. 2006. *Daniel' Shtain, perevodchik* [Daniel Stein, Translator]. Moscow: Eksmo.

Ulitskaia, Liudmila. 2001. "Golubchik" [Darling]. *Veselye pokhorony*, 282–306. Moscow: Vagrius.

Ulitskaya, Ludmila. 2011. *Daniel Stein, Interpreter: A Novel*. Arch Tait (trans.). New York: Overlook.

Uman, Deborah. 2012. *Women as Translators in Early Modern England*. Lanham, MD: University of Delaware Press.

Uspensky, Boris. 1973. *A Poetics of Composition. The Structure of the Artistic Text and Typology of a Compositional Form*, V. Zavarin and S. Wittig (trans.). Berkeley and Los Angeles: University of California Press.

Vail', Petr and Aleksandr Genis. 1998. *60-e. Mir sovetskogo cheloveka* [The Sixties. The World of the Soviet Person]. Moscow: NLO.

Veidle, Vladimir. 1973. "O neperevodimom" [On the Untranslatable]. In *O poetakh i poezii* [On poets and poetry], 147–164. Paris: YMCA Press.

Venclova, Tomas. 1979. "Translations of World Literature and Political Censorship in Contemporary Lithuania." *Lituanus* 25(2). Available online at: http://www.lituanus.org/1979/79_2_01.htm (accessed 16 Nov 2014).

Venuti, Lawrence. 2002. "The Difference that Translation Makes: The Translator's Unconscious." In *Translation Studies: Perspectives on an Emerging Discipline*, A. Riccardi (ed.), 214–241. Cambridge: Cambridge University Press.

Venuti, Lawrence. 1999. *The Scandals of Translation. Towards an Ethics of Difference*. London and New York: Routledge.

Venuti, Lawrence. 1995. *The Translator's Invisibility. A History of Translation*. London and New York: Routledge.

Venuti, Lawrence. 1992. Introduction. In *Rethinking Translation: Discourse, Subjectivity, Ideology*, L. Venuti (ed.), 1–17. London and New York: Routledge.

Veresaev, Vikentii. 2000. Introduction "Safo." In *Safo. Lira, lira sviashchennaia* [Sapho. Lyre, Holy Lyre], V. Veresaev (trans.), 5–16. Moscow: Letopis'.

Vitkovskii, Evgenii. 2000. Introduction. In *Oskar Uail'd. Polnoe sobranie stikhotvorenii i Poem* [Oscar Wilde. Complete Collection of Verses and Poems], 7–25. St. Petersburg: Evraziia.

Vojvodić, Jasmina. 2011. "Transfery Danielia Staina" [Daniel Stein's Transfers]. *Russian Literature* LXIX.1: 141–155.

Vol'pert, Larisa I. 2010. *Lermontov i literatura Frantsii* [Lermontov and the Literature of France]. Third edition, O. Palikova (ed.). Tartu: Internet-Publikatsii.

Von Flotow, Luise. 1997. *Translation and Gender. Translating in the "Era of Feminism."* Manchester: St. Jerome.

Wachtel, Andrew. 1999. "Translation, Imperialism and National Self-definition in Russia." *Public Culture* 11.1: 49–73.

Wakabayashi, Judy. 2011. "Secular Translation: Asian Perspectives." In *The Oxford Handbook of Translation Studies*, Kirsten Malmkjaer and Kevin Windle (eds), 23–36. Oxford: Oxford University Press.

Wall, Wendy. 1993. *The Imprint of Gender*. Ithaca, NY: Cornell University Press.

Wanner, Adrian. 1996. *Baudelaire in Russia*. Gainesville, FL: University Press of Florida.

Watt, Richard. 2005. *Packaging Post/Coloniality: The Manufacture of Literary Identity in the Francophone World*. Lanham: Lexington Books.

White, Micheline. 2011. "Introduction: Women, Religious Communities, Prose Genres, and Textual Production." In *English Women, Religion, and Textual Production, 1500–1625*, Micheline White (ed.), 17–36. Farnham, Surrey, and Burlington, Vermont: Ashgate.

White, Micheline. 1999. "Renaissance Englishwomen and Religious Translations: The Case of Anne Lock's *Of the Markes of the Children of God* (1590)." *English Literary Renaissance* 29: 375–400.

Wierzbicka, Anna. 1992. *Semantics, Culture, and Cognition: Universal Human Concepts in Culture-specific Configurations*. Oxford: Oxford University Press.

Wilde, Oscar. 1994. *The Complete Works of Oscar Wilde*. New York: Harper Collins.

Williams, Raymond. 1983. *Keywords. A Vocabulary of Culture and Society*. Revised Edition. New York: Oxford University Press.

Winter, Werner. 1964. "Translation as Political Action." In *The Craft and Context of Translation: A Critical Symposium*, W. Arrowsmith and R. Shattuck (eds), 295–301. Garden City, NY: Anchor Books.

Witt, Susanna. Forthcoming. "Byron's Don Juan in Russia and the Soviet School of Translation." *Translation and Intepreting Studies* 11(1).

Witt, Susanna. 2011. "Between the Lines: Totalitarianism and Translation in the USSR." In Contexts, Subtexts, and Pretexts: Literary Translation in Eastern Europe and Russia, Brian James Baer (ed.), 149–170. Amsterdam and Philadelphia: John Benjamins.

Wolff, Larry. 1994. *Inventing Eastern Europe. The Map of Civilization on the Mind of the Enlightenment*. Stanford: Stanford University Press.

Wolff, Tatyana and John Bayley. 1986. *Pushkin on Literature*. London: Athlone Press.

Wood, Elizabeth A. 2009. "The Woman Question in Russia: Contradictions and Ambivalences." In *A Companion to Russian History*, Abbott Gleason (ed.), 353–367. New York and London: Wiley Blackwell.

Zabolotsky, Nikita. 1994. *The Life of Zabolotsky*, R. R. Milner-Gulland (ed.), R. R. Milner-Gulland and C. G. Bearne (trans.). Cardiff: University of Wales Press.

Zaitseva, Valentina. 2006. "National, Cultural, and Gender Identity in the Russian Language." In *Gender and National Identity in Twentieth-century Russian Culture*, Helena Goscilo and Andrea Lanoux (eds), 30–54. DeKalb: Northern Illinois University Press.

Zemskova, Elena. 2013. "Translators in the Soviet Writer's Union: Pasternak's Translations from Georgian Poets and the Literary Process of the Mid-1930s." In *The Art of Accommodation: Literary Translation in Russia*, Leon Burnett and Emily Lygo (eds), 185–212. Oxford and Bern: Peter Lang.

Zerbe, Noah. 1997. "Russia." In *Censorship*. Vol. 3, L. Amey et al. (eds), 694–696. Ipswich, MA: Salem Press.

Zetlin, Mikhail. 1958. *The Decemberists*. Madison, CT: International Universities Press.

Zhukovskii, Vasilii. 1960. Letter to N. V. Gogol', 6(18) Feb. 1847. In *Sobranie sochinenii v chetyrekh tomakh* [Collected Works in Four Volumes]. Vol. 4. *Odisseia, Khudozhestvennaia proza, kriticheskie stat'i, pis'ma*, I. D. Glikman (ed.), 543–545. Moscow and Leningrad: Khudozhestvennaia Literatura.

Zhukovskii, Vasilii. 1818. "Listok" [The leaf]. *Für Weinige. Dlia nemnogikh* 2:25.

Zhukovskii, Vasilii. (1810) 1985. "O perevodakh voobshche, i voosobennosti o perevodakh stikhov" [On Translation in General, and in Particular on the Translation of Verse]. In *Zhukovskii – kritik* [Zhukovsky as Critic], Iu. M. Prozorova (ed.), 81–85. Moscow: Sovetskaia Rossiia.

Zinger, G. 2001. "Ot perevodchika" [From the Translator]. In *Zhan Zhene. Torzhevstvo pokhoron* [Jean Genet. Funeral Rites]. Moscow: Tekst.

Zolotonosov, Mikhail. 1999. "Kniga o 'golubom Peterburge' kak fenomen sovremennoi kul'tury" [A Book on "Gay Petersburg" as a Phenomenon of Contemporary Culture]. *Novyi mir* 5: 185–191.

Zverev, Aleksei. 2000a. "Improvizator Akroid" [Akroyd, the Improviser]. In *Petr Akroid. Zaveshchanie Oskara Ual'da* [Peter Ackroyd. The Last Testament of Oscar Wilde], L. Motyleva (trans.), 5–16. Moscow: GSB Press.

Zverev, Aleksei. 2000b. "Predislovie. Preodolenie bar'era" [Foreword. Overcoming a Barrier]. In *Dzheims Bolduin. Drugaia strana* [James Baldwin. Another Country], V. Bernadtskaia (trans.), 3–10. Moscow: Informaishn Grup, Geleos, and ACT.

Zverev, Aleksei. 2000c. "Uail'd: 'Naslazhdenie stikhiinost'iu'" [Wilde: The Pleasure of the Elemental]. Review of Richard Ellman's *Oscar Wilde, A Biography*. *NLO* 46: 373–378.

Zverev, Aleksei. 1999. "Nespasaiushchaia krasota" [Beauty That Doesn't Save]. In *Oskar Ual'd*, Jacques Laglande (ed.), 5–14. Moscow: Molodaia Gvardiia and Palimsest.

Zverev, Aleksei. 1993. Review of *Piter Akroid. Zaveshchanie Oskara Uail'da* [Peter Ackroyd. The Last Testament of Oscar Wilde], L. Motyleva (trans.). *Unostrannaia Literatura* 11: 5–7.

Index

Note: Locators followed by the letter "n" refer to notes.

Ackroyd, Peter 135, 146
Acquinis, Thomas 121
aestheticization 142, 144–8, 153
aesthetics 119, 155, 166
agency 49, 94, 133, 149, 154–5, 164
  authorial 113, 115, 122
  creative 103
  translator 169
Akhmatova, Anna 115, 118
Aksyonov, Vasily 175
Akunin, Boris. *See* Chkhartishvili,
  Grigorii
Alekseev, Mikhail 130
All-Union Book Chamber 61
Altman, Denis 136
Alvarez, Román 49
Anderson, Benedict 2, 7, 9, 69, 85
Appiah, Anthony 164
Apter, Emily 13, 15–16, 52, 71
Arnault, Antoine-Vincent 17, 28,
  35–6, 40, 42–4
Arrojo, Rosemary 2
Asimakoulos, Dmitri 49
authorship 88–9, 91, 108, 113, 116,
  118–19, 122, 125–6, 130
  de-individualization of 19, 123–4,
  126, 130

Baker, Mona 12–13
Bakhtin, Mikhail 5, 9, 15
Baldwin, James 144, 151–2, 154, 157–9
Bal'mont, Konstantin 127–9
Balzac, Honoré de 7, 14, 55, 91
bardic authorship 123–6
Barta, Peter 89
Barthes, Roland 120, 126
Bassnett, Susan 49

Bayley, John 38
belatedness 3–4, 171
Belinsky, Vissarion 1, 4–5, 14
belles infidèles 87
Benjamin, Walter 2, 119
Béranger, Pierre-Jean de 17, 28, 35–6,
  38–40
Berdyaev, Nicolas 89, 110, 153
Berlina, Alexandra 139, 144
Bermann, Sandra 16, 67
Bestuzhev-Marlinsky, Aleksandr 51
Bhabha, Homi 178
bilingualism 15
Binyon, T. J. 58
Blackledge, Adrian 69
Bogdanov, Konstantin 125
Bogomolov, Nikolay 116
Borenstein, Eliot 165
Boym, Svetlana 89, 171, 173, 175
Brodsky, Joseph 43, 63, 152
Browning, Frank 178
Buden, Boris 5
bukvalizm 126, 130
Bulgakov, Mikhail 115, 153
Bullock, Philip Ross 139–41, 147–8, 156
Bunin, Ivan 12
Burnett, Leon 1, 8, 16, 55
Burroughs, William 144
Burson, Jeffrey 22
Burt, Richard 116
Butashevich-Petrashevsky, Mikhail.
  See Petrashevsky, Mikhail
Byron, George (Lord) 11, 26, 29,
  34–5, 38

Casanova, Pascale 137, 163, 166
Cassin, Barbara 52

Caucasus 8, 12, 50–1, 56–9, 61
censors 21, 23–5, 28, 30–1
censorship 17, 22, 24–5, 28, 126, 142,
        144, 153
Chaikovsky, Petr 148
Chamberlain, Lori 18, 87–8
Chartier, Roger 13
Chekhov, Anton 123
Chénier, André 17, 28, 35–8, 60
Chernyshevsky, Nikolai 13, 109
Chester, Pamela 89
Cheyfitz, Eric 49
Chkhartishvili, Grigorii 101, 147,
        153, 156–8, 164
chronotope 9
Chukhno, Valerii 145–6, 148–50, 154
Chukovsky, Kornei 79, 122, 127, 139,
        149
Clark, Katerina 119, 122–3, 126–7,
        130–1
Clowes, Edith 6
colonization 49, 56, 60
Colonna, Vittoria 145
Condee, Nancy 6, 83, 165
Condivi, Ascanio 144
Condren, Dustin 173
Constant, Benjamin 4
Cooper, James Fenimore 62
Costlow, Jane 89
Crane, Mary Thomas 121, 212
Creese, Angela 69
Cronin, Michael 16, 49, 93, 97
Cummings, William 88

Damrosch, David 16, 134, 168, 179
Danilin, Iurii 35, 38
Dante 29, 64
Debreczeny, Paul 21
Decembrist Revolt 17, 32, 38, 96
Decembrists 21–2, 24, 26, 29–36,
        38–40, 42, 44, 46–7
Decembrist uprising 31, 37–8, 44–5
Delabastita, Dirk 163
de Noailles, Anna 103–5

Derrida, Jacques 2, 53–4, 125
Derzhavin, Gavrila 9
Dobrenko, Evgeny 115, 122
Dolack, Thomas 90
Dollimore, Jonathan 141, 155
Dontsova, Darya 97
Dostoevsky, Fyodor 10, 14, 18, 54–5,
        69, 73–82, 85–6, 89, 91–6, 124,
        152–3, 155, 171, 173, 176
    Crime and Punishment 18, 54–5,
        91–2, 95–6, 102, 109, 112, 153,
        155
    "Peasant Marei" 18, 69, 73–9,
        81–2, 85
Douglas, Alfred 146, 154
Dovlatov, Sergei 65
Dowler, Wayne 82
Doyle, Conan 141
Dreiser, Theodore 62, 140
Dzhabaev, Dzhambul 65, 124–6

Efros, Abram 143
Egolin, A. M. 93
Eliseev, G. Z. 54, 92
Elliot, George. *See* Evans, Mary Jane
Enikeeva, Dilia 176
Erlich, Iza S. 73–4, 78
Essig, Laurie 151, 178
Etkind, Alexander 6, 25, 33, 43, 46,
        50, 117, 131, 178
Etkind, Efim 17, 117
Evans, Mary Jane 93
exile 29, 34, 36–8, 40, 42–4, 46, 55,
        92, 131

Fadeev, Aleksandr 62, 116
Fateev, I. S. 26–7, 47
Fedorov, Andrei 17, 122, 127
Felch, Susan M. 113, 122
feminism 109, 137
foreign words 53, 55, 70–4, 111
forgery 49, 53, 57, 59, 61, 63, 65, 67
formalism 19, 62, 126, 129
Forrester, Sibelan 89

Foster, David 154
Frank, Joseph 55, 79–80, 95
Freidberg, Maurice 17
Freud, Sigmund 18, 70–1, 84–5, 178
Fridshtein, Iurii 147–8, 150, 154
Friedberg, Maurice 65

Gabrielyan, Nina 18, 102, 104, 106–9
Galsworthy, John 140
Gasparov, Mikhail 121, 142
Gavchuk, Iurii 130
Genis, Aleksandr 42
Gentzler, Edwin 49
Gheith, Jehanne 110, 113
globalization 101, 164
Gnedich, Tatyana 117, 129, 131
Goethe 25, 131, 179
Goff, Ellen I. 108
Gogol, Nikolai 10–12, 27, 134
Goldberg, Jonathan 88, 113, 122
Goodrich, Jaime 113, 122
Goriachkina, M. S. 109
Gorky, Maxim 123
Goscilo, Helena 89
Gosse, Étienne 42
Grafton, Anthony 120
Gray, Thomas 1, 10–11
    "Elegy Written in a Country
    Churchyard" 1, 11
Grebnev, Naum 125–6
Greenblatt, Stephen 121
Greene, Thomas 119
Greenfeld, Liah 7
Greenleaf, Monica 21, 26, 33, 37–8, 59
Grutman, Rainer 163
Gutbrodt, Fritz 4, 88

Haber, Erika 83–4
Habermas, Jurgen 133
Harussi, Yael 90
Harvey, Keith 136
Hayes, Julie Candler 113, 122
Heilbron, Johan 13
Heine, Heinrich 14, 27, 93

Hemingway, Ernest 62
Herder, Johann Gottfried 81
Hermans, Theo 3, 121
Herzen, A. I. 40, 47, 123
Hirsch, Francine 6
Hobsbawn, Erik 6, 69–70
Hofstede, Geert 87
Holmgren, Beth 137
Holquist, Michael 25n, 28
Holub, Miroslav 21, 23, 28–9
homosexuality 89, 98, 100, 135–8,
    140–9, 151, 153–5, 157–61,
    174–7, 180
Hosking, Geoffrey 6, 50, 79
Hughes, Langston 62

Imagined Communities 69, 85
Imitatio 115, 119, 121
imitation 3, 5, 19, 35, 44, 88–9, 95, 102,
    107, 109, 112, 119, 121–4, 132
individualism 4, 89, 94, 113, 127–9,
    131, 171
Inostrannaia Literatura 147, 157
Intelligentsia 17–18, 22, 46, 64, 70,
    81, 98, 119, 131–2, 172–3
interpreter 49, 52, 148, 166, 169–71
    ad hoc 97
Irving, Washington 62
Iskander, Fazil 18, 69, 82–6
    Pshada 18, 69, 73, 83–5
Ivanov, Viacheslav 65, 142–3

Jaffe, Alexandra 7
James, Henry 172
Jedamski, Doris 88
Jusdanis, Gregory 10

Kálmán, G. C. 54
Kanzer, Mark 73
Karamzin, Nikolai 1, 10
Karlinsky, Simon 23, 104
Kashkin, Ivan 127, 129
Kelly, Catriona 90
Kervi, Aleks 144

Kholmskaia, Ol'ga 21–2
Khotimsky, Maria 123, 130
Khramov, Evgenii 158
Khrushcheva, Nina 134–5
Khvoshchinskaya, Nadezhda 18,
    107–10, 112–13
Kipling, Rudyard 99–100
Kiukhel'beker, Wilhelm 34, 44–6,
    132, 171
Komissarov, Vilen 17, 170
Kon, Igor 142
Kopper, John M. 64
Kratsev, Nikolai 159
Kristeva, Julia 178
Kronitiris, Tina 113, 122
Kurpatov, Andrei 151n. 25
Kutuzov, A. M. 32
Kuzmin, Mikhail 115–16, 138, 152

Laird, Sally 83
Lakoff, George 53
Lamartine, Alphonse de 35
Langlade, Jacques 135, 146, 148
Lanoux, Andrea 89
Layton, Susan 51–2, 57–8, 60
Lefevere, André 13, 15
Leighton, Lauren 17, 26, 30, 32–3,
    35, 62
Leites, Aleksandr 13
Lemontov, Mikhail 17
Lermontov, Mikhail 8, 40, 44, 49–52,
    56–61, 176
Levantovskaya, Margarita 167
Levin, Iurii 17
Lewis, Phillip 53
Lipovetsky, Mark 165
literary history 13–14
literature, translated 11, 13, 23, 25,
    28, 47, 142
Littau, Karen 163–4
Liubimov, Nikolai 130
Longfellow, Henry Wadsworth 27,
    62, 93n
Loseff, Lev 22, 24–6
Lotman, Juri 14, 26, 32, 34–5

Lowen, Alexander 143
Lunin, Mikhail 40
Lyden, Jacki 133
Lygo, Emily 1, 8, 16, 55

Makanian, Eva 168, 172
Malmstad, John E. 116
Mandel'shtam, Osip 115
Marinina, Aleksandra 18, 97–102,
    106, 164
Marrese, Michelle Larouche 15
Marsh, Rosalind 97, 107, 166
Marshak, Samuil 126, 169
Martin, Henri-Jean 13
Martin, Terry 65
Mason, John 22
Maugham, Somerset 140
Medvedev, Kirill 10, 159
memoirs 26, 158
Mendelson, M. 46
Mephistopheles 153
Merkle, Denise 22
metanarrative 170
metaphor 12, 33, 37, 42–5, 113, 118,
    121
Meyer, Priscilla 61, 176
Meylaerts, Reine 15
Michelangelo 139, 143–5
Mikhailov, Mikhail 14, 26–7, 46–7
Miller, Robin Feuer 94
Mishima, Yukio 147, 153, 156–8
    Death in the Middle of Summer
    158
    Golden Temple 156, 157
mistranslation 17–18, 52–3, 55–61,
    67, 86, 164
Mochizuki, Tetsuo 165
Mogutin, Yaroslav 144, 151
monolingualization 13–15
Monticelli, Daniele 115
Moore, David Chioni 3, 50, 164
Moore, Thomas 47
Morozova, Elena 158n. 31
multilingualism 6–7, 15, 49–50,
    70–1, 163, 168, 177

Murashov, Iurii 125
Murav, Harriet 63, 67, 93, 116
Murav'ev, Aleksandr 44, 46, 79, 132
Murray, Stephen O. 136

Nabokov, Vladimir 2, 5, 8, 23–4,
    56–8, 66, 69, 83, 133–5, 139
Nadezhdin, Nikolai 153
Nafisi, Azar 133–5
Nandy, Ashis 74
nationalism 2, 7, 20, 69, 72, 81, 85–6,
    124
Nekrasov, Nikolai 79, 109
Newman, John 145
New Russians 98–9, 101
Nietzsche, Friedrich 104
Niranjana, Tejaswini 49, 53–5
Noiriel, Gerard 14

Obratsova, A. G. 139, 146, 149–50,
    152, 154
Odoevsky, A. I. 34
Offord, Derek 81
Ogarev, N. P. 40, 47
originality 3–5, 12, 19, 88–9, 96,
    102, 107–8, 113, 118, 122,
    124–5
Ozkirimli, U. 69

packaging 139–41, 156, 160–1
Padunov, Vladimir 165
palimpsests 28–9
Pal'tsev, Nikolai 149, 153
parapraxis 70–1, 73–4, 80–1, 83, 86
paratext 19, 28, 36, 138, 140, 154
Parris, David 22
Pasternak, Boris 14, 115–17, 130
Pavić, Milorad 134, 168, 179
Paz, Octavio 12
Peeters, Tine 165–6
Peletier du Mans, Jacques 121
Pelevin, Vladimir 165
Perry, Catherine 104–5, 107
Petrashevsky, Mikhail 55n, 92–3n. 4
Petrashevsky Circle 55n, 77

Petrashevsty 38
Pevear, Richard 71–2
Poe, Edgar Allen 62
Polish Uprisings 40, 79–80
polyglossia 5, 12, 15, 108
positivism 89, 100, 120
postcolonialism 3, 6, 49–50, 164
postmodernism 12, 20, 120, 163–73,
    177–9
post-Soviet Russia 19, 97, 99, 101,
    133, 135–6, 142, 149, 151,
    155–6, 158, 167, 177–8
pseudo-translations 22, 25, 54, 65
Pushkin, Alexander 1–2, 4–5, 8, 10,
    12, 26, 34, 36–8, 40, 59–60, 94,
    96, 123–4, 171, 173
    Eugene Onegin 2n. 3, 8, 56
translations 4

Rafael, Vincente 2–3, 21, 49, 52, 56,
    67, 86, 118
Rait-Kovaleva, Rita 159
Rancière, Jacques 115
Ranger, Terence O. 6, 70
Reinach, Théodore 143
Renan, Ernst 6, 69–70
repression 54, 70, 73, 80, 84, 116–17,
    133
Rice, James 73, 75, 77–9, 81
Richter, Eva 88–9
Roger, Terence 69
Rogers, Margaret 49
Romanticism 2–5, 12, 15, 22, 34–5, 56,
    59, 70, 89, 91, 94, 110, 113, 131
Romantics 4–5, 10, 16, 27, 60, 69, 78,
    86, 96, 113, 116, 131, 171
Rosenholm, Arja 109
Rosenthal, Randy 166
Rossel's, Vladimir 62
Rosslyn, Wendy 30, 90–1
Rotikov, Kostia 138
Rousseau, Jean-Jacques 1–2, 4–5,
    93–4
    Confessions 93–4
    Social Contract 2n. 2, 94

Rowe, John Carlos 134
Rozanov, Vasily 89, 143
Roziner, Felix 18, 49, 52, 61, 63–5, 116
   A Certain Finkelmeyer 17, 49, 52,
      61–7, 116
Rufeisen, Oswald 172
Russification 142, 147, 151, 153
Ryleev, Kondraty 5, 34

Saburoff, Ivan 137
Said, Edward 50
Salinger, J. D. 159
Saltykova, Vera 97
Sandler, Stephanie 30, 36, 38, 89
Sandomirskaia, V. B. 36–7
Santaemilia, José 87
Savonarola, Girolamo 145
Schiller, Friedrich 11–12, 35, 82
Scott, Walter 11–12
Scotto, Peter 50–1, 59
Seidman, Naomi 9, 17
Seldon, Raman 164
Selim, Samah 16
Semevskii, V. I. 55, 93
Semyonovna, Pelageya 111
Senderovich, Savely 33
Serman, Ilya 17
sexuality 136–7, 141–2, 161, 178–9
Shakespeare, William 14, 25, 44–5,
      109–12, 116, 131
Shalamov, Varlam 9
Sharova, Veronika 177
Shatalov, Aleksandr 144, 151, 158–9
Shcherbakov, Sergei 152, 154
Sherer, Anna 72
Sherry, Samantha 142
Shmakov, Gennadii 151, 157
Shneidman, N. N. 83–5
Shread, Carolyn 92
Siberia 30, 63–6, 75
Simon, Sherry 87, 102
Sinyavsky, Andrei 131
Sirotkina, Irina 55, 152
socialism 27, 47, 149, 155–6

Solov'ev, Vladimir 1–2, 10–11, 98–102
Solzhenitsyn 43
Song, Bailin 88
Sorokin, Vladimir 165
Soviet school of translation 62, 123,
   126, 129–30
Staritsyna, Zoia 35, 38–40
Steiner, George 169
Stewart, Susan 120
Strakhov, Nikolai 79, 82
Suleiman, Sarah Rubin 178
Sutcliffe, Benjamin 166, 174

Tarkovsky, Arsenii 62, 129–30, 154
Taylor, Juliette 56
Tertz, Abram 43
Thompson, Eva 50, 52, 63–4
Tolstoy, Leo 5, 51–3, 55, 71–3, 123,
   172–3, 176
   War and Peace 53, 55, 71, 73, 172
Toury, Gideon 65
translatability 9–10, 12, 53–4, 59, 164
translation
   total 53–5
   zero 53–5
translator-activist 47
translator-forger 52, 67
Trivedi, Harish 49, 88
Trofimova, Elena 108
Tsvetaeva, Marina 23, 104, 115
Tuller, David 178
Tumanik, E. N. 45–6
Turgenev, Andrei 1, 40, 123
Turgenev, Ivan 80
Twain, Mark 61
Tymoczko, Maria 49, 115
Tynianov, Iurii 45
Tyulenev, Sergey 91

Ulitskaya, Liudmila 19, 164, 166–8,
      170–7, 179–80
   Daniel Stein: Interpreter 19, 163–77
   "Golubchik" 175–6, 180
Uman, Deborah 113, 122

Vail, Petr 42
Vasari, Giorgio 145
Venclova, Tomas 1, 3
Venuti, Lawrence 49, 53, 84–6
Veresaev, Vikentii 142–3
Veselovsky, Alexander 64
Viazemsky, Prince V. A. 39–40
Vidal, M. Carmen África 49
Vidocq, Eugène François 26
Viktiuk, Roman 151
Vol'pert, Larisa 29, 40, 42
Von Flotow, Luise 87
Von Kotzebue, Auguste 27
von Mahlsdorf, Charlotte 158
Vowles, Judith 89
Vygotsky, Lev 5

Wachtel, Andrew 2, 11–12, 49, 96,
    171
Wakabayashi, Judy 88
Wall, Wendy 120–1
Watt, Richard 140
Western gay literature 133, 135–6,
    138–9, 151, 159, 161
Whitman, Walt 62, 127–9, 139
Wierzbicka, Anna 154

Wilde, Oscar 19, 128, 134–5, 138–42,
    144–56, 159, 161
    Ballad of Reading Goal 19, 147–8,
        151
    De Profundis 19, 147–50, 153–5
    The Portrait of Dorian Gray
        140–1, 153–4
    "The Soul of Man under
        Socialism" 149, 155–6
Williams, Raymond 78
Witt, Susanna 125, 129–30
Wolff, Larry 4
Wolff, Tatyana 38
Wood, Elizabeth 109

Young, Edward 5, 32

Zabolotsky, Nikolai 115, 117
Zerbe, Noah 31
Zetlin, Mikhail 35
Zhukovsky, Vasilii 1–2, 4–5, 10–12,
    28, 33, 40, 43, 90, 171
Zinger, G. B. 153
Zolotonosov, Mikhail 138
Zverev, Aleksei 135, 144, 146–8,
    150–1, 154, 157–9